1972

University of St. Francis
GEN 842.709 A257
Affron
A stage for poets

3 0301 00033997 4

W9-ABR-569

A Stage for Poets

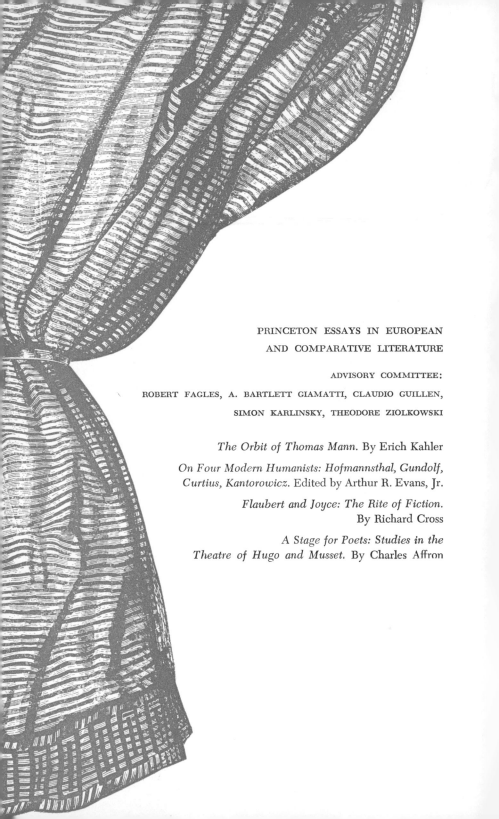

PRINCETON ESSAYS IN EUROPEAN
AND COMPARATIVE LITERATURE

ADVISORY COMMITTEE:
ROBERT FAGLES, A. BARTLETT GIAMATTI, CLAUDIO GUILLEN,
SIMON KARLINSKY, THEODORE ZIOLKOWSKI

A Stage for Poets

STUDIES IN THE THEATRE OF
HUGO & MUSSET

by Charles Affron

PRINCETON UNIVERSITY PRESS
PRINCETON, NEW JERSEY, 1971

LIBRARY
College of St. Francis
JOLIET, ILL.

Copyright © 1971 by Princeton University Press

ALL RIGHTS RESERVED

Library of Congress Card: 75-153847

International Standard Book Number: 0-691-06201-3

This book has been composed in Linotype Caledonia

Printed in the United States of America
by Princeton University Press, Princeton, New Jersey

LIBRARY
College of St. Francis
JOLIET, ILL.

842.709
Q257

"À *des oiseaux envolés*"

FOR M., M., B., N.B.

62483

Preface

THE subject of this book grew out of a common and deep-seated prejudice. Throughout my education, the French romantic theatre was treated with enormous condescension by my teachers, fellow-students, and eventually colleagues, and smugness was an attitude all too easy to appropriate. The prospect of actually having to teach *Hernani* was a fortuitous shock. Necessity forced me to extract the play from beneath a heavy accumulation of *idées reçues* and literary history. The resulting pleasure seemed worth sharing, and it was with that purpose in mind that I extended my inquiry.

The translations of texts drawn from Musset's plays were found in a rendering by Raoul Pellissier, published in 1908 by James L. Perkins and Company, New York. They are quite accurate, and since literalness was the prime requirement they seemed suitable. The other translations are my own. The standard, turn-of-the-century versions are puzzlingly frivolous and often incomprehensible. I have consistently sacrificed sonority and grace to clarity and fidelity, and hope that these leaden efforts will send the reader scurrying back to Hugo's French.

PREFACE

I am delighted to be able at last to express my gratitude to those who helped me during the preparation of this manuscript: Bernard Garniez and Ralph Tarica, friends and colleagues who read the introductory chapters and offered valuable suggestions and encouragement; Gloria Vilardell, for her excellent typing of the manuscript; Henri Peyre, whose unstinting aid has been acknowledged by scores of his students, and who read this manuscript at a time when his kind praise was particularly appreciated. My greatest debt is to my wife, Mirella, for her infinitely meticulous reading, her keen editorial sense and taste, and her patience in all things.

C.A.
New York City
January 11, 1971

Contents

Illustrations

ILLUSTRATIONS

11. Camille. An illustration by Eugène Lami for *On ne badine pas avec l'amour*. Photograph courtesy of Bulloz, Paris.
12. Poster for *Lorenzaccio* with Sarah Bernhardt, by A. M. Mucha. Courtesy of la Bibliothèque de l'Arsenal.

A Stage for Poets

one

INTRODUCTION:
The Problem of a Poetic Theatre

THE stage belongs to the poet. Guaranteed by the oldest literary and critical traditions, it is his birthright. The theatrical genre and the diction of poetry create a set of complements that draws into tension the formal time of the play and the reciting voice. A poem's texture is released from the space of the reader's mind and inhabits the movement of a theatrical dialectic. Speech, the common radical of social activity, is drastically altered, and the new pattern is consciously opposed to the spectator's idiom. While seeing men perform inside the frame of a proscenium the public perceives its own vocabulary arranged in various artificial series. The poet-dramatist's voice is heard because it is different; a play is not a conversation. French romantic theatre loudly enunciates this voice. At the beginning of the nineteenth century the lyric poets impose their diction on the theatrical genre, and in doing so illuminate the essence of both poetry and theatre. A variable focus is provided into the artist's dual identity—poet and playwright.

A. ROMANTICISM AND THE THEATRE

An examination of the French romantic theatre is

complicated by the character of its practitioners and its own noisy publicity. The novelty and the revolutionary aspects of romanticism are expressed in the genre most fully defined by classical criticism, most obviously and insistently before the public's eyes. The history of romanticism is punctuated with important dates related to the theatre: Constant's version of *Wallenstein* (1809), Stendhal's *Racine et Shakespeare* (1823), the visit of the Kemble-Smithson troupe (1827), Hugo's Preface to *Cromwell* (1827), Dumas' *Henri III et sa cour* (1829), Vigny's version of *Othello* (1829), and the *bataille d'Hernani* (1830). In their quarrel with the classics, the romantics unleashed their loudest voice in the theatre. The novel and lyric poetry are of course genres exploited during the period, but they did not offer the same opportunity for direct confrontation of the old manner. Any controversy aroused by the publication of a *recueil* or a *roman noir* is paled by the shouting matches attendant upon a controversial première.

The unities and the notion of *bienséance* continue to rule dramaturgy at the beginning of the nineteenth century. In 1809 Benjamin Constant succinctly characterized the kind of stylistic rigor that seemed to be essential to French dramatic art. "We have a need for unity which makes us reject all which, in the personality of our tragic characters, mitigates the single impression we wish to produce. We eliminate everything from the previous life of our heroes which is not absolutely related to the principal action."[1] The taste for French classical theatre, this "need for unity," was consistently challenged by the cult of Shakespeare, the

[1] Benjamin Constant, "De la Guerre de Trente Ans, de la tragédie de 'Wallstein,' par Schiller, et du théâtre allemand," *Oeuvres*, Bibliothèque de la Pléiade (Paris, 1957), pp. 901-902.

most dangerous representative of the romantic manner. It is hardly necessary here to reitcrate the story of Shakespeare's reputation in France, the bastardized versions, the fiasco of Penley's troupe in 1822, the furor over mention of the *mouchoir* in Vigny's *Le More de Venise*.[2] For the romantics, Shakespeare is the prime example of mixed form and tone. Vigny, too seldom credited with his initiatory role in the history of romanticism, projected the scope of such a mixture: "a modern tragedy suggesting in its conception, a wide panorama of life instead of a narrow rendering of the plot's catastrophe; in its composition, characters, not roles, peaceful scenes with peripeties, mixed with comic and tragic scenes; in its execution, a style that is familiar, comic, tragic, and sometimes epic."[3] In a similar vein, Stendhal and Hugo based their apologies on a sense of reality, and a corresponding flexibility of style which supposedly presented life in its roundness.

The polemic fire burns brightly, and its brilliance perhaps diverts the eye. The acclaimed precursors, Shakespeare, Schiller, Scott, and Byron, help us date French romanticism, provide useful models for particular scenes and characters, but are foreign to the true originality of French romantic theatre. The distance between art and propaganda is so great that the merits of the first suffer from the bombast of the second. In their unceasing efforts to score obvious distinctions the playwright-theoreticians barely analyze the works them-

[2] Maurice Descotes, in *Le Drame romantique et ses grands créateurs* (Paris, 1955), evokes the theatrical world in the heyday of *le drame romantique*. There is a succinct discussion of these first years and the influence of the English troupes, pp. 36-43.

[3] Alfred de Vigny, "Lettre à Lord *** sur la soirée du 24 octobre 1829 et sur un système dramatique," *Oeuvres complètes*, Bibliothèque de la Pléiade (Paris, 1950), i, 280.

selves. Hugo, in particular, falls victim to a fuzziness of definition which can be ascribed to excessive enthusiasm. "Lyric poetry is especially suited to drama. Without impeding, it follows all its caprices, manifests itself in all of its forms, at turns sublime as Ariel and grotesque as Caliban. Our epoch, dramatic above all, is for just that reason eminently lyric." (Préface de *Cromwell*, i, 424)[4] Where is poor Miranda? Her ecstatic reaction to nature seems just as appropriate to Hugolian lyricism as the fantasy of Ariel or the grotesquerie of Caliban. Herein lies the difficulty which inhibits an accurate reading of romantic theatre. *Hernani's* battle was to rage over the wrong issues.

B.   HYBRIDIZATION IN ART:
ROMANTIC THEATRE AND OPERA

The problems of a poetic theatre are double because of its double allegiance. Lyric poetry and theatre are to some extent mutually exclusive. The solitude of the first is at odds with the dialectic of the second; timelessness is compromised by the proscenium and the audience. Unlike the classical theatre, whose poetry is fundamentally theatrical, the romantic theatre, with typical bravado, introduces its lyricism into an apparently inimical genre. The solutions it finds represent a certain faith in art's flexibility, an attempt to realize poetic conceits in a theatrical context. Attention to this has been scant. Critics have been distracted by the purely historical importance of the genre, and possibly discouraged because of the intermittent favor the ro-

---

[4] The extracts cited from Hugo's works, unless otherwise indicated, are drawn from the edition of his *Théâtre complet* published by the Bibliothèque de la Pléiade, 2 vols. (Paris, 1963-64). Prose passages will contain the page reference. Poetry will be indicated by verse numbers.

mantics have enjoyed with the theatre-going public. That other barometer of approval, the literature course, has also been unsympathetic. Even the token deference to the exemplary *Hernani* is often replaced by the date of the "*bataille.*" Musset has fared better, but only because one can pretend his plays are not really theatrical. Taste has been unkind to this extroverted manifestation of romanticism. Readers who savor lyric poetry do not necessarily appreciate its translation into gesture, décor, and character.

The only form of romantic theatre which has survived on the stage is opera. The public still goes to the opera to achieve that wordless transport effected through song. Absurdities of plot and character, incongruence between face, physique and identity are forgotten because a singer makes beautiful sounds. It becomes vitally important that a gypsy hag mistakenly threw her son into the fire while her mother was being burned at the stake; it seems appropriate that advanced tuberculosis has not impaired the strength of a character's lungs or that a shapely soprano impersonates an adolescent boy. All of these improbabilities contribute to the degree of stylization in opera. Disbelief is suspended because it cannot for an instant be engaged. As soon as characters sing rather than speak a vital pact has been made between the public and art, one which gives the creator license to violate the common notions of time and substitute a universe where characters address each other in extremes of pitch quite unlike those of normal speech. This new modality lightens the gypsy hag's burden of absurdity. The tone of her passion and torment are self-sufficient and transcend her caricatural being. The soprano bares the soul of the adolescent boy more accurately than he could himself. The death of the tubercular victim is granted a span appropriate to art, not medicine. Music is the principal factor in the metaphorical structure of an opera. Obviously, it can never be ignored. In opera, the combination of its essential character and its conventions extends the time of the lyric without compromising its power of transport.

Opera is an analogy useful for gaining insight into romantic theatre. It is a mixed genre; its center is lyric. The French call it *théâtre lyrique*. The perception of song governs the theatrical expectations of its public. These characteristics are shared by some examples of the *drame romantique*.[5] Their lyric qualities are cited even by adverse critics.[6] They grudgingly grant it poetic value even if it fails as theatre. A strictly theatrical

[5] Opera composers were quick to see the appropriateness of the *drame romantique* as a source of libretti. From Hugo alone Verdi drew *Ernani* (*Hernani*) and *Rigoletto* (*Le Roi s'amuse*), Donizetti turned *Lucrèce Borgia* into *Lucrezia Borgia* (and was sued by Hugo), and Ponchielli managed to fashion *La Gioconda* out of *Angélo, tyran de Padoue*. The list is far from complete.

[6] A propos of *Marion de Lorme* F.W.M. Draper asserts that "the language of the play makes a favorable impression on the reader and perhaps blinds him to the fact that the lyric treatment of the subject is developed at the expense of its dramatic effectiveness." *The Rise and Fall of the French Romantic Drama, with special reference to the influence of Shakespeare, Scott and Byron* (New York, n.d.), p. 180. Zola, in "Nos Auteurs dramatiques," *Oeuvres complètes*, édition établie sous la direction de Henri Mitterand, Club du Livre Précieux (Paris, 1968), xi, 559-822, opposes his own naturalistic theatre to the lyricism of the romantics. ". . . the poet's dramas are very bad theatre draped in very beautiful poetry." p. 589. "Lyricism on the stage, beyond everything, beyond truth and good sense, lifts the public aloft. It is enchanted out of the mundane, it applauds with transport." p. 595. Pierre Nebout, in *Le Drame romantique* (Paris, 1895), p. 267, adds a slight nuance to his reproach. "Romantic drama has often been challenged for its lyricism. It would be more accurate to say that romantic theatre is not precisely faulty for being lyric, but for being too lyric, and essentially lyric."

8

definition of the *drame romantique* seems inappropriate however in light of its hybrid nature. Is it not possible to redesign the framework of a play in order to accommodate the voice of the lyric poet?

The reaction of Francisque Sarcey to Sarah Bernhardt's performance of the Queen in *Ruy Blas* indicates the kind of impression romantic theatre was capable of making. "That delectable cantilena was breathed forth in a sad voice by Mlle. Sarah Bernhardt. She did not seek nuance; it was a long caress of sounds which had in its very monotony something sweet and penetrating. She only added the music of her voice to the music of the poetry."[7] These effusions hardly explain or justify that "something sweet and penetrating." The reasons for the relish felt by Sarcey are not however impervious to analysis. They are located in his inarticulated perception of poetry and theatre. This mixture of genres presents an intriguing challenge to the poet, an opportunity to test the resonance of his song and to examine dramatically his urge to sing.

Hugo and Musset are poets who write plays and novels reflective of poetic movement. It is absurd to expect Hugo to write a play structured like *Phèdre* or to conceive of character as Shakespeare does in *Hamlet*. He searches for harmony and metaphor rather than the measure of the five-act classical tragedy and the imitation of psychological complexity. Hugo's novels bear witness to the same concern for pattern, vibrant antithesis, and integrity of image that we find in his theatre. *Notre-Dame de Paris* is an ingenious amplification of object through a series of metaphorical extensions. Plot and character, the usual coin of the novelist, are con-

---

[7] Francisque Sarcey, *Quarante ans de théâtre* (Paris, 1907), IV, 54.

sumed by the organic image of the cathedral. The grossness of characterization and the mechanics of coincidence are designed to put *Notre-Dame de Paris* in a variety of foci. The development of Esmeralda, Quasimodo, or Claude Frollo beyond their emblematic configurations would be a violation of the novelist's pattern. In the same way, a more subtle definition of character or a less florid rhetoric would mitigate the resonance of *Hernani*. Hugo's principal consideration is always the fullness of image and song.[8]

Musset's theatre has other claims, yet it too is governed by poetic concerns. His most important plays are written in prose, but this does not prevent them from manifesting his serious interest in poetic style, inspiration, perception, and harmonics. Musset's theatrical voice does not quite have the volume and range of Hugo's, but it sets off bittersweet echoes of Lucie and la Malibran. Obsessed with the character and tone of verse, he allegorizes people in a manneristic theatrical dialectic.

The three major genres tempt Hugo and Musset, and their readiness to write novels, plays, and poems betrays a romantic attitude. The desire to combine contrasting moods and various levels of diction within a single work is symptomatic of a freely manipulated formal spectrum. Musset writes *Contes d'Espagne et d'Italie*, consisting of short stories and dramatic pieces in verse. Versatility and generic hybridization tend to make clear-cut distinctions arbitrary and of relatively limited use. Is *Don Paez* a poem, a play, or a short story? It is all three at

[8] Jean Gaudon, in *Victor Hugo, dramaturge* (Paris, 1955), noting the absence of a Corneillian or Racinian treatment of character in Hugo's theatre, points instead to "That marvellous integrity of the Hugolian hero." p. 73.

once. The pictorial qualities of Hugo's poetry are obvious, his sense of the dramatic is conveyed by the overriding antithetical structure present in whatever genre he uses, his narrative technique is displayed as early as the *Odes et Ballades* (1826). Therefore the concept of poetry must be taken in its broadest sense in order to accommodate these particular poets. In their avidity to explore the various dimensions of art they project their imagination into formal combinations that wrench poetry from its immediately recognizable contexts. In both Hugo and Musset there appears a basically poetic consciousness which shapes ballads and *drames*.

At the risk of simplistic definition we must attempt to locate the matrices of this poetic consciousness, to discover why a poem is essentially different from a play, beyond distinctions of rhyme, meter, and form. It will be useful to sketch the nature of three overlapping categories: time, voice, and metaphor. I will first signal those characteristics of romantic lyric poetry which facilitate an understanding of the theatre of Hugo and Musset, in the hope that this review will furnish a framework for the subsequent textual analyses. Consideration of the epic will be postponed until the discussion of *Les Burgraves*. The purely lyric qualities of poetry seem to be a functional point of departure, since they bring us closest to the most singular attitudes of these poets.

C. LYRIC TIME

The time of the theatre is fundamentally existential, the time of moments which in their passage govern the rhythm of the play. Theoretically, there is no going back and no stopping. To elicit attention and concentration the playwright may exploit this anguishing inexorability of movement, and the spectator's virtual captivity. There is no place to go and nothing else to listen to. The classical theatre insisted upon the perception of chronological time. The *unité de temps* is derived from the shape of a day. This shape may be more or less apparent, but its finiteness is exposed in plays whose rhythms differ as much as *Bérénice* and *Phèdre*. Five acts and a dénouement are elements that impose time upon a play. Even plays that openly flaunt the rule of unity are trapped by their mode of presentation. Nothing can really alter the fact that actors answer each other sequentially, that the sequence is linear, and that in two or three hours the public will have seen and heard the whole play. This texture of time spent is not appreciably transformed by devices such as flashback, or the rapid episodic passage of years. The medium of the actor stamps a play with lived time. Encounter and conflict are punctuated by varying temporal spans whose tracings are immediately distinguished by the spectator. Patterns of character and incident are underlined by conventions of coincidence, the *coup de théâtre*, the scene of recognition. The theatre's clock can be accelerated, slowed, and syncopated, but its tick is basically unrelenting.

Poetry can achieve what is impossible in the theatre: it can abolish time. All art effectively does so in that it provides a repeatable experience. A play can be reseen, a novel reread. In fact, the author's decision to write a play is a gesture against time even if that very time is a mandatory element of his genre. Among literary genres only the poem, and more precisely the lyric poem, can actually give a single perception of timelessness, a moment that stops in its tracks and contains an immutable impression which profits from reiteration. This is perhaps its major goal. The following lyric of Hugo illustrates the poet's unique command over time.

MES DEUX FILLES

Dans le frais clair-obscur du soir charmant qui tombe,
L'une pareille au cygne et l'autre à la colombe,
Belles, et toutes deux joyeuses, ô douceur!
Voyez, la grande soeur et la petite soeur
Sont assises au seuil du jardin, et sur elles
Un bouquet d'oeillets blancs aux longues tiges frêles,
Dans une urne de marbre agité par le vent,
Se penche, et les regarde, immobile et vivant,
Et frissonne dans l'ombre, et semble, au bord du vase,
Un vol de papillons arrêté dans l'extase.

(Les Contemplations)

MY TWO DAUGHTERS

In the cool chiaroscuro of the enchanting nightfall, one like the swan and the other like the dove, beautiful, and both joyful, oh sweetness! Behold, the older sister and the younger sister are seated on the threshold of the garden, and upon them, a bouquet of long-stemmed, white sweet williams shaken by the wind, in a marble urn, immobile and living, leans over and gazes upon them, and shivers in the darkness, and seems, on the brim of the vase, a flight of butterflies stopped short in ecstasy.

The element of time is loudly signaled by the poet. Firmly anchored in the day, it is the time of an instant preserved. The gestures are frozen in immobility, suggested by the two seated girls. The flowers moving in the wind are first qualified by the stationary marble urn and then the living, vibrant stasis of butterflies in flight.

13

This is the time basic to lyric poetry, the eternalization of an epiphany-like impression, an invitation to partake in the wonder now, in its totality. Nothing need happen in a poem. The reader's participation is gauged by the patently false time which is the rhythm of verse, removing the slightest confusion between it and existential time. The magic of the impression is inherently opposed to the logic of chronology, thus relieving both poet and reader from the force of its grip. Even the formality of the poem's time conspires to transport. The lyric élan exploits the possibilities of simultaneity, the merging of various strands in an infinitely expandable instant. Art always transports to an altered temporal sphere. In the theatre this may become the eternal day of the tragic hero. The transport of lyric poetry surpasses reality's essential pattern of time. As the glance repeats and penetrates the landscape without disturbing its stability, the reader makes sense out of two girls forever seated beneath a marble urn filled with flowers.

D. THE LYRIC VOICE

Unless the dramatist presents himself incarnated in a character, and therefore played not by himself but by an actor, his voice is absent. This is perhaps an absurd reduction to the obvious, for in a sense the only voice one ever hears is that of the playwright; but its absurdity does not alter the quality of the impression made upon the public. One consistently feels the presence of people other than the creative artist. There is a transfer of voice whose completeness depends on the intention of the author and perhaps the technique of the actor. There will be cases where the characters seem to disappear as entities and are palpably inhabited by their creator, but these are rare, and as we

will demonstrate, are indicative of structures contrary
to the theatrical tradition. The fragmentation that is a
play usually stills the single voice of the dramatist,
breaks it up into a progressive dialectic, renders an
imitation of people talking in a definable time context.

The poet's voice is of course related to the poet's time.
Its cadence is regulated by the integral structure created
in the poem, removed from the contiguity of ungov-
ernable and exterior rhythms, safely locked in an auto-
generated system. Here, the surface of the poem is no
longer a convention but a tangible manifestation of a
separate linguistic phenomenon. The poet encloses himself in a space completely filled by the sound of his own
voice. There is nothing else. He expects no answer since
the plenitude of his utterance leaves room for none.
The resonance of his self instantly transforms all the
matter of his perception, appropriates it in an oral
arrangement, imposes on it an unadulterated audible
imprint. The lyric poet is permitted this because time
and space are contained in the rhythm and tone of his
voice. There is no need for exteriorization and for the
surrogates that people a stage. The success of a poem
often hinges upon the immediacy of its voicing, the
rapidity with which its elements are juxtaposed so as
to convey the composite instant upon the reader-lis-
tener. *Mes deux filles* has a sound of wonder, is animated
by the enormous sigh of Hugo's voice which takes in the
impression's complexity. In the texture of this poem the
common rhetorical invitation "voyez" effectively sounds
the call to vision.

The syntax of the poem reinforces its power of com-
pression. It is really one sentence. The exclamation
point after "ô douceur" signals an affective interjection
that does not interrupt the single breath. The phrase

15

is spun out, and through its disproportion to the shape of normal, apoetical assertions puts into tension the poem's shortness. The resulting ambivalence, the great length of the sentence coincidental with the brevity of the completed form, distorts the precise measure of the poem's time and sustains the poet's voice in an infinity of ten lines. This example is particularly vivid, but similar effects are created in markedly different poems. The lilt of rhyme and rhythm can produce the same transport, effecting a suspension in the new and total universe of poetry. The voice substitutes a realm where traditional avenues of communication are useless. The poet need not concern himself with logic or persuasion, but rather devote his being to the transportive power of his incantation. Thus, he sings himself out of time and provides escape and vision for all who listen.

E. THE METAPHOR AND THE LYRIC

A metaphor remains a metaphor whether it is found in a poem or a play. The distinguishing factor is its frequency. It is rare for an artist to do without metaphor, from the most common figures of speech to the most personal and hermetic symbology. Yet normally there are categories of choice and appropriateness in the various genres.

In a play, metaphor functions on two perceptible levels. The more obvious is the area of exchange between characters, the means they use for communication. Depending on the degree of stylization, the characters' speech resembles the speech of men, and will contain metaphorical figures in roughly the same proportion. Even plays written in verse do not by definition present characters who predominantly speak in metaphors. On the other hand, the playwright, through certain patterns of reference in dialogue, may wish to make apparent a metaphorical movement. This does not however impose upon the exchanges an exclusively metaphorical cast. These patterns comprise the second and more important level of metaphor in the theatre. It is that area unaffected by the action involving characters in verbal conflict or complement, such as the historical and mythological bases of *Andromaque* and *Phèdre*. It would be incorrect to interpret these plays from any single angle of abstraction and thus deny the characters their integrity. Only morality plays and similar allegories are intended to be viewed in this manner. Most plays freely mix the two levels of metaphor, and even offer the spectator the choice of disregarding the second. It is difficult but possible to see *Phèdre* exclusively as an odd dramatic quadrangle. It remains a play even if the mythical and purely thematic material is ignored.

Metaphor is the very fabric of lyric poetry. The compactness of its time and voice are guaranteed by the mode of metaphorical change, the stamp of poetic authority, the ability to transform objects at will. Here the poet expresses his greatest power, focusing upon the mechanics of creation. In poetry the metaphor transcends rhetoric. A poem like *Mes deux filles* clearly demonstrates the priority of metaphor in Hugo's imagination. He equalizes the two main factors of the poem, the girls and "un bouquet d'oeillets blancs," placing them in a tension so strong that it produces something else altogether. Initiating the metaphorical movement by comparing the sisters to birds, he continues the sequence of metamorphoses to merge the bird-like creatures and living, vibrating flowers in a

17

miraculous anomaly, the frozen flight of butterflies. The linkages are infinite and include the poet himself in the poem's final word, "l'extase." He has celebrated his own ecstasy, a state produced by his metaphorical power. Given the strategic position of the butterflies, there is no doubt about the hierarchy of interest. The objects are only meaningful in their combination and rebirth. The swiftness of change once again affirms the time and voice of lyric poetry in the immediacy of an image. Metamorphosis is perhaps the clearest model of transport, for that is exactly what it demonstrates.[9] Here transport is not the result but the movement itself. The poet adds girls and flowers, and suddenly existence is fixed in the eternal perception of butterflies' flight. The reader relates to this pattern, partakes of the new rhythm. He is sung out of reality.

F. OMISSIONS AND DIRECTIONS

The plays chosen for study here are not meant to represent the history of French romantic theatre. They are pertinent to an understanding of the poet's adventure on the stage but do not primarily illustrate

[9] The first stanza of "Dicté en présence du glacier du Rhône" (*Les Feuilles d'automne*) contains a remarkably explicit description of this process.

> Souvent, quand mon esprit riche en métamorphoses
> Flotte et roule endormi sur l'océan des choses,
> Dieu, foyer du vrai jour qui ne luit point aux yeux,
> Mystérieux soleil dont l'âme est embrasée,
> Le frappe d'un rayon, et, comme une rosée,
>   Le ramasse et l'enlève aux cieux.

> *Often, when my spirit rich in metamorphoses floats and rolls asleep upon the ocean of things, God, abode of that true light which does not shine for the eyes, mysterious sun which sets the soul ablaze, strikes it with a ray, and, like the dew, picks it up and carries it off to heaven.*

trends or developments in the genre. The omissions include plays worthy of serious consideration were one to treat the complexity of the genre and epoch. The historical significance of Alexandre Dumas is well-known. His sure intuition of stagecraft is proof of theatrical expertise, and *Antony* is a remarkable demonstration of the *coup de théâtre*. An arsenal of coincidences, gestures, and encounters, tonally intensified by their rapidity and the enormity of their dimensions, the play faithfully portrays aspects of the romantic sense of passion and doom. An even more regrettable omission is Vigny's *Chatterton* with its silent love scenes and its original theatrical metaphor, Kitty Bell's *dégringolade*. Despite its poet-hero, it does not qualify linguistically or structurally as an exercise in poetic theatre. Vigny addresses himself to the poet's relationship to society, a familiar romantic theme which receives an ingenious but fundamentally prosaic treatment in *Chatterton*. *Ruy Blas* is absent, and this is perhaps surprising given Hugo's importance in this inquiry. One can even argue that *Ruy Blas* is Hugo's most thoroughly realized play. It is certainly more faithful than the others to the author's published aesthetics. The play displays some of the elements which make Hugo's theatre poetic, yet less forcefully than *Hernani*. In *Ruy Blas* the playwright seems to take precedence over the poet. Despite its excellence the play lacks Hugo's initial fervor and the excitement of his subsequent theatrical experiments. In Musset's *oeuvre* I have not slighted major plays, but the bulk of charming theatrical *proverbes* which keep him consistently in the standard French repertoire. *L'Âne et le ruisseau*, *Il ne faut jurer de rien*, *Le Chandelier*, and *Carmosine* are only a few of the titles that represent Musset's substantial output, and whose apparent frivolity does not reflect pejoratively upon the quality of the dramatist's talent. These plays do betray, however, a shift in his interest. The singular concentration on poetic attitudes disappears after *Lorenzaccio* and *On ne badine pas avec l'amour*. I therefore limit the analysis principally to plays written in 1833-1834, the period in which Musset's theatre focuses obsessively on the mechanics of poetic inspiration and expression.

Hugo will be discussed first. Aside from his chronological priority, he manifests with particular clarity the qualities of the poetic imagination, from the lyric to the epic, that characterize the best examples of French romantic theatre.

two

THE TIME OF THE LYRIC:
Hernani

THE opening night of *Hernani*, February 25, 1830, is the most famous date of French romanticism. Théophile Gautier's *gilet rouge*, an *enjambement* from the first line to the second, and a trimeter, securely locate its place in the history of literature. This is precisely what Hugo intended in his eagerness to promote the literary cause he had so verbosely championed in *Cromwell* and its preface three years previously. The plays of his youth[1] are followed by the unstageable *Cromwell* (1827), the fiasco of *Amy Robsart* (1828), and the censured *Marion de Lorme* (1829). *Hernani* finally gives Hugo his anticipated *succès de scandale*. It follows the furor created by Dumas' *Henri III et sa cour* and Vigny's *Le More de Venise*. But if the swordplay, the booming canon, the tomb of Charlemagne, and the bandit's horn contributed to the event's panache, then as today, they obscured the essential qualities of the play. An incredible plot,[2] absurd coincidences, and

[1] *Irtamène* (1816), the uncompleted *Athélie ou les Scandinaves* (1816?), *A.Q.C.H.E.B.* (1817-18) and *Iñez de Castro* (1818-20?).

[2] Brief plot synopses will be provided for all the plays which are

preposterous characters, tend to obscure the fact that *Hernani* is part of a poet's consciousness.

The shape of *Hernani* reveals Hugo's lyric élan. Each of the first three acts contains an extended love duet for Hernani and Doña Sol. Act IV appears to break the pattern, but it too, as I shall demonstrate, contributes to the play's coherence. Act V is a reprise of the first three, completing a theatrical poem whose parameters are projected in Act I and consistently carried through to the climax. The characters, ungoverned by traditional norms of psychological development, reflect this lyricism. The lovers do not evolve towards self-understanding. Their progression is not analogous to the logic of classical tragedy. The *péripéties* of the plot contribute superficial surprise which leaves intact the essential and fixed pattern of relationships between the characters. This pattern is created by the imposition of lyric values on the theatrical genre. The distinctions made in the introductory chapter between the voice, the temporal movement, and the metaphorical structure peculiar to lyric poetry are of course arbitrary since they are part of the same inspiration. Yet their enunciation in regard to *Hernani* will perhaps return the tomb, the picture gallery, and the horn to the poet, and in the process, reveal the play's unity.

A. Perception of the Voice

The play's first scene, an encounter between Doña Josefa and Don Carlos, is meant to be funny. Much has been made of the presence of comic elements in roman-

---

extensively discussed. In order to avoid disproportionate interruptions in the analyses, these synopses will be found in an appendix.

tic theatre, a presence that Hugo himself, in the frequently quoted Preface to *Cromwell*, makes a requirement for the new kind of play.

> What would romantic drama achieve? It would compress and artistically mix these two kinds of pleasure. From one moment to the next it would make the public go from the serious to laughter, from paroxysms of mirth to heart-rending emotions, from the grave to the sweet, from the pleasant to the severe. As we have already established, drama is the grotesque with the sublime, the soul inside the body, tragedy inside comedy. Alternating one impression with another, at turns sharpening the tragic on the comic, the cheerful on the terrible, if need be even employing the fascinations of opera, it is apparent that these spectacles, while constituting only one play, would be worth many. (I, 450)

The ambitions outlined here are high, and they will remain largely unrealized. *Cromwell* attempts to illustrate the theory: politics and plottings are animated by an ugly duenna, an inept young poet, and an array of clowns. But *Cromwell* must be disqualified from consideration as a functioning *drame romantique* because of its dimensions. While *Hernani* fleetingly manifests the comic-serious polarity, it hardly reflects the tonal mixture Hugo advocates for the new theatre.[3] The only intentionally comic moments are found in the by-play between Josefa and the swaggering Carlos. These are set to the chopped up alexandrines that Hugo uses to stress rapidity of movement.

---

[3] The most successful example of a comic element in a serious play by Hugo is the character of Don César de Bazin in *Ruy Blas*.

DoÑA JOSEFA.
    Qui.
DON CARLOS.
       Cache-moi céans.
DoÑA JOSEFA.
               Vous!
DON CARLOS.
                   Moi.
DoÑA JOSEFA.
                    Pourquoi?
DON CARLOS.
                       Pour rien.
                          I.i.18

This pattern of quick ripostes dominates the first scene. It functions as a verbal and temporal transition to the second. The rushing about of Josefa and Carlos is temporarily resolved in the stasis of Hernani and Doña Sol. At the end of the first love duet, another few moments of farce recall the opening tempo. The lyric transport of Hernani and Doña Sol is interrupted by Don Carlos' precipitous exit from the already much-exploited closet, and this eruption sets off a chain reaction of half-verses which suggest a parody of time accelerated. Paradoxically, the comic speed is sluggish and earthbound compared to the expansion of lyric time. However it does serve as a spur which gives the spectator a heightened consciousness of the true center of interest. Thus, if Hugo abandons the lyric flight of the protagonists it is only to send them winging anew. The pertinent clocks in *Hernani* are lyric ones. The hour of songs engulfs the hours of forced doors and quick entries.

Hernani and Doña Sol carefully define this hour of songs, and appropriate it as their destiny. "Pourquoi le sort mit-il mes jours si loin des vôtres?/ J'ai tant besoin de vous pour oublier les autres!" *Why has destiny riven my days from yours? I need you to forget my intolerable life!* (I.ii.39-40) Through Doña Sol, Hernani seeks a transport out of the banality of chronological time. One aspect of the play's movement will be the abolition of the intolerable days without her through the substitution of a never-ending song and its promise of oblivion. It is Doña Sol who marks the beginning of this unique lyric span

DOÑA SOL.   Oui, cette heure est à nous.
HERNANI.   Cette heure! et voilà tout. Pour nous, plus
    rien qu'une heure!
    Après, qu'importe? Il faut qu'on oublie ou qu'on
    meure.
    Ange! une heure avec vous! une heure, en vérité,
    À qui voudrait la vie, et puis l'éternité! (I.ii.58-62)

DOÑA SOL.   *Yes, this hour is ours.*
HERNANI.   *This hour, and that is enough. For us,*
nothing more than an hour! Afterwards, what matters? To forget or to die. Angel, an hour with you,
only an hour, for him who wants a life of it, and
then eternity!

The words that follow "voilà tout" constitute an emphatic recapitulation of "cette heure," time that is theirs alone. The significant value of time is distorted, stretched through repetition; the hour is merely a pretext to sing about timelessness. In Act II, Hernani adds physical stasis to temporal stasis.

HERNANI, *revenant sur ses pas.*
    Eh bien, non! non, je reste,
    Tu le veux, me voici. Viens, oh! viens dans mes bras!
    Je reste, et resterai tant que tu le voudras.
    Oublions-les! restons.   (II.iv.682-85)

62483

LIBRARY
College of St. Francis
JOLIET, ILL.

HERNANI, turning back. *Ah, no, no, I'll stay, if you wish it, I am yours. Come, oh come into my arms! I'll stay, and I shall stay as long as you wish it. Let us forget the others, let us stay.*

In Act I Doña Sol's presence stops time; here it stops motion. But there is no real distinction between the two. Time and motion are aspects of the same phenomenon, as they are integrated into the protagonists' lyric identities. In both passages Hernani is evoking eternity, the time of lyricism.

The lovers strive for a reappraisal of time's value, or more accurately, a new arrangement of time concordant to their state of transport.

DOÑA SOL.
                                        Écoutez.
Allez où vous voudrez, j'irai. Restez, partez,
Je suis à vous. Pourquoi fais-je ainsi? Je l'ignore.
J'ai besoin de vous voir et de vous voir encore
Et de vous voir toujours.   (I.ii.153-57)

DOÑA SOL. *Hear me. Go where you wish, I will follow. Stay, leave, I am yours. Why is it thus? I do not know. I must see you, and see you once more and see you forever.*

Doña Sol admits that she has abandoned all logic and capacity for conventional distinction. She is swept up by the presence of Hernani, and is able to forget time and place. This is expressed in the contiguity of "restez" and "partez." The only coherence is Hernani, amplified by "vous voir" three times. This sequence is not a normal progression of tenses, but rather the shape of time passing. Present, future, and eternity meld in this song, obliterating phenomenonological movement through time. The various states of "vous voir" are secondary to its repetition, a pattern that here demonstrates the concept of lyric time during its clear articulation. The repetition effectively neutralizes the logical time evolution from present to *toujours*. The song explains its own tempo—a lyric now and forever.

Hugo insistently makes apparent the beauty of the protagonists' voices. Their beings are their voices, their mutual presence is a guarantee of song, and each time they are together the play's tone increases in sonority. They are inspired to sing instead of speak, to use a mode of expression appropriate to their exultation at being united. Whenever they greet each other the key of the play changes. The language takes on a poetic tension quite different from what precedes, as exemplified in the transition between the play's first two scenes.[4] As soon as the protagonists appear on stage the audience expects to hear their song.

The quality of their voices is governed by readily discernible elements: strong rhythms, frequent interior rhyme, accentuated harmonics. They are united by the presence of sound, the fact that they hear each other's voices. This is an elementary but vital distinction between dramatic and non-dramatic lyricism. Hernani first identifies Doña Sol by the sound of her voice, a source of enchantment and song. "Doña Sol! Ah! c'est vous que je vois/ Enfin! et cette voix qui parle est votre voix!" *Doña Sol! Ah! It is you that I see at last, and this voice which speaks is your voice!* (I.ii. 37-38) These lines are intentionally simplistic. The words are merely an extension of the name, Doña Sol. She is identified by the pronoun *vous*, by the verb *vois*, and by the repeated

4 See above, p. 24.

noun *voix*. The conceptual link in the pattern of identification is reinforced by the rhyme. The initial consonance of the three factors, bolstered by the assonance
of *vois* and *voix* is of a sort frequent in Hugo's rhetoric.
Vois and *voix* are homonyms, but in this case the dis-
similarity of meaning is blurred. The rhyme, which produces coincidence in sonority, describes conceptual
coincidence as well. This is partly achieved by the
amplification and expansion of the rhyme within the
verse itself. One need not wait until the end of the
next line before encountering the echo of *vois*. It comes
at the first opportunity for traditional stress, at the
caesura, only to be taken up again on the final stress
of the line. The sound, echoed and reechoed, is a familiar device in Hugo's theatre. It creates harmony and
concentrates attention on the final element in the series.
Seeing and hearing Doña Sol become one phenomenon.
The rhyme partially obliterates the distinction between
the two senses, and gives the dominant position to the
aural impression. Doña Sol is light and song throughout
the play, but the light she represents is in turn rendered
by her voice, her song. Her identity is a lyric one.

The dramatist's problem in this play is to convince the
audience that the characters are singing. The rich harmonics of Hugo's verse help create this impression. Harmonics however are not necessarily theatrical, and it is
a mark of Hugo's dramatic talent that he finds the means
to put the lyric voice into discernible relief. The love
duets are nuanced by shifts of tone and changes of diction. If Doña Sol and Hernani both have a talent for
song, they are not always prepared to exhibit it at the
same time. The lovers learn the songs from each other, a
process that provides an element of movement in their
essentially static relationship. They remind each other

of the characteristics of their song. Their own lyric consciousness makes the audience aware of their singing.

DOÑA SOL, *touchant ses vêtements.*
    Jésus! votre manteau ruisselle! Il pleut donc bien?
HERNANI.
    Je ne sais.
DOÑA SOL.
              Vous devez avoir froid!
HERNANI.
                              Ce n'est rien.
DOÑA SOL.
    Ôtez donc ce manteau.
HERNANI.
        Doña Sol, mon amie,
    Dites-moi, quand la nuit vous êtes endormi,
    Calme, innocente et pure, et qu'un sommeil joyeux
    Entr'ouvre votre bouche et du doigt clôt vos yeux,
    Un ange vous dit-il combien vous êtes douce
    Au malheureux que tout abandonne et repousse?
                              (I.ii.41-48)

DOÑA SOL, touching his clothing.
    Heavens! Your cloak is drenched! Is it raining so
    hard?
HERNANI.
    I do not know.
DOÑA SOL.
    You must be cold!
HERNANI.
    It is nothing.
DOÑA SOL.
    Take off this cloak.
HERNANI.
    Doña Sol, my beloved, tell me, when at night

29

> *you sleep, peaceful, innocent and pure, and a*
> *pleasant slumber half parts your lips, and with its*
> *finger shuts your eyes, does an angel tell you how*
> *sweet you are to this unfortunate being, abandoned*
> *and rejected by all?*

Her banal concern for physical well-being is countered by his plea for transport and detachment from time and place. He is oblivious to cold and rain, she repeatedly refers to them. This antithetical pattern describes a poetic distance between the lovers at the beginning of this scene. Hugo gradually brings Doña Sol into verbal proximity with the hero, extending Hernani's unchanging state of rapture through the time necessary to achieve a harmony of perception. The timelessness of the lyric mode is integrated into the time of the stage by the presence of a contrasting voice. In this exchange the lovers do not yet hear each other's words. They achieve consonance as their voices and responses become more and more alike. Movement is expressed through sound.

A development of this technique is found in the cadence which signals the end of the love duet in Act II. Hernani has just evoked the magic power of Doña Sol's voice. "Oh! laisse-moi dormir et rêver sur ton sein,/ Doña Sol! mon amour! ma beauté!" *Oh, let me sleep and dream upon your breast, Doña Sol, my beloved, my beauty!* (II.iv.695-96) At this point Doña Sol interrupts the song with her cry, "Le tocsin!/ Entends-tu? le tocsin!" *The alarm bell! Do you hear the alarm bell?* (II.iv.-696-97) The sound of the alarm seems to be a facile effect, consistent with Hugo's bent for melodrama and violent contrast. In fact, this *coup de théâtre* is not the end of the lyric exchange but a new rhetorical pivot.

The poet Hernani transforms the foreign element, a potential barrier to his quest for transport, and succeeds in making it an integral factor in that very transport. He does not hear alarm bells, but wedding bells, an additional aural element which sustains their song. "Eh non! c'est notre noce/ Qu'on sonne." *Ah, no! Our wedding is being tolled.* (II.iv.697-98) The lovers develop the bell image together.

DOÑA SOL.
          Lève-toi! fuis! Grand Dieu! Saragosse
S'allume!
HERNANI, *se soulevant à demi.*
          Nous aurons une noce aux flambeaux!
DOÑA SOL.
C'est la noce des morts! la noce des tombeaux!
                       (II.iv.697-99)

DOÑA SOL. *Arise! Flee! Almighty God! Saragossa is alight!*
HERNANI, half rising. *We will have a torch-lit wedding!*
DOÑA SOL. *It is the wedding of the dead, the wedding of graves!*

Doña Sol finally participates in the song, and her version is the definitive one, the wedding in death that fully anticipates Act V.[5] This is another example of

[5] In *Les Travailleurs de la mer*, Édition Ollendorff (Paris, 1911), A, VII, 441, the wedding of Déruchette and Ebenezer is also given funereal characteristics. "Déruchette le matin en se levant, désespérée, pensant au cercueil et au suaire, s'était vêtue de blanc. Cette idée de deuil fut à propos pour la noce. La robe blanche fait tout de suite une fiancée. La tombe aussi est une fiançaille." (*Upon rising in the morning, Déruchette, desperate, thinking of the coffin and the shroud, dressed herself in white. This notion of mourning was appropriate for the wedding. The white dress immediately suggests a bride. The tomb*

dramatic lyricism in which an initial counterpoint is resolved in the harmony of two voices singing together.

By striving to join voices in unison Hugo radically alters orthodox theatrical dialectic. One character states a musical theme, the other sings its variations, embroiders it with elaborate fioritura, using it as a pretext to show off the beauty of his voice. The passage previously discussed in reference to the particular "heure"

---

also is a betrothal.) A closer approximation of the love-death imagery occurs in *Marion de Lorme*.

> DIDIER. Laisse-moi suivre seul ma sombre route; hélas!
> Après ce dur voyage, et quand je serai las,
> La couche qui m'attend, froide d'un froid de glace,
> Est étroite, et pour deux n'a pas assez de place.
> —Va-t'en!
> MARION. Didier, je veux dans l'ombre et sans témoins
> Partager avec vous . . . —oh! celle-là du moins! (III.vi)

DIDIER. *Let me follow my dark route alone, alas! After this hard voyage, and when I will be tired, the icy-cold bed which awaits me is narrow, and does not have room for two. Away!*
MARION. *Didier, in the darkness and without witnesses I wish to share with you, oh, at least that one!*

An interesting prose version of this death wish is found in Dumas' *Antony, Nineteenth Century French Plays*, edited by Joseph L. Borgerhoff (New York City, 1931), p. 178. The hero is consistently associated with death. In the play's final moments this is explicitly stated as a wedding in death. "Eh moi, aussi, je veux mourir! . . . mais avec toi; je veux que les derniers battements de nos coeurs se répondent, que nos derniers soupirs se confondent. . . . Comprends-tu? . . . une mort douce comme un sommeil, une mort plus heureuse que toute notre vie. . . . Puis, qui sait? par pitié, peut-être jettera-t-on nos corps dans le même tombeau." *And I too wish to die, but with you. I want our last heart beats to answer each other, our last sighs to meld. . . . You understand? . . . a death as sweet as sleep, a death happier than our whole life. . . . Then, who knows, perhaps in pity our bodies will be thrown into the same tomb.* (V.iii)

of Doña Sol and Hernani, is a useful example of the technique of musical restatement.[6]

DOÑA SOL.

> Oui, cette heure est à nous.

HERNANI.

> Cette heure! et voilà tout. Pour nous, plus rien
> qu'une heure!
> Après, qu'importe? il faut qu'on oublie ou qu'on
> meure.
> Ange! une heure avec vous! une heure, en vérité,
> À qui voudrait la vie et puis l'éternité! (I.ii.58-62)

(See p. 25)

The half line statement of the first voice is stretched into four lines by the second through repetition and interior rhyme. Hernani begins by echoing "cette heure." The "nous" of Doña Sol is taken up at the beginning of the second hemistich, and linked to "tout" and "pour" which give a particularly sonorous center of gravity to the line. The symmetry of Hernani's first alexandrine, shaped by *heure-tout-nous-heure*, exaggerates its musical quality and diminishes the significant value of the words. The effect is similar to that of a bel canto aria, where words function only as a point of departure and serve as an excuse for repetition and melody. Indeed, why bother to repeat the words in refrains, in reprises, in cadenzas, if not to distort or surpass their habitual connotation?[7] The value of "heure"

---

[6] See above, p. 25.

[7] Examples of this phenomenon in opera are infinite. In *Rigoletto*, the Duke and Gilda sing the word "Addio" eighteen times in a passage that lasts approximately one minute. Verdi is certainly not interested simply in reminding the public that the lovers are taking leave of each other. That fact is absurdly apparent. The composer uses the

is severely modified by its reiteration. Hugo places it in a pattern which exhibits the richness of the hero's voice and reinterprets the word's meaning according to the play's projection of timelessness. The same technique of embellishment is applied to the verbs *suivre*[8] and *rester.*[9] In all these cases the song is shared, the word is passed from one character to the other. Identities are blurred as the two voices unite.

Doña Sol.

Quand le bruit de vos pas
S'efface, alors je crois que mon coeur ne bat pas,
Vous me manquez, je suis absente de moi-même;
Mais, dès qu'enfin ce pas que j'attends et que j'aime
Vient frapper mon oreille, alors il me souvient
Que je vis, et je sens mon âme qui revient!
(I.ii.157-62)

Doña Sol. *When the sound of your footsteps grows dim, I feel that my heart beats no longer. When you are gone I am absent from myself. But as soon as the step I await and love sounds in my ear, then I remember that I am alive, and my soul returns to me!*

The concord of soul is demonstrated by the concord of voice, and both will be manifested in the play's climax.

Rhythm is a second element in awakening the audience's perception of voice. By establishing an individ-

---

repeated word to link them, to express their oneness, their excitement, their agitation, their joy at being together. The sense of "Addio" is effectively abolished by its incessant repetition.

[8] I.ii.124-25, 139, 146, 147, 165-66.

[9] II.iv.682-85.

ual pattern of beat Hugo further separates the sound of Hernani and Doña Sol from the conventional shape of the alexandrine and gives them a vocal personality. This occurs most noticeably in the Act II duet. Here the ternary figure gives their song an identifiable rhythm and is integrated into the definition of their character. Hernani initiates the beat with the simple repetition of a conjunction. "Car vous m'avez aimé! car vous me l'avez dit!/ Car vous avez tout bas béni mon front maudit!" *For you have loved me! For you have uttered it to me! For you have softly blessed my cursed brow!* (II.iv.663-64) Were it not for the subsequent development of the scene, this pattern would be unexceptional. A moment later Hernani transforms it into an aural event, the famous romantic trimeter that contributed to the play's notoriety. "Je suis banni! je suis proscrit! je suis funeste!" *I am banished! I am outlawed! I am deathlike!* (II.iv.681) Capitalizing on the triplet described by the "car" series, Hernani extends "maudit" into three distinct aspects of his identity. He wishes to denote lack of congruence with the established order. He is outside society and beyond the law.[10] But these first two modes of separateness and uniqueness are subordinate to the third factor, that state described by "funeste." Hernani is a stranger to life. His presence is fatal to others, and particularly to Doña Sol. It is a factor necessary to their ecstasy. The lovers isolate themselves from space, time, and life, they penetrate a

[10] The hero who is at odds with society is a constant in Hugo's imagination, appearing in the major novels: *Notre-Dame de Paris* (Quasimodo), *Les Misérables* (Jean Valjean), *Les Travailleurs de la mer* (Gilliatt), and the plays: *Marion de Lorme* (Didier), *Angélo, tyran de Padoue* (Rodolfo), *La Grand'mère* (Charles), *L'Épée* (Slagistri), *Mille francs de récompense* (Glapieu), *Mangeront-ils?* (Aïrolo).

35

realm where nothing matters but the purity of their song. This is established by the trimeter, a variation on the previously introduced ternary figure, and a rhythm relatively alien to the tradition. It jolts the listener, announcing the passage of Hernani and Doña Sol to their private sphere. A moment later the sense of the triplet reaches its fullest expression. "<u>Chante</u>-moi quelque <u>chant</u> comme parfois le soir/Tu m'en <u>chantais</u>, avec des pleurs dans ton oeil noir." *Sing me a <u>song</u> as in the evening you sometimes <u>sang</u> to me with tears in your dark eyes.* (II.iv.687-88) Hugo further varies the first ternary figure enunciated by "car," whose value has already been enhanced by the interceding trimeter. This final syncopation, where the organizing factor is redistributed through the lines, utilizes the established rhythm to sound the principal word, "chante," thus capping Hernani's *banni-proscrit-funeste* with an evocation of the beloved. Through a shared pattern of beat he succeeds in linking their two presences, uniting them in the all-encompassing song.

Hernani's bliss is effected by a love song, a hypnotic *cantilena*, defined in a reprise of the "heure" duet.

> HERNANI.
>> Soyons heureux! buvons, car la coupe est remplie,
>> Car cette heure est à nous, et le reste est folie.
>> Parle-moi, ravis-moi! N'est-ce pas qu'il est doux
>> D'aimer et de sentir qu'on vous aime à genoux?
>> D'être deux? d'être seuls? et que c'est douce chose
>> De se parler d'amour la nuit quand tout repose?
>> Oh! laisse-moi dormir et rêver sur ton sein,
>> Doña Sol! mon amour! ma beauté!   (II.iv.689-96)

> HERNANI. *Let us be happy! Let us drink, for the cup is full, for this moment is ours, and all else is*

madness. Speak to me, enrapture me! Is it not sweet to love and to know that you are adored? To be together, to be alone, and is it not sweet to speak of love at night when all is at rest? Oh, let me sleep and dream upon your breast, Doña Sol, my beloved, my beauty!

The apposition of "parle-moi, ravis-moi" puts into relief the transportive power of the word. The entire action of the play unfolds at night, that part of the day when time does not perceptibly pass and which suggests eternity and death.[11] The words of the night song are never heard distinctly. Murmured by Doña Sol they bring sleep and oblivion.

B. Metaphors of Love-Death

Hugo tends to reduce the area of the play's projection, concentrating it through the single focus of love-death. This theme is announced in Act I as the lovers evoke eternity. It is reiterated in their continuous song, and acted out in the play's final moments. The poet relates the play's principal elements to this center. Doña Sol's voice sings death to the hero; the voice of Hernani is a theatrical metaphor for death. His voice

[11] Young love and death are obsessively linked by Hugo throughout his career. The love scene between the arch-innocents, Marius and Cosette, takes place in a dark garden in which Marius has already appeared as a shadow. He seems as if inhabited by death. "Il avait, sous un voile d'incomparable douceur, quelque chose de la mort et de la nuit. Son visage était éclairé par la clarté du jour qui se meurt et par la pensée d'une âme qui s'en va." (*Beneath a veil of incomparable sweetness, he had something of death and the night. His face was illuminated by the light of a dying day and by the thought of a departing soul.*) *Les Misérables*, Bibliothèque de la Pléiade (Paris, 1951), p. 958.

is his horn, an image that clusters around it aspects of
banditry essential to the hero's identity.[12]

HERNANI.
                        Parmi mes rudes compagnons?
Proscrits dont le bourreau sait d'avance les noms,
Gens dont jamais le fer ni le coeur ne s'émousse,
Ayant tous quelque sang à venger qui les pousse?
Vous viendrez commander ma bande, comme on
    dit?
Car, vous ne savez pas, moi, je suis un bandit!
                                    (I.ii.125-30)

HERNANI. *Among my rough companions? Outlaws
whose names are already known by the executioner, men whose swords and courage are never
blunted, who all are spurred by some blood to
avenge? You would come to lead my band? For
you do not know. I am a bandit!*

The cliché bandit, an obsession Hugo shares with
other romantics such as Schiller, Byron, and Scott, is
amplified by the dramatic-poetic coherence of *Hernani*.
In addition to denoting the distance between the hero
and society at large, the outlaw figure suggests violence
and death. These are controlling factors in the love of
Hernani and Doña Sol. Their passion is fatal by definition, and such fatality is nourished by the echoes of
a bandit's life and death. It is fitting that Doña Sol
accept Hernani's invitation to command a band of men
whose names are already known to the executioner.
The hunted men in the mountains allow a sonorous
rendering of Hernani's identity.

[12] Michel Butor, in "Le Théâtre de Victor Hugo," *NRF* (Nov.
1964), 878, comments on the importance of the horn. "The sound
of the horn becomes his true name."

HERNANI.

Parmi ses montagnards, libres, pauvres, et graves,
Je grandis, et demain trois mille de ses braves,
Si ma voix dans leurs monts fait résonner ce cor,
Viendront . . .   (I.ii.135-38)

HERNANI. *I grew up among its free, poor, solemn*
mountaineers, and tomorrow, if my voice sounds
this horn in their mountains, three thousand of the
bravest will come . . .

The horn, Hernani's voice, is a constant symbol for the
hero. The most appropriate death for Hernani is one
announced by his own horn. The horn shall be detached from its standard linkage to banditry, and trans-
ferred to the particular cast of this hero's destiny. Hugo
changes the function of the object itself, a procedure
characteristic of his theatre. The horn is conventional
only in its first evocation, when the audience relates to
it banditry and mountains. Subsequently it is con-
fined to the play's organism, governed by its logic. The
image itself undergoes metamorphosis until its sense is
quite distant from its habitual connotation. The horn
we hear at the play's climax is one fashioned by five
acts of *Hernani* and its sound is different from that of
the Act I prototype.[13]

Hernani does not abandon the image of banditry.
Like so many other elements in the play, it is used as a
theme whose variations are more interesting, and even

[13] In *Amy Robsart* the sound of a horn is important to the melodramatic finale. In addition, the heroine nostalgically remembers the
sound of her lover's horn. "Vous souvient-il Mylord, dans les premiers
temps de nos amours, c'est le son de votre cor qui m'annonçait votre
présence au bois de Devon." *Do you remember Mylord, in the first*
days of our love, the sound of your horn announced your presence to
me in Devon wood. (V.iii.387)

39

more significant than the original statement. The motif is progressively drawn into the special relationship of the lovers. "Me suivre dans les bois, dans les monts, sur les grèves,/ Chez des hommes pareils aux démons de vos rêves," *You will follow me through the forests, to the mountains, on the beaches, to the lair of men like the demons of your dreams.* (I.ii.139-40) Hernani's social identity as a leader of doomed men is made a function of Doña Sol's sleep, her dream life, which is in turn a prefiguration of death, and a link to the beginning of the duet.[14] "Pareils" makes the connection in the most direct way possible. Doña Sol is in love with one of her dream demons, and she will literally follow him into the timeless dream world that he inhabits.

This is signaled a moment later as she seeks to identify Hernani. "Êtes-vous mon démon ou mon ange?" *Are you my demon or my angel?* (I.ii.152) This recalls the first angel which Hernani projected into Sol's dreams: "Un ange vous dit-il combien vous êtes douce/ Au malheureux que tout abandonne et repousse?" (See p. 29) (I.ii.47-48) She incorporates the time of dreams and establishes their pertinence to her existence, blissfully confusing angels and devils.[15] The angel-devil polarity offers Hugo a standard, easily recognized set of indices for character transformation.[16] The particu-

[14] "Doña Sol, mon amie/ Dites-moi, quand la nuit vous êtes endormie." *See p. 24.* (I.ii.43-44)

[15] It is not within the scope of this study to investigate the angel-demon polarity as a romantic convention. Some extended examples are found in Vigny's *Eloa*, Lamartine's *La Chute d'un ange*, and Balzac's *Séraphita*.

[16] Jean Gaudon, p. 69, discusses the emblematic value of metaphors. "Words in fashion, such as angel, demon, serpent, metaphorically describe the profound being of the character as surely as an emblem or the letter printed on the forehead of a criminal designate those who

lar transformation involved suggests vertical movement away from earthly contingency. Hernani is almost indiscriminately described as angel and/or devil; Doña Sol is inevitably an angel. She does not care if Hernani is angel or devil as long as he is otherworldly and guarantees transport through his presence. Her effect upon him is identical, expressed in his response, the single syllable, "Ange!" (I.ii.163)

Hugo prefers the use of conventional metaphors in characterization. In addition to being simple enough for immediate assimilation by the audience, they are easily recapitulated and integrated into the love-death pattern. Another one of these is Hernani's sword.

> DoÑa Sol, *lui défaisant son manteau.*
> Allons! donnez la cape, —et l'épée avec elle.
> Hernani, *la main sur son épée.*
> Non. C'est mon autre amie, innocente et fidèle.
> (I.ii.55-56)

> DoÑa Sol, unfastening his cloak. *Come! Give me your cape, and your sword with it.*
> Hernani, his hand upon his sword. *No. It is my other beloved, innocent and faithful.*

The sword is invested with Doña Sol's being, linking the bandit's violent existence to his love. At the same time there is the hint that the beloved will be an instrument of death. The standard connotation of the sword is thus qualified by the play's dénouement; Hernani will receive death from the hand of Doña Sol. Part of circumstance, plot, banditry, and the politics of Spain, it also prefigures the exact nature of the lovers' destiny.

---

are condemned socially. Let us add that, in the same way, they designate dramatic coordinates."

Through the process of metaphoric abstraction Hugo increases the distance between the lovers and reality, and further defines their otherworldliness. The Act III love duet contains the two most famous lines in the play, both of them illustrative of this method of identification. Hernani declares, "Je suis une force qui va!" *I am an unchecked force!* (III.iv.992) This is significant in that it reveals the extent to which the hero accepts his own abstraction. Hernani is never more accurate than when describing himself as "une force qui va." He thus ties his presence to the play's movement, suggesting that he is not really a person at all but part of a design. On this occasion Doña Sol demonstrates a consonance of perception: "Vous êtes mon lion superbe et généreux!" *You are my proud and noble lion!* (III.iv. 1028)[17] The lion image is a complement to Hernani's "Je suis une force qui va!" It makes vivid the progressive abstraction of the hero. Again, the movement of the play is away from plot, temporal contingency, and conventional portraiture, towards a purely lyric sphere. Doña Sol transforms her lover into an image, allegorizes his presence. It is Hernani the lion, "une force qui va," the angel of death that she loves. Multiplying and blurring identities, Hugo has Hernani transfer death back to Doña Sol.

> DOÑA SOL, *se jetant à son cou.*
> Vous êtes mon lion superbe et généreux!
> Je vous aime.

[17] Mlle. Mars, who created the role of Doña Sol, found the line so shocking that during rehearsals she said instead, "Vous êtes, mon seigneur, vaillant et courageux!" (*You are, my lord, valiant and courageous.*) Hugo threatened to relieve her of the role unless she promised to be faithful to his version.

HERNANI.
>Oh! l'amour serait un bien suprême
>Si l'on pouvait mourir de trop aimer!

DOÑA SOL.
>Je t'aime!
>Monseigneur! je vous aime et je suis toute à vous!

HERNANI, *laissant tomber sa tête sur son épaule.*
>Oh! qu'un coup de poignard de toi me serait doux.
>(III.iv.1028-32)

DOÑA SOL, throwing herself upon his neck. *You are my proud and noble lion! I love you.*
HERNANI. *Oh! Love would be a supreme boon if one could die of too much loving!*
DOÑA SOL. *I love you! My lord! I love you and I am completely yours!*
HERNANI, letting his head fall upon her shoulder. *Oh! A dagger thrust from you would be so sweet.*

The rich harmonics of the reiterated verb *aimer*, heavily accented by the *vous-tu-vous-tu* pattern, gives an aural identity to this restatement of the death wish, and signals the lovers' full acceptance of their common fate.[18]

[18] Because of its importance in literary history, its Spanish locale, the youth of its protagonists, etc., *Hernani* has often been compared to *Le Cid.* Robert Champigny, in *Le Genre dramatique* (Monte Carlo, 1965), pp. 153-54, precisely links the two plays in regard to the purely superficial quality of dramatic conflict they exhibit. This comparison makes particular sense in relation to the Act III encounter of Rodrigue and Chimène, and the use of the sword as an analogy for love. Hugo's explicit interest in Corneille is manifested in *Marion de Lorme,* written shortly before *Hernani,* which contains many references to the seventeenth-century playwright. Marion and Didier join a troupe of actors, and she is chosen to play the role of Chimène. In addition, Hugo wrote four scenes of a play entitled *Corneille* (1825).

43

C. Plot and Poem

1. Silva: The Spectre and the Portrait

The love duets of Doña Sol and Hernani most clearly demonstrate the unchanging relationship of the lovers, their vocalization of timelessness. This is not, however, a two-character play. Its subtitle, *Tres para una*, announces the presence of four principal characters, and in terms of the plot, Don Carlos and Silva are not really subordinate to the lovers. Hugo proliferates situations ripe for jealousy and conflict. Three men love Doña Sol; two of them are political enemies of the third. These oppositions contribute to the play's coincidental and melodramatic nature. Yet this subtitle is a clue to the other scheme operating, that which conspires to the play's density—the reduction of elements and the abolition of conflict. Carlos and Silva are integrated into the poem of love-death. Their voices and their time contribute to its definition; they are metaphorical extensions of the lovers.[19] Through them the source of comparison is expanded. This development is vital if the play is to have theatrical coherence. Carlos and Silva are necessary to the poetry of Hernani and Doña Sol. Silva is first transformed by Hernani.

[19] An inability to relate the various factors of the play is demonstrated by Georges Lote in *En Préface à "Hernani"* (Paris, 1930), p. 99. "*Hernani* does not have the kind of tightness which classical tragedies exhibit. All those great effusions of Don Carlos or of Hernani himself, as well as many parts of the dialogue, have no direct relationship to the question of finding out which of the three suitors will marry Doña Sol. They only slow down the progress of the play, which they swell with all kinds of parasitic growths." Lote falls into the familiar trap of trying to judge *Hernani* according to norms pertinent to classical tragedy.

Ô l'insensé vieillard, qui, la tête inclinée,
Pour achever sa route et finir sa journée,
A besoin d'une femme, et va, spectre glacé,
Prendre une jeune fille! ô vieillard insensé!
Pendant que d'une main il s'attache à la vôtre,
Ne voit-il pas la mort qui l'épouse de l'autre?
Il vient dans nos amours se jeter sans frayeur!
Vieillard! va-t-en donner mesure au fossoyeur!

(I.ii.79-86)

*Oh, the crazed, bent old man who needs a wife to
help him finish his journey and the course of his day;
this frigid ghost is going to take a young girl! Oh,
crazed old man! While he clasps you with one hand,
does he not see Death marrying him with the other
one? He disturbs our love without the slightest dread!
Old man, give your measurements to the grave-
digger!*

The hero evokes the spectral nature of his rival in a fore-
warning of Silva's role in Act V when he announces the
doom of Hernani. But Hernani's anger is not merely
prophetic; it integrates the time of death into this important first love scene. Silva's proximity to death contrasts naturally with the youth of the lovers. Further-
more, with the precise reference to the marriage in
death, Hernani clearly places himself in the shadow of
Silva. Anticipating the play's outcome, this first evocation of the old man is one in a series of metaphoric links
that lead to the final wedding night.

The analogy between Hernani and Silva is strength-
ened at the end of Act I when the bandit identifies himself with his aged rival through ironic projection. Carlos
is included in the bargain.

45

Va! je suis là, j'épie et j'écoute, et sans bruit
Mon pas cherche ton pas et le presse et le suit.
Le jour tu ne pourras, ô roi, tourner la tête
Sans me voir immobile et sombre dans ta fête;
La nuit tu ne pourras tourner les yeux, ô roi,
Sans voir mes yeux ardents luire derrière toi!

(I.iv.409-14)

*Go! I am there, I spy and listen, and my step noise-
lessly seeks after yours and closes upon it and follows
it. O king, by day you will be unable to turn around
without seeing me, immobile and grave amidst your
festivities. O king, at night you will be unable to turn
your gaze without seeing my burning eyes aglow
behind you!*

Here is another prefiguration of the play's final act,
with the substitution of Hernani for Silva as avenger,
and Carlos for Hernani as victim. The reference to "ta
fête" is a further link to the "nuit de noces." Hugo suggests the presence of the three suitors while blurring
their individual identities; plot becomes a pretext and
framework for the love-death motif and lyric movement. At the end of Act I the protagonist makes a
poem out of the play's climax. He transforms himself
into a diabolic presence, superimposes the end upon
the beginning, changes roles, and even more significantly, reveals himself as the author of his own doom.
He prepares the role of avenger for Silva. Silva thereby
becomes an extension of Hernani. The molding of the
play is controlled by the realization of a poetic destiny,
not a political one.

Silva's fullest development occurs in Act III. His
transport is controlled by tradition, and is distinct from
the hero's rhapsodic style.

Oh! mon amour n'est point comme un jouet de verre
Qui brille et tremble; oh! non, c'est un amour sévère,
Profond, solide, sûr, paternel, amical,
De bois de chêne ainsi que mon fauteuil ducal!
Voilà comme je t'aime, et puis je t'aime encore
De cent autres façons, comme on aime l'aurore,
Comme on aime les fleurs, comme on aime les cieux!
De te voir tous les jours, toi, ton pas gracieux,
Ton front pur, le beau feu de ta fière prunelle,
Je ris, et j'ai dans l'âme une fête éternelle!

(III.i.765-74)

Oh, my love is not a glass bauble which glistens and trembles! Oh, no! This love is grave, profound, solid, sure, paternal, friendly, made from oak like my ducal throne! That is how I love you, and I love you in yet a hundred other ways, as one loves the dawn, as one loves the flowers, as one loves the sky! At seeing you every day, you, your graceful step, your pure brow, the lovely fire of your proud eyes, I laugh, and there is eternal rejoicing in my soul!

This is a love poem whose conventions are common to renaissance lyrics. The Petrarchian catalogue of love is a chain of similes. Doña Sol is dawn, flowers, the firmament. Yet this little poem surpasses its renaissance conventions in its particular relevance to the play. Silva paradoxically thrusts Doña Sol back into life, in direct opposition to the movement which links her to Hernani. Silva wants to see her every day; Hernani wishes to share eternity with her. The hero's desire for union with his beloved suggests death; the old man finds in this woman a reason for living.

SILVA.

> Et puis, vois-tu? le monde trouve beau,
> Lorsqu'un homme s'éteint, et, lambeau par lam-
> beau,
> S'en va, lorsqu'il trébuche au marbre de la tombe
> Qu'une femme, ange pur, innocente colombe,
> Veille sur lui, l'abrite, et daigne encor souffrir
> L'inutile vieillard qui n'est bon qu'à mourir.
>
> (III.i.775-80)

SILVA. *And then, you see, when a man stumbles on a tombstone, failing and disappearing bit by bit, everyone admires the woman, a pure angel, an innocent dove, who watches over him, protects him, and deigns to tolerate the useless old one who is only good for dying.*

The ambiguity of the familiar angel is significant. Hernani casts Doña Sol in that role as he describes their inevitable death. Silva employs the same image to imply a contradictory phenomenon. The opposition of Hernani and Silva, youth and age, vitality and decrepitude, is resolved however by the presence of the angel they both adore. Doña Sol is the medium through which their identities are refracted, and eventually rendered indistinguishable.

It is in Act III that Silva dramatizes his familiarity with death by conversing with the dead.

SILVA. *(Il fait lentement trois pas dans la salle et promène de nouveau ses regards sur les portraits des Silva.)*

> Morts sacrés! aïeux! hommes de fer!
> Qui voyez ce qui vient du ciel et de l'enfer,
> Dites-moi, messeigneurs, dites, quel est cet homme?

Ce n'est pas Hernani, c'est Judas qu'on le nomme!
Oh! tâchez de parler pour me dire son nom!
(Croisant les bras.)
Avez-vous de vos jours vu rien de pareil?
(III.v.1063-68)

SILVA. (He slowly takes a few steps in the room
and again passes his gaze over the portraits of the
Silvas.) *Sacred dead! Ancestors, men of iron, who
see what emerges from heaven and from hell, tell
me, my lords, tell me, who is this man? It is not
Hernani. His name is Judas! Oh, try to speak so
that you can tell me his name!* (Crossing his arms.)
*In your lifetimes, have you ever witnessed such
as this?*

The stage decor is drawn into the poem. At the beginning of the act Silva opposes the time of mortality,
youth and age, to the timelessness of death. He erases
these differences as he addresses the gallery of portraits.[20] This is a self-reflecting device, a way of analo-
gizing his identity, giving it the particular aspect of
quasi-legendary time. He asks his ancestors for judgment on Hernani, thus leading the young man through
the picture-frames and back through time. It is not
coincidental that a moment later he hides Hernani in a
secret compartment behind one of the portraits. In
earlier plays of Hugo this sort of device is simply
guignolesque. *Amy Robsart* and *Cromwell* are full of
secret passages and trap doors. Here the convention is
related to the play's core.

At the end of Act III Hernani stages his own death so
as to have the opportunity for revenge on Don Carlos.

[20] Michel Butor (Dec. 1964), 1075-77, discusses the use of portraits
as stage decor in *Hernani.*

49

HERNANI, *lui présentant le cor qu'il détache de sa ceinture.*
Écoute. Prends ce cor. —Quoi qu'il puisse advenir,
Quand tu voudras, seigneur, quel que soit le lieu, l'heure,
S'il te passe à l'esprit qu'il est temps que je meure,
Viens, sonne de ce cor, et ne prends d'autres soins.
Tout sera fait!

SILVA, *lui tendant la main.*
Ta main.
(Tous deux se serrent la main. —Aux portraits.)
Vous tous, soyez témoins!
(III.vii.1292-96)

HERNANI, presenting him the horn which he detaches from his belt. *Listen. Take this horn. Whatever happens, sir, whenever you wish, in whatever place, at whatever time, if you decide that I should die, come, sound this horn, and take no other measures. It will be done!*

SILVA, offering him his hand. *Your hand.* (They both shake hands. To the portraits.) *Bear witness, all of you!*

This is a meeting of the characters' poetic identities—the horn and the portraits. The two men, in this moment of great stress, project themselves by the images that best characterize them. They substitute a realm of analogy for one of circumstance. Hernani's death is in the song played upon the horn. Silva's death is in the accumulation of ancestral tradition, manifested in the sum of portraits. The conflict between these characters is essentially resolved as they counter death with death.

2. *Carlos: The Emperor and the Tomb*

Act IV is probably the most controversial part of the play. The election of Carlos as emperor, his confrontation with the spirit of Charlemagne, and the pardon he grants Hernani, seem to interrupt the pattern maintained by the lovers' encounters. The audience's attention is focused now upon the king-to-be-emperor. The comic vulgarian of the Act I closet scene is replaced by the sensitive visionary who somberly enters the tomb of Charlemagne. Yet the transformation of Carlos is not sudden. His diction begins to change as early as Act II when he compares Doña Sol's eyes to a variety of light-giving sources: windows, mirrors, rays, torches, the day itself.[21] These conventions are also exploited by Hernani: "Des flammes de tes yeux inonde ma paupière." *Engulf my eyes with the flames from yours.* (II.iv.686) "La flamme de tes yeux dont l'éclair est ma joie!" *The flame of your eyes whose flashing is my joy!* (II.iv.1022) Carlos' participation in the poem-making is continued in Act III. "Un homme devient ange ou monstre en vous touchant." *A man becomes an angel or a monster by touching you.* (III.vi.1215) This notion reiterates the Hernani-Sol relationship, while the heroes are brought into closer identity than before. The process is continued a moment later as Carlos approaches the realm of imagery created by the lovers. "J'étais grand, j'eusse été le lion de Castille!/ Vous m'en faites le tigre avec votre courroux." *I was great. I might have become the lion of Castille! With your anger you make me its tiger.* (III.vi.1218-19) In Act IV Carlos adds his variation to the design. As the lovers prolong their lyric transport

[21] II.i.415-18, 431-32, 465-66.

unto death, and the old man stands on its threshold, Carlos goes through a complete metamorphosis. His new being is possessed by the shade of Charlemagne. He emerges from the tomb reborn, offering a vivid example of the transcendence to which the others aspire.

In a scene which corresponds to Silva's Act III confrontation of his ancestors' portraits, Carlos apostrophizes the tomb of Charlemagne. Going counter to a texture created by the mixing of voice and the absence of the extended monologue, Hugo suddenly includes a gigantic *tirade*, one of the longest in the French theatrical tradition. Carlos, the least eloquent character until Act IV, is granted a scene which lasts 167 lines, far surpassing in length any individual pronouncement of Hernani, Doña Sol, or Silva. The rhetoric follows a conventional but quite complicated logic. Carlos begins by addressing the physical reality of the tomb, and wondering if its dimensions are commensurate with the stature of Charlemagne. The notion of dimensions is expanded into that of Europe itself, and its leaders, the pope and the emperor. The function of this cliché-ridden oratory becomes apparent once the pan-European superstructure is drawn into the play's fabric.

> Le pape et l'empereur! ce n'était plus deux hommes.
> Pierre et César! en eux accouplant les deux Romes,
> Fécondant l'une et l'autre en un mystique hymen,
> Redonnant une forme, une âme au genre humain,
> Faisant refondre en bloc peuples et, pêle-mêle,
> Royaumes, pour en faire une Europe nouvelle,
> Et tous deux remettant au moule de leur main
> Le bronze qui restait du vieux monde romain!
> (IV.ii.1485-92)

The pope and the emperor were no longer two men.
Peter and Caesar! The two Romes were coupled in
them. Making each other fecund in a mystical mar-
riage, giving back a form, a soul to humankind, mas-
sively recasting and jumbling peoples and kingdoms
to make a new Europe, they both shaped in the mold
of their hands the bronze which remained of the old
Roman world!

It is the image of the "hymen" which reminds us of
Hernani and Doña Sol. As Carlos contemplates the
transformation of king into emperor, he conceives of it
in terms of coupling and collaboration. The result is a
new form, made manifest as a work of art in the references to the mold and the bronze. Carlos assumes the
mythic stature of emperor, relating first to the ghost of
Charlemagne, and then to the historical yet mystical
marriage of pope and emperor. He appropriates the
methods of the lovers and the old man, marriage and
history, the lyric and the legend.

The passage from *grandeur* to *décadence* is dictated
by the conventional flux of the rhetoric and suggested
by the proximity of the tomb and the Emperor Charlemagne who lies there. Earthly power and magnificence
are replaced by the image of death. Again we are struck
by the similarity of movement here and in the love
scenes. Hernani and Doña Sol find their true identities
by abandoning the world, translating their lives into
death. Carlos relates his own destiny to that of Charlemagne, polarizing himself between life and death,
greatness and nothingness.[22] The lovers approach eter-

[22] Pierre Albouy, in *La Création mythologique chez Victor Hugo*
(Paris, 1963), p. 187, notices how Carlos appropriates the mythological identity of Charlemagne.

nity; he transcends himself and becomes the enlight-
ened emperor, capable of infinite grace and understanding. When Carlos evokes the "tocsin" *warning bell*
(IV.ii.1528), the spectator cannot fail to remember the
importance of this image in the Act II love duet.[23] He
addresses the ghost of Charlemagne: "Verse-moi dans
le coeur, du fond de ce tombeau,/ Quelque chose de
grand, de sublime et de beau!" *From the bottom of this
tomb, pour into my heart something great, sublime and
beautiful!* (IV.ii.1563-64) Death is a source of beauty
and grandeur for him as it is for the lovers. And then,
in the simplest of theatrical gestures, Carlos prefigures
the end of the play. Dying to the world, he walks into
the tomb.

After the meeting of the conspirators the cannon shots
are heard, announcing Carlos' election.[24] The author has
found a purely aural, theatrical way to signal the character's transformation. The three cannon shots not only
dramatize but represent his new identity, just as the
"tocsin" and the horn are sonorous counterparts of Doña
Sol and Hernani. Further parallels are apparent even
to the characters themselves. Doña Sol pleads for the
life of Hernani. "Il est à moi, comme l'empire à vous!"
He belongs to me as the empire belongs to you! (IV.iv.
1752) The empire is an analogy for her love. Destinies
which were initially separate and in conflict are now
complementary. "L'empereur est pareil à l'aigle." *The
emperor is like the eagle.* (IV.iv.1770) Carlos has become one with the abstraction, abandoned contingency,
joined the force/lion and the picture gallery.

[23] See above, p. 30.

[24] Considering the frequent use of the triplet, it is not gratuitous
that three votes are decisive, and three cannon shots indicate his
election.

54

D. The Theatricalization of Transport

Act V opens with the appearance of Silva in a domino, the very presence of death. "Si les morts/ Marchent, voici leurs pas." *If the dead walk, these are their footsteps.* (V.i.1870-71) The wedding festivities and death are juxtaposed at the beginning of the play.[25] Now they are acted out. Moreover, Silva is here the final extension of the portrait scene and the confrontation with Charlemagne's ghost. Hugo presents to the audience a character who is both theatrically and symbolically death.

The final modulation in the love duet is the most ample development of the themes and images already introduced: the night, the song, love and death. It is the last variation on the familiar motifs, and particularly vivid because the resolution is at hand, the moment when music and action become one. It begins on a note of promise and joy.

HERNANI.

    Mais je ne connais pas ce Hernani. —Moi, j'aime
    Les prés, les fleurs, les bois, le chant du rossignol.
    Je suis Jean d'Aragon, mari de Doña Sol!
    Je suis heureux!

DOÑA SOL.

    Je suis heureuse!   (V.iii.1924-27)

HERNANI. *But I do not know this Hernani. I love the meadows, the flowers, the woods, the song of the nightingale. I am John of Aragon, husband of Doña Sol! I am happy!*

DOÑA SOL. *I am happy!*

[25] See above, p. 31.

Hernani is victim of an illusion. He thinks he has become Jean d'Aragon whereas his identity remains that of the bandit, the horn, the mountains. It is as Hernani the outlaw, not as the noble Jean, that he will marry Doña Sol.

HERNANI.
Je ne suis plus que joie, enchantement, amour.
Qu'on me rende mes tours, mes donjons, mes bastilles,

. . . . .

Je n'ai rien vu, rien dit, rien fait. Je recommence,
J'efface tout, j'oublie! Ou sagesse ou démence,
Je vous ai, je vous aime, et vous êtes mon bien!
(V.iii.1934-41)

HERNANI. *Now I am nothing but joy, enchantment, love. Let them give back my towers, my keeps, my fortresses. . . . I have seen nothing, said nothing, done nothing. I am beginning again, I am cancelling out everything, I am forgetting! Be it wisdom or madness, I possess you, I love you, and you are my treasure.*

Hernani takes up the triplet rhythm that characterizes so many of his previous declarations. The beat of the lines is incessant, with groups of three nouns and three verbs. They herald the last line of this passage which itself recapitulates Doña Sol's declaration in Act III: "Je t'aime!/ Monseigneur! je vous aime et je suis toute à vous!" (*See p. 43.*)   (III.v.1030-31)

At this moment the lovers' voices mingle with special sonority. Doña Sol initiates the night song, fulfilling the destiny Hernani prescribed for her in Act II.[26]

[26] See above, p. 37.

DoÑA SoL.

Un moment! —Vois-tu bien, c'est la joie! et je
    pleure!
Viens voir la belle nuit.
    (Elle va à la balustrade.)

> Mon duc, rien qu'un
>   moment.
>
> (V.iii.1948-49)

DoÑA SoL. *Just a moment! Do you not see that I
am crying for joy! Come see the beautiful night.*
(She goes to the balustrade.) *My duke, only a moment more.*

The tears of joy well from her eyes, so closely identified
with her song. Doña Sol seizes upon the coherence of
nature and her personal universe. "Tout s'est éteint,
flambeaux et musique de fête./ Rien que la nuit et
nous." *Everything is fading—the torches and the fes-
tive music. There is nothing but the night and ourselves.* (V.iii.1951-52) The music that accompanies the
marriage of Doña Sol and Don Jean d'Aragon has given
way to the music of the night, the heroine's own
voice, the dark tone of their previous duets. And it is
in the full acceptance of the night that the lovers find
themselves.

DoÑA SoL.

Dis, ne le crois-tu pas? sur nous, tout en dormant,
La nature à demi veille amoureusement.
Pas un nuage au ciel. Tout, comme nous, repose.
Viens, respire avec moi l'air embaumé de rose!
Regarde. Plus de feux, plus de bruit. Tout se tait.
La lune tout à l'heure à l'horizon montait;
Tandis que tu parlais, sa lumière qui tremble
Et ta voix, toutes deux, m'allaient au coeur en-
    semble.

57

Je me sentais joyeuse et calme, ô mon amant,
Et j'aurais bien voulu mourir en ce moment.

(V.iii.1953-63)

DOÑA SOL. *Do you not believe that sleeping nature
is half watching over us with love. There is not a
cloud in the sky. Everything is at rest like ourselves. Come, breathe with me the rose-scented
air! Look. There are no more fires, there is no more
noise. All is quiet. A moment ago the moon was
climbing over the horizon; while you were speaking both its trembling light and your voice went
together to my heart. Oh, my beloved, I felt joyful
and calm, and I would have liked to have died in
that instant.*

Doña Sol announces her own doom.

In this lyric, the self is a double presence, and that
constitutes its theatricality. Hernani focuses attention
upon the singing of his beloved. "Ah! qui n'oublierait
tout à cette voix céleste?/ Ta parole est un chant où
rien d'humain ne reste." *Ah! Who would not forget
everything at this heavenly voice? Your speech is a
song in which nothing human remains.* (V.iii.1963-64)
But Doña Sol's song is not complete, for Hernani cannot accompany her in music and flight with his voice.
The horn is his aural counterpart. In order to break the
silence that surrounds her own voice, she elicits music.
She finally recognizes the appropriate accompaniment
in Hernani's horn.

Mais un oiseau qui chanterait aux champs!
Un rossignol perdu dans l'ombre et dans la mousse,
Ou quelque flûte au loin! . . . Car la musique est douce,

Fait l'âme harmonieuse, et, comme un divin choeur,
Éveille mille voix qui chantent dans le coeur!
Ah! ce serait charmant!
  (*On entend le bruit lointain d'un cor dans l'ombre.*)
          Dieu! je suis exaucée!
                      (V.iii.1974-79)

*But a bird who would sing in the fields! A nightingale
lost in the shadows and the moss, or some distant
flute! . . . For music is sweet. It makes the soul harmonious, and like a divine choir, awakens a thousand
voices which sing in the heart! Ah! it would be lovely!*
(The far-off noise of a horn in the darkness is heard.)
God! My prayer is being answered!

This is a reprise of Act II when Hernani incorporated
the bell into the fabric of his poem.[27] Here it is Doña
Sol's turn.

DOÑA SOL, *souriant.*
    Don Juan, je reconnais le son de votre cor!
HERNANI.
    N'est-ce pas?
DOÑA SOL.
          Seriez-vous dans cette sérénade
    De moitié?
HERNANI.
          De moitié, tu l'as dit.
DOÑA SOL.
                      Bal maussade!
    Oh! que j'aime bien mieux le cor au fond des
      bois! . . .[28]
    Et puis, c'est votre cor, c'est comme votre voix.
                      (V.iii.1982-86)

[27] See above, p. 31.
[28] This is, of course, a variation on Vigny's *Le Cor*. "J'aime le son
du cor, le soir, au fond des bois." (*I love the sound of the horn, at
night, from the depths of the woods.*)

> Doña Sol, smiling. *Don Juan, I recognize the sound of your horn!*
> Hernani. *Do you?*
> Doña Sol. *Do you have some part in this serenade?*
> Hernani. *Some part, you said.*
> Doña Sol. *A gloomy ball! Oh, how I would prefer the horn deep in the woods! . . . And yet, it is your horn, it is like your voice.*

The irony of this rather facile play on words is effaced by the final line, the complete acceptance of the identity between voice and horn. The pattern of identity in music, projected in Act I, is now complete, and all that remains is its dramatization.

The second appearance of the spectre-like Silva signals the final cadence. Again, Hugo disappoints with the bad taste of his invention as Doña Sol declares, "Je suis bien pâle, dis, pour une fiancée?" *I am quite pale, do you not think, for a bride?* (V.vi.2148) Exploiting all the possible variations of the wedding-night/death notion he diverts attention away from the simplicity of the nexus. The last words of Doña Sol, however, achieve a perfect correspondence between the object and the metaphor because Hugo allows the character to accept these factors without embellishment. The lovers have entered fully into their poetic universe, they have loved for death.

> Doña Sol, *échevelée, et se dressant à demi sur son séant.*
>
> Mort! non pas! nous dormons.
> Il dort. C'est mon époux, vois-tu. Nous nous aimons.

Nous sommes couchés là. C'est notre nuit de noce.
(D'une voix qui s'éteint.)
Ne le réveillez pas, Seigneur duc de Mendoce.
Il est las.
(Elle retourne la figure d'Hernani.)
      Mon amour, tiens-toi vers moi tourné . . .
Plus près . . . plus près encor . . .   (V.vi.2161-66)

DOÑA SOL, disheveled, half rising from her place. *Dead! No, we are sleeping. He is sleeping. He is my husband, you see. We love each other. We are lying here. It is our wedding night.* (With a failing voice.) *Do not wake him, Duke of Mendoce. He is tired.* (She turns Hernani's face.) *My beloved, turn towards me . . . closer . . . closer still . . .*

The poem, the song and the play become one when love becomes death. The reiteration, "Plus près . . . plus près encor . . ." reaches towards the analogy of being, the union that is the ultimate goal of lyric transport.

three

THE TIME OF THE EPIC:
Les Burgraves

THE success of *Hernani* and the fiasco of *Les Burgraves* date Hugo's career in the theatre and exemplify different modes assumed by his poetry on the stage. *Hernani* projects a lyric transport, an abolition of existential time, a blurring of episode and character; *Les Burgraves* does the opposite. The ecstasy and rapture of the earlier play is replaced by an epic sweep; timelessness gives way to a monumental and explicit representation of time. In both cases Hugo transcends conventional theatrical time. If *Hernani* reduces the stage to a threshold between life and death, *Les Burgraves* turns it into a book of years, a calendar, a family tree. Its organization is controlled by a chronology expanded beyond normal proportions.

How does one act out time? There are certainly no clues to be found in the classical tradition. Seventeenth-century theatre orients the play's movement towards the inevitable present. Andromaque evokes "la nuit éternelle" and consults with Hector's ghost, but not even she can escape the immediate confrontation of the other characters as they are locked in the two hours of the play's duration. The same is true of Phèdre despite her projected encounters with Apollo and Minos. This contingency of the present goes far deeper than the familiar *unité de temps*. It is an understanding of the theatre's principal strength, its ability to deal with the actual on its own terms, its power to recreate the moment as a moment, and to thrust the spectator into painful contact with that moment.

In *Les Burgraves* Hugo juggles the present and the past, and achieves a new order. The duration of the performance is a frame in which past time is evoked. The play spreads out and back, using voices and gestures to go beyond their conventional imitation of life and invade domains usually foreign to the theatre. In effect, the events which transpired prior to the play's first line constitute the poet's major concern. Hugo must find devices that will give a semblance of theatricality to a time structure basically incompatible with the genre. *Les Burgraves'* universally poor reception, and its infrequent revival appear to prove his inability to integrate the vision and the form.[1] The play's failure, however, is due to a strict interpretation of the tradition of the genre, and of the timeworn standard of verisimilitude. "This melodrama is a cheap illusionist's bag of tricks, with its plot where everything goes beyond the limits of improbability, from magic potions which take away or give back life in five minutes, phantoms wandering in lost tombs, slaves who drag their hate with their chains for sixty years without tiring, to burgraves who never die, and resuscitating

[1] See Olga W. Russell, *Étude historique et critique des Burgraves de Victor Hugo, avec variantes inédites et lettres inédites* (Paris, 1962), for a discussion of the play's critical reception and destiny, pp. 224-61, and specific remarks on the difficulties of staging an epic, pp. 231-35.

emperors!"[2] It is clear that this critic's indignation is a result of his disbelief. It is also clear, after reading a few words of the play, that Hugo does not for a moment wish to elicit belief, in the accepted sense of that word. The play is emphatically *invraisemblable*.[3] While this cannot be overlooked, it must be understood, and related to the fabric of the play. The curtain rises and we encounter a disheveled hag, carrying her chains. This is burden enough to alienate those who dismiss the apparatus of melodrama out of hand. Yet such distaste is premature. If the play is outrageous it is also daring.

A. The Stage and the Myth

The differences between *Les Burgraves* and Hugo's previous plays are apparent even in its preface. Hugo as self critic is often amusing and almost always inaccurate.[4] It is thus surprising to find a relevant self-

[2] Claude Roffat, *La Croix* (1943), cited in Hugo, *Théâtre complet*, Bibliothèque de la Pléiade, II, 1827-28.

[3] It is ironic that Dumas' *Antony*, undoubtedly one of the most *vraisemblable* of romantic plays, is virtually unperformable today for just that reason. Despite its convincing portrayal of the romantic personality, the hero's dilemma and his destiny are controlled by social conventions that have lost their meaning. The play is doomed by its sociology.

[4] The measure of his inaccuracy is apparent in the preface to *Angélo, tyran de Padoue*. There the author piously describes his work, a rattling potboiler, as a story of human suffering.

> I must nail all this human suffering to the back of the cross. . . . In order to satisfy that need of the spirit which always seeks the past in the present and the present in the past, I must mix in this work the human element with the eternal, the historical element with the social. Prompted by this idea, I must paint not only a man and a woman, not only these two women and these three men, but a whole century, a whole atmosphere, a whole civilization, a whole people. (II, 556)

What follows is a melodrama whose excesses can be best appreciated

appraisal in the preface to *Les Burgraves*. Beneath the elephantine prose and the grandiose references to Aeschylus there is an understanding of the myth in the theatre. The Greek poet was inspired by the landscape of Thessaly, and found there the imprint of gods and giants; the landscape of the Rhine suggests the same to Hugo. It is a place for giants, for creatures exempt from the laws of ordinary men. One has no right to expect a play about giants to sound and look like a play about men.

> One may surmise that we wish to describe the banks of the Rhine. There, in fact, as in Thessaly, everything is thunderstruck, desolate, uprooted, destroyed: everything bears the imprint of a profound, bitter, implacable war. There is not a rock which is not also a fortress, not a fortress which is not also a ruin; extermination has passed through. But this extermination is so vast one feels that the combat must have been colossal. There, in fact, six centuries ago, other Titans struggled against another Jupiter. Those Titans are the burgraves; that Jupiter is the Emperor of Germany.   (II, 14)

The dimensions are clearly defined, the links between locale and character fixed. Hugo will be true to this projection. The myth extends men through metaphor into the superhuman, into a realm of total relevance where analogies are not hidden but manifest, and magic is the common mode of action. It is the kind of system Hugo establishes for *Les Burgraves*. The evocation of Aeschylus is not gratuitous. Hugo is fascinated

---

by comparing it to the relatively less preposterous libretto that Arrigo Boito drew from the play, and which was to become Ponchielli's *La Gioconda*.

by the Greek poet whose legitimate source is the body of myths which is the foundation of the European tradition. The sort of belief exemplified by Aeschylus is translated into Hugo's own terms; the cosmic vocabulary, the pantheism of his philosophically oriented poetry. Titans, gods, god-like men, the river and the rock, the Bible (one of the play's main characters is named Job, and is accordingly Job-like), the obsessive paternity theme, *ananké*, and the working out of destiny all meet in this play. Such a collection of *hugolismes* would be unexceptional were it not for the fact that *Les Burgraves* is a play rather than a novel or epic poem. The author has here an opportunity to test the relationship between epic, myth, and the theatre.[5]

Hugo's nostalgia for the age of myths reflects the need to construct a personal myth, prompted by his search for grandeur, the very size of his vision, and personal experience. *Les Burgraves* seems to be the play most directly inspired by an identifiable set of circumstances. During a trip along the Rhine with Juliette Drouet he is particularly struck by the ruined castles and their appearance at different times of the day.[6] In the preface these impressions are recounted in

[5] It is not surprising to find an apology for *Les Burgraves* in Pierre Albouy's *La Création mythologique chez Victor Hugo*. "*Les Burgraves* is drawn in fact from myth rather than dramatic symbolism. That is why it must be judged by criteria pertinent to the epic genre and not those which are applicable to psychological theatre," p. 183. Another discussion of the preface's reference to myth is found on pp. 83-85. Richard B. Grant, in *The Perilous Quest, Image, Myth, and Prophecy in the Narratives of Victor Hugo* (Durham, North Carolina, 1968), pp. 96-121, discusses the mythic elements in *Les Burgraves* and their prefiguration in earlier poetry of Hugo, as well as in *Le Rhin*.

[6] The first extended expression of this interest is shown in *Le Rhin* (1842).

the third person. ". . . and there, alone, pensive, forgetting everything, surrounded by the song of birds, beneath the rays of the rising sun, seated on some basalt green with moss, or buried up to his knees in high grass wet with dew, he deciphered a Roman inscription or measured the gap of a gothic arch, while the bushes inside the ruin, joyously stirred by the wind over his head, released upon him a rain of flowers." (II, 15) This is a familiar mixture, the irresistible juxtaposition of natural setting, ruins, history and love, all linked by the falling flowers.[7] He finally decides "that from this trip he had to fashion a work, that from this poetry he had to extract a poem." (II, 16) These are precious words from an author whose analyses are wont to be gross mystifications. How precious they are is made apparent at the end of the preface where Hugo returns to his usual rhetoric. The conclusion is a baldly schematic description of the play, a didactic abstract in which the author seeks to evoke the power of "fatality and providence." (II, 17) The play suffers from some of the faults of the preface. It too reveals Hugo's sincerity and his capacity for self-delusion, his grasp of history and time, and his appalling lack of taste. These qualities and defects must be sifted to produce a clear reading.

B. Magnification: Time, Character and Place

Les Burgraves is divided into three *parties* rather than acts.[8] The first part is, by far, the most interesting of the three, and perhaps the most original theatrical

---

[7] Ruins provide a fertile source for the poet's inspiration as early as the *Odes*: "La Bande noire" (1823), "Aux Ruines de Montfort-L'Amaury" (1825).

[8] Hugo states in the preface (II, 19) that this division is an homage to the *Oresteia* trilogy.

statement in all of Hugo's plays. It is here that he fashions a technique to represent pseudo-mythic time and to establish the play's movement. The first scenic reference indicates a picture gallery in the castle. The portraits are turned towards the wall, reminiscent of Silva's gallery, his age, his embodiment of historical time and death. The function of this new gallery is somewhat different from that of the earlier play. Silva's gallery is a metaphor for the passage of historical time in a play whose time is the eternity of the lyric. The gallery in *Les Burgraves* is but the first signal of a process that increasingly expands the limits of chronological time.

Guanhumara is a characterization of this phenomenon. She appears on stage immediately, and with her Hugo risks the play's success. This withered hag, dragging her chains and her years, is indeed a striking heroine. In his notes to the play Hugo describes Mme. Mélingue, the first interpreter of the role, as having embodied "the ideal of the author, the statue who walks." (II,1841) Such flattery is common to Hugo, but here it contains an important clue to the understanding of the character. She is not really a human being. With unaccustomed accuracy the author suggests the essence of his creation. Her *roman noir* aspect notwithstanding, Guanhumara is a bold theatrical personage, a realization on the stage of extended time and monumental place. As such, she expresses her relationship to the castle, "le burg," the true center of the play.

> GUANHUMARA.   Le burg, plein de clairons, de
>   chansons, de huées,
> Se dresse inaccessible au milieu des nuées;
> Mille soldats partout, bandits aux yeux ardents,
> Veillent, l'arc et la lance au poing, l'épée aux dents.

Tout protège et défend cet antre inabordable.
Seule, en un coin désert du château formidable,
Femme et vieille, inconnue, et pliant le genou
Triste, la chaîne au pied et le carcan au cou,
En haillons et voilée, une esclave se traîne.—
Mais, ô princes, tremblez! cette esclave est la haine.

(I.i.25-34)

GUANHUMARA. *The burg, filled with clarions, songs and shouts, stands inaccessible amidst the clouds. A thousand soldiers, bandits with fiery eyes, bows and lances ready, armed to the teeth, keep watch everywhere. All conspires to protect and defend this unapproachable retreat. Alone, in a deserted corner of the formidable castle, a slave, a woman, a stranger, old, bent, and sad, drags herself along with a chain at her feet and an iron collar at her neck, in rags and veiled. But, o princes, tremble! This slave is hatred.*

Her coherence to the castle is the result of her objectification. Guanhumara refers to herself in the third person, stressing her dehumanization and thus her function in the enormous object, the castle. This personification of hatred belongs to "cet antre inabordable."

Guanhumara's abstract quality is intensified as Hugo multiplies her identities. One of the play's conventions is mystery and its gradual clarification. Guanhumara consciously adds to the mystery by confusing the issue of her identity. "Enfin si je suis corse, ou slave, ou juive, ou maure?/ Je ne veux pas répondre et je ne dirai rien." *Am I a Corsican, a Slav, a Jewess or a Moor? I do not wish to answer and I will say nothing.* (I.iv.498-99) But this aspect of mystery, the unravelling of an infinitely complicated plot, and the movement of discovery are particularly appropriate conventions. The time and space of this play are stretched by the elaboration of multiple identities. Guanhumara is many women, many nationalities, many epochs, who has wandered endlessly over the face of the Earth. In refusing to be one woman she inhabits the stage both alone and with a host of her projected images. She brings the fullness of the past into contact with the theatrical present. Space is expanded as well. "J'ai vu le Nil, l'Indus, l'Océan, la tempête,/ Et les immenses nuits des pôles étoilés." *I have seen the Nile, the Indus, the Ocean, the storm, and the endless nights of the starry poles.* (I.iv. 554-55)

Hugo is fond of explicating his own works as he writes them, granting to his characters his own omniscience, making neat little summaries so as to avoid the slightest possibility of ambiguity. Should the spectator have not yet grasped the extent of Guanhumara's realization in stone and the transformation of her human traits, she herself spells it out.

> Je n'ai plus rien d'humain,
> *(Mettant la main sur son coeur.)*
> Et je ne sens rien là quand j'y pose la main.
> Je suis une statue et j'habite une tombe.
> Un jour de l'autre mois, vers l'heure où le soir tombe,
> J'arrivai, pâle et froide, en ce château perdu;
> Et je m'étonne encor qu'on n'ait pas entendu,
> Au bruit de l'ouragan courbant les branches d'arbre,
> Sur ce pavé fatal venir mes pieds de marbre.
> (I.iv.559-66)

There is nothing human left within me, (Putting her hand on her heart.) *and I feel nothing when I place my hand here. I am a statue and I inhabit a tomb. One*

*day last month, towards dusk, I arrived, pale and
cold, at this God forsaken castle. And I am still surprised that no one heard, amidst the noise of the
storm bending the branches, the sound of my marble
feet on this fatal floor of stone.*

Guanhumara's stone-like nature is a function of the
burg. Hugo states one of his goals in the preface: "To
reveal in the burg the three things it contained: a
fortress, a palace, a burial vault." (II, 16) This division
corresponds to the three parts of the play, but more important, it suggests a richness and variety within the
image, again swelling the play's space. Guanhumara
merges with the castle, expresses it, inhabits all three
levels, and particularly the final one. The stone castle,
a place for giants, is haunted by this woman of stone
who carries the chains which link her to the burg. Her
chains announce the theme of imprisonment and en-
closure which permeates the play.[9] It is she who ties
the others together, and it is she who most fully suggests
petrification. As she apostrophizes the night, the castle,
and her own chains she projects herself metaphorically
throughout the play.

Ô vastes cieux! ô profondeurs sacrées!
Morne sérénité des voûtes azurées!
Ô nuit, dont la tristesse a tant de majesté!
Toi qu'en mon long exil je n'ai jamais quitté,
Vieil anneau de ma chaîne, ô compagnon fidèle!
Je vous prends à témoin; —et vous, murs, citadelle,
Chênes qui versez l'ombre aux pas du voyageur,
Vous m'entendez, —je voue à ce couteau vengeur

[9] Victor Brombert, in "Victor Hugo, la prison et l'espace," *Revue
des Sciences Humaines*, CXVII (Jan.-Mar. 1965), 70, refers to the
caveau perdu in a discussion of imprisonment and escape.

Fosco, baron des bois, des rochers et des plaines,
Sombre comme toi, nuit, vieux comme vous, grands
   chênes!   (II.iii.971-80)

*O vast heavens! O holy depths and dismal serenity of
azured vaults! O night, filled with such majestic sadness! You whom I never abandoned during my long
exile, old link of my chain, O faithful companion,
bear witness. And you, walls, citadel, chains which
cast a shadow on the voyager's steps, hear me. To this
avenging knife I promise Fosco, baron of the forests,
the rocks and the plains, as dark as you, night, as old
as you, great oaks!*

We can appreciate how object takes precedence over
character. Guanhumara uses the particular links of the
chain placed on her wrists the night of Job's terrible
crime, to fit together the protagonists and the superhuman forces that guide their destinies. They are transplanted into appropriately grandiose metaphors which
reflect back on the burg and its century.

Hugo also uses more specific references in his effort
to divest the characters of a conventional theatrical personality. Readers familiar with *Hernani's* ephemeral
brand of metaphor are surprised by the specificity of
Les Burgraves. Reminding us of her capacity for change,
her embodiment of transformation, Guanhumara explains her name.

Oui, mon nom est charmant en Corse, Ginevra!
Ces durs pays du Nord en font Guanhumara.
L'âge, cet autre Nord, qui nous glace et nous ride,
De la fille aux doux yeux fait un spectre livide.
                                        (III.ii.1591-94)

*Yes, my name, Ginevra, is charming in Corsican.
Those hard northern countries have turned it into*

*Guanhumara. Old age, that other north, which freezes
and wrinkles us, has made a livid ghost out of the girl
with gentle eyes.*

It is this very insistence upon detail, on a well defined
polarity of identity, that closely associates her with objects and events. Like the other characters, her will is
controlled by the weight of time and place. Hugo denies the protagonists freedom to exist in the moment. In
Les Burgraves we look backwards rather than into the
present, through a perspective which minimizes the
importance of what happens on the stage. The play is
designed to make us participate in the monumental past
of Guanhumara, Job, and Barberousse, rather than in
the coincidental working out of their present.

Job and his son, Magnus, explicitly illustrate the use
of character as an historico-legendary manifestation.
Magnus interrupts the feast of Hatto with the word
"Jadis" *(In other times)* and then proceeds to evoke the
old ways. The appearance of the two old men, who are
compared to statues as they stand motionless amidst
the laughter, the movement and the fanfare, expresses a
gulf between what they represent and what is happen-
ing before our eyes. During this scene, four generations
inhabit the stage simultaneously, incarnating the play's
temporal dimension and further marking a separation
between the aged and the young, the reflective and the
active. Job's first words distinguish between present bad
manners and ancient hospitality. A moment later he reiterates the gothic manner introduced by Guanhumara,
reminding us that his identity is engulfed by the burg.

Qui que vous soyez, avez-vous ouï dire
Qu'il est dans le Taunus, entre Cologne et Spire,

73

Sur un roc près duquel les monts sont des coteaux,
Un château renommé parmi tous les châteaux,
Et dans ce burg, bâti sur un monceau de laves,
Un burgrave fameux parmi tous les burgraves?

(I.vii.797-802)

Whoever you may be, have you heard that in the
Taunus, between Cologne and Spire, upon a rock be-
side which mountains seem mere hills, there stands a
castle renowned among all castles, and that within
this burg, built upon a pile of lava, there sits a bur-
grave famous among all burgraves?

The priority of place, the elimination of all that we
habitually call "psychological," the merging of character and landscape are typical of *Les Burgraves.* The
titan and his unattainable rock are proportionate to the
statue who drags her chains across Europe. The rock is
made from the violence and destruction of lava, a rock
out of time, indicating by its inaccessibility all the
temporal forces that have tried to penetrate it. The
rock is the measure of the characters whose lives are
subject to its violence, its dimensions and its age.

Hugo maintains a superhuman measure by frag-
menting and enlarging the identities of the individual
characters. Guanhumara-Ginevra is not the only one
who enjoys a multiple personality. Job-Fosco, Barbe-
rousse-Donato, and Otbert-Yorghi complete the pattern
of dual names. The repeated scenes of recognition
dramatize this expansion of identity, effectively distinguishing the different epochs in which a character
bears name A and name B. The theme of resurrection
is an echo of this process. The characters return to life
miraculously, thus exhibiting another mythic quality.
In addition to the participants in the original vendetta,

74

Yorghi, the long-lost son of Job, is eventually revealed to be Otbert, and the young heroine, Régina, quite literally dies and is resurrected on the stage. The best justification for the presence of these rather pale lovers in a play about giants is their shadow effect on the principal trio of ancients. The awakening of Régina and the rediscovery of Yorghi are partially redeemed, despite their triteness, because they help dramatize mythic and epic time, the play's central issue. The action involving the young lovers is treated cursorily by Hugo; the poetry allotted them is without distinction. His lack of interest betrays impatience with what amounts to be traditional stagecraft and characterization. The dénouement which involves Régina and Otbert is subordinate to the events described in the exposition. The most interesting dramatic encounters take place decades before the action begins.

C. The Exposition and Epic Time

The patterns described by the resurrected and multinamed characters constitute the poetic fabric of *Les Burgraves*. Hugo does not articulate the passage of years with words. He makes a time configuration out of characters placed in a contrapuntal relationship. The episodes of the past, and the succession of generations are in turn made theatrically accessible by the play's décor and central image, the burg. This concentration of time and place is accentuated by the image of chains. Guanhumara carries her chains as a reminder of the original crime, the terrible moment when Fosco supplied the first link in the chain of years. At the end of the play's second part, as Barberousse reveals himself, Job and the other burgraves allow themselves to be chained like slaves as a sign of obeissance to the resurrected Emperor. This spectacular gesture, typical of the epic theatre Hugo is trying to create, joins the private image of Guanhumara's slavery to the massed burgraves and the political reality of the burg. This collection of chains reminds us of the slaves that dominate the play's first part, and who embody Hugo's most original theatrical invention.

It falls to the slaves to enunciate the play's exposition. Exposition, however, seems a woefully conventional term for describing the background of *Les Burgraves*. The hundred years which precede the play's beginning, years of attempted fratricide, betrayal, wars, petrified emperors, abducted children, and pillage are the true body of the play, and must be made theatrical. The exposition is not simply gotten out of the way, summarized or integrated gracefully into the play's present. It is boldly amplified and pushed out of traditional proportion, voiced and fragmented in a scene involving nine different speaking characters. The story is given weight by the suffering of these slaves carrying their chains, and dramatic tension by the succession of reactions, and speculations about whether the circumstances are legend or fact. The slaves continue the epic movement as they transmit elements of the story passed on to them by previous narrators who do not appear in the play. Thus they add yet another temporal dimension to the exposition. And throughout this ensemble retelling of past events, whose order in time is clear neither to the audience nor the narrators, Guanhumara prowls the stage. She embodies the past that is being recounted by the quasi-bardic voices. The elements of the exposition are given a theatrical life of their own in this exchange between the slaves. The different episodes seem to become characters themselves as they are juxtaposed and rearranged in the free flow of this scene.

The pattern is consciously scrambled by Hugo. It will perhaps be useful to indicate its shape schematically and thus distinguish the time relationships between the fragments of narration. Each roman numeral denotes a new speaker or group of speakers.

I. Present	The nine slaves describe the situation of Guanhumara, Magnus, Job, Otbert, and Régina.
II. One month, then twenty years previous	Karl recounts the meeting of Max Edmond (a character who does not appear in the play) with Barberousse.
III. Unspecified time previous	Jossius relates Barberousse's apparent death in battle.
IV. Approximately eighty years previous to the present	Teudon describes Sfrondati, Donato's squire (another absent character), who in a madhouse told him the story of the rivalry between Donato and Fosco, and the subsequent crime.
V. The war of giants, an epoch nearer the present	Jossius tells of the battle between the masked Emperor and an unnamed bandit.

No one slave knows all the details. Each voice contributes to piecing together the many elements drawn from hearsay and personal experience, each new aspect is signaled by a new voice. The events are prevented from assuming the linear thrust common to storytelling. The burg, and the characters governed by its myth, are recalled and evoked by a series of slaves. In effect, the dimensions of place and character are amplified by this accumulation of reference.

Hugo divides the legend into seemingly disconnected parts by repeatedly reminding us a story is being told. One of the slaves interjects, "Parlons d'autre chose, hein?" *Change the subject, eh?* (I.ii.140) and "Tiens, Karl, finis-nous ton histoire." *Look here, Karl, finish your story.* (I.ii.141) Hermann, the voice of disbelief, ironizes the story with "Le conte est beau!" "Barberousse est l'objet de cent contes." "Un conte de grand-mère!" etc. *That's quite a story! Barberousse is the hero of many tales. An old-wives' tale!* (I.ii.189,235,358) This type of reaction is vital to the theatricality of the legend, rooting the narration of the past in a vivid present, compounding it with an alien tone that gives it yet another degree of relief. The parts will ultimately fit together. At this point Hugo puts them in a cyclical rather than progressive time structure. All the elements of the past are presented in a circle, beginning and ending in the present, a circle whose form is only faintly perceived at the close of the scene. The design is confused by the lapses of time, the changing of names, the variety of narrators, the references to absent narrators. The tale is made present by the burg and Guanhumara while it stretches through the ever-expanding past as the scene progresses. Hermann, the sceptic, has the final word, compromising the veracity of the collective story.

Bah! Songes d'un fiévreux qui voit dans son cerveau,
Où flottent des lueurs toujours diminuées,
Les visions passer ainsi que des nuées! (I.ii.360-62)

*Bah! They are dreams of a feverish mind. Its faculties
diminishing, it sees visions pass like clouds!*

This is an accurate description of the scene's structure,
of its poetic quality. The visions which pass like clouds
capture the freedom and fluidity of movement, a series
of cinematic dissolves from one sequence to another.
The originality of the exposition lies in the manner in
which is preserved the integrity of each transformation.
The bloody night in the *caveau perdu*, the battle of the
Titans Job and Barberousse, the sleeping Emperor and
the roving witch are melded in this chorus of slaves,
evoked in their various guises and identities through a
century whose duration is itself a factor in their conflict.

To appreciate Hugo's full intention in the opening
scene one must refer to the play's prologue, almost
completed but discarded in the final version. The scene
is a mountain gorge, and the slaves are voyagers prior
to their capture by Hatto and his men. Before the capture there is a sudden appearance of the burg in the
distance, an effective theatrical image which is reminiscent of the scenic effect at the end of *Marie Tudor*.[10]
In the prologue the elements of the exposition are presented in a much expanded form. The author gives the
battle of giants its full breadth, and a framework whose
proportions are worthy of the subject. In the staged
version the story of the final encounter between Job

[10] The Queen draws a curtain and reveals an illuminated night
view of London and the Tower, "dont la réverbération éclaire le
théâtre." *Whose reverberation lights the theatre.* (III.ii)

and Barberousse is allotted only three lines, while in the prologue it fills out twenty-eight. Much is sacrificed in the reduction, not least of which is the amplitude of the bardic voice. The missing details are significant for they posit the stature of the adversaries.

> JOSSIUS. L'empereur frémissant poussa deux cris hor-
> ribles.
> Il saisit le géant entre ses poings terribles,
> Et l'étreignit si fort sur son corset d'airain
> Que son talon fit choir deux créneaux dans le Rhin.
> II, 1843-44)

> JOSSIUS. *The trembling emperor let forth two hor-*
> *rible cries. He seized the giant between his ter-*
> *rible fists, and clasped him so firmly upon his*
> *bronze corset that his heel knocked two pieces of*
> *the battlements into the Rhine.*

This passage successfully links the fury of the struggle with the size of the castle, and helps explain the importance of place in *Les Burgraves*. During the combat the brothers recognize each other, an important omission in the final version where in other instances the mechanics of the recognition scene are repeatedly exploited.

D. THE FAILURE OF *Les Burgraves*

At the end of the prologue's exposition we find the passage most sorely missed in the play as it was finally performed.

> JOSSIUS. Et nous restâmes là, tous, croyant voir un
> rêve,
> Comme si saint Michel, debout, tenant le glaive,

Terrible, l'oeil en flamme et le pied sur Satan,
Soudain jetait l'épée et lui disait: Va-t'en!

(II, 1844)

JOSSIUS. *And all of us were riveted there, thinking
we saw a dream, as if Saint Michael, upright, hold-
ing his sword, terrible, his eyes aflame and his foot
on Satan, suddenly threw away his blade and said
to him: Away!*

The reaction of the soldiers, who transform the warriors
into quasi-celestial beings of cosmic dimensions, should
be our reaction as well. This is Hugo at his myth-mak-
ing best, writing as he does in *La Légende des siècles*,
turning men into giants. This is the crux of *Les Burgraves*, as expressed in the preface and as realized in
certain scenes. But the finished play does not fulfill the
promise. The battle of giants, so excitingly recounted by
others, is enfeebled by a conventional conclusion. Here
Hugo succumbs to one of his obsessions as he shifts from
the realm of myth to a banal treatment of the theme of
paternity characteristic of many of his dénouements.[11]
He sets the audience to wondering whether Job will reveal to Otbert that he is his father, whether the son will
commit parricide. Our attention is irretrievably shifted
away from the legendary matter that is the true core
of the play. The fault is compounded by the conventionality of the poetry throughout. The verbal magic that
invests the best scenes of *Hernani* is absent. What dis-
tinguishes the two plays is an almost complete reversal
of emphasis. In *Hernani* the poetry is song; in *Les
Burgraves* the poetry is vision. While we can hardly

[11] In *Cromwell* the son almost kills the father; Triboulet is directly
responsible for the death of Blanche, his daughter, in *Le Roi s'amuse*;
Lucrèce Borgia and Gennaro, her son, kill each other.

expect lyric transport from characters one hundred years old, something other than the cliché rhetoric of *Les Burgraves* would have given it a sound commensurate with its shape.

The defects reveal Hugo's uneasiness at a task perhaps doomed from the start. He is victim of a theatrical tradition at odds with a particular theatrical vision.[12] Abandoning the projected prologue with its distant castle and its extended descriptions is obviously a concession to the "well-made play," a play more in line with the expectations of the public. The gesture is a futile one for enough is left of the epic-mythic play to clash gracelessly with the standard dramatics of the finale. The initial images of the Rhine, the burg, the wandering crone, Saint Michael, and Satan, granted unexpected theatrical viability, are reduced in size and interest as they become increasingly involved in the dénouement. The theatrical myth becomes a melodramatic situation, and the disproportion is ruinous to the play's integrity. We are left to marvel at the uniqueness of Hugo's point of departure, and with some doubt as to whether there was a satisfactory way to complete the design.

[12] Michel Butor, in "Le Théâtre de Victor Hugo" (Jan. 1965), p. 112, makes an eloquent case for Hugo's theatrical vision in *Les Burgraves*. "He thus makes a kind of demonstration of the technical insufficiencies of the theatre of his time, suggesting a new theatre which could only come about in a new society. Due to this constant defiance of the limits of traditional theatre, today it would only be possible to give justice to that part of Hugo's works by signaling him as the precursor of all our attempts at total theatre, in the most spectacular way imaginable."

1. The Death of Hernani, by Louis Boulanger. From the collections of la Maison de Victor Hugo.

2. (*above*) Dishevelled Romans at the First Performance of *Hernani*, by Granville. From the collections of la Maison de Victor Hugo.

3. (*left*) Mounet-Sully as Hernani. From la Bibliothèque de l'Arsenal collection.

4. (*right*) Madame S.-Weber as Guanhumara in *Les Burgraves*.

Daumier caricature of
the failure of *Les
Burgraves*

Hugo, lorgnant les voûtes bleues,
Au Seigneur demande tout bas
Pourquoi les autres ont des queues
Quand les Burgraves n'en ont pas.

*Hugo, gazing into the blue
vaults of heaven, asks
the Lord in a whisper why
the others* [falling stars]
have tails [box-office lines]
*when Les Burgraves
doesn't have any.*

5. (*top left*) Les Burgraves, by Daumier. From the collections of la Maison de Victor Hugo.

6. (*bottom left*) *Les Burgraves*, Part III, scene 3 of La Comédie-Française production. From the March 2, 1902 issue of *Le Théatre*.

7. (*above*) A Study for le Burg à la Croise, by Victor Hugo. From the collections of la Maison de Victor Hugo.

8. (*above*) Geneviève Page
and Gérard Philipe in
Les Caprices de Marianne.
Photograph courtesy of
Studio Lipnitzki, Paris.

9. (*below*) Marie Bell
(Elsbeth) and Pierre Fresnay
(Fantasio) in Musset's
Fantasio. La Comédie-
Française, 1925.

10. (*above*) Gérard Philipe and Suzanne Flon in *On ne badine pas avec l'amour*. Photograph courtesy of Studio Lipnitzki, Paris.

11. (*below*) Camille. An illustration by Eugène Lami for *On ne badine pas avec l'amour*. Photograph courtesy of Bulloz, Paris.

12. Poster for Lorenzaccio with Sarah Bernhardt, by A. M. Mucha. Courtesy of la Bibliothèque de l'Arsenal.

four

LYRIC ECHOES:
Nostalgia and Parody
Torquemada and *Mangeront-ils?*

THE fiasco of *Les Burgraves* irrevocably signals Hugo's retirement from the Parisian stage, but does not mark the end of his career as a dramatist. No writer with his penchant for schemes of antithesis could resist the theatre indefinitely. There is however a hiatus of more than twenty years before he engages seriously in theatrical activity once again. *La Forêt mouillée* is written in 1854, and it marks the beginning of Hugo's commitment to armchair theatre, a sub-genre skillfully exploited by Musset before him. Aside from an interesting excursion into pseudo-realistic theatre, *Mille frances de récompense* (1866), the poet devotes himself to a theatre of fantasy, giving dramatic expression to themes and images without regard for the requirements of the proscenium. The fiasco of *Les Burgraves* is often cited as the reason for Hugo's abandonment of orthodox theatre, but this seems to be only one of the responsible factors. Discouragement following the clamorous failure is probably intensified by a basic dissatisfaction with the inherent strictures of the form. The boldness of *Les Burgraves,* and its impatience with theatrical conventions, predict a break between an establishment constituted by actors, directors, and spectators, and an author whose vision becomes increasingly personal. Scenes and full-length plays not meant for stage representation are found in several of the poet's later *recueils*: *La Légende des siècles* (1859-1883), *Quatre vents de l'esprit* (1881), and the posthumous *Toute la lyre* (1888) and *Dernière gerbe* (1902).

Torquemada and *Théâtre en liberté*, published respectively in 1882 and 1886, were largely composed between 1865 and 1870, and they represent the most interesting examples of Hugo's later theatre. The interval that separates them from the playwright's first efforts gives them a shadow-like cast, as if they were remembrances of youth's excitement—the flush of adolescent love, the undisguised polemic of the young revolutionary. Yet in the case of *Mangeront-ils?* these poses are affectionately ironized. Hugo's renewed interest in the theatre offers a useful perspective into his art. From the summit of his years and the privacy of his living-room the author examines himself and the genre he so fiercely defended.

A. ADOLESCENCE: VARIATION AND REFRAIN

Torquemada returns Hugo to the land of his great successes, the Spain that nourished *Hernani* and *Ruy Blas*.[1] It is the Spain of love and politics which lends familiarity to *Torquemada* and helps bridge the chronological gap between it and the earlier plays. This gap is superficial, for it does not mark a change in theatrical style. The armchair format does little to distinguish it from the plays of the *Hernani-Ruy Blas* period. *Torquemada* is interesting not for its innovations, but for its

[1] *Iñez de Castro* (1818) is his first play which boasts a Spanish locale.

purity. It contains a distillation of some of the author's best theatrical notions, combined with the skill of experience and hindsight. The excitement of invention that marks *Les Burgraves* is absent, but in its place stands, ironically enough, a stage-worthy piece whose occasional eloquence has not been heard since *Hernani*. The play's movement is governed by four characters, interlocking in circumstance and conflicting in essence. Torquemada is an enemy to life because of his religious fanaticism; King Ferdinand simultaneously menaces life and represents vitality through his selfish hedonism; the young lovers Sanche and Rose embody life's freshness and innocence. The system described by these related characters is dramatically sound; the encounters are sharp and offer opportunities for clashes of rhetoric as well as situation.

The first act of Part One most effectively exploits the play's potential for confrontation and introduces its significant imagery. The meeting between the King and the Prior quickly posits Ferdinand's disregard for the life of others. It is followed by a monologue that opens conventionally enough with an expression of the King's passion and energy but evolves into a chilling description of his relationship with Queen Isabelle: "deux larves,/ Deux masques, deux néants formidables, le roi,/ La reine; elle est la crainte et moi je suis l'effroi." *Two wraiths, two masks, two formidable nothingnesses, the king, the queen; she is fear and I am fright.* (I.I.ii.184-86) The notion of coldness is lengthily developed, providing the expected contrast to life's burning passion. Finally Ferdinand links the two extremes.

En revoyant demain mon regard froid,
Tu trembleras, doutant et prenant pour un songe
L'ivresse où maintenant devant toi je me plonge,

Fournaise où sous tes yeux brûle et bout mon passé,
Mon rang, mon sceptre, et d'où je sortirai glacé!
(I.I.ii.234-38)

*Tomorrow, on seeing my cold eyes, you will tremble,
doubting and taking for an illusion the intoxication
which now possesses me; a furnace burning and boil-
ing my past, my rank, my sceptre, and from which I
will emerge frozen!*

This self-description is related to imagery henceforth associated with Torquemada. The renaissance freeze-burn
conceit belongs to the whole arsenal of fire and furnaces
that characterizes the demoniacal priest.

Gucho, the King's fool, announces the play's dialectic
with images also suggestive of Torquemada.

J'ai deux marottes. L'une est en or, l'autre en cuivre.
L'une s'appelle Mal, l'autre s'appelle Bien.
Et je les aime autant l'une que l'autre. Rien
Est mon but.
    (Il considère le gazon des fosses.)
            Là des fleurs, là des feuilles séchées.
                        (I.I.ii.268-71)

*I have two baubles. One is gold, the other copper,
one is called Evil, the other Good. I love them equally.
I have no goal. (He looks down on the turf of the
graves.) Here there are flowers, there dry leaves.*

Here, the bare dramatic conflict is twice presented
symbolically, through the baubles and the prefigurative
flowers and leaves. This constitutes an interesting transition of imagery, creating a series of levels that is typical
of Hugo's verse. The play is conceived in very basic
terms, as a simplistic conflict between Good and Evil.
This scheme is familiar; the assorted prefaces reveal

Hugo's penchant for abstraction, the desire to explain dramatic conflict as moral conflict. But Hugo is a better dramatist than even he himself realizes. Good and Evil are immediately transformed into flowers and dry leaves, they are vested and colored, and become recognizable characters. Sanche and Rose will be more closely identified by the references to flowers than by the equally applicable abstractions like Virtue, Innocence, and Good. The dry leaves are evocative of Torquemada's personality. Thus, the characters escape the banality of their moral genesis and are woven into a coherent poetic system. Sanche and Rose may represent Good, but they function dramatically as flowers. Torquemada embodies Evil, but he is the theatrical manifestation of an all-consuming fire, obliquely approached through the dry leaves image. Having thus created a rhetorical and symbolic relationship between Torquemada and the lovers, Hugo will proceed to present them dramatically in a conventional plot.

The first encounter of Sanche and Rose takes up the voice of *La Grand'mère* (1865) and *Mangeront-ils?* (1867), a voice which sings youth's love and the praises of nature. This is not the heroic love-death chanted by Hernani and Doña Sol, but rather the naïve effusions of adolescence. It is the creation of a tonality absent in the theatre of the young Hugo—a fresh lyricism made poignant as it echoes in the old poet's ear.[2] It is also the best example of theatrical lyricism in Hugo's theatre since *Hernani*. The love song of death initiates his career as a dramatist; the love song of life brings it to

[2] An extended example of this nostalgia is found in the first Marius-Cosette episodes of *Les Misérables*, where Hugo lavishes patience and pages on the glances exchanged in the Luxembourg gardens.

a close. In between, the muffled exchanges of Ruy Blas and the Queen, of Otbert and Régina, seem low-keyed and furtive.

In presenting Sanche and Rose, Hugo imposes upon himself very definite rhetorical limits. He is careful not to go beyond the borders of a diction appropriate to these characters whose existence is defined by youth, sequestration, and contact with nature. Without the variety of metaphor employed by Hernani and Doña Sol, Sanche and Rose recall the earlier play as their voices meld, weaving a single poem out of their double presence. Even the structures of the respective love scenes have a measure of similarity; a series of quick exchanges is followed by an extended thematic development made by one of the characters.

It is Rose who initiates the poetic by-play. "Écoute, partageons./ À toi les fleurs, à moi les papillons." *Listen, let us share. The flowers for you, the butterflies for me.* (I.I.v.490-91) She gives impetus to the entire scene as Hugo pursues the flowers and butterflies, weaving them together, transforming them into appropriate euphemisms, and of course capitalizing on the fact that his heroine happens to be named Rose. This last effect strikes one as being simplistic at first, but then seems singularly congruent to the kind of adolescent love scene in progress.

Sanche responds to Rose's invitation with an élan fundamental to Hugo's lyricism. "Il passe/ On ne sait quoi de tendre et de bon dans l'espace." *Something tender and good is passing in space.* (I.I.v.491-92)[3] It suggests the innocent faith of these characters, a quality of their

---

[3] This flight is reminiscent of the passing angels' wings and the "quelque chose de bleu" (*Something blue*) of "Booz endormi."

lyricism which will later be exploited in the plot. Their love is projected into a flower, a butterfly, and the firmament.[4] This constitutes a metaphoric cycle, and exemplifies Hugolian transcendentalism. The latter element will be effectively thrust into contact with Torquemada's dogmatic religious fanaticism.

The duet continues along familiar lines, the voices and the gestures are mutually inspirational. While Rose tries to capture the butterflies, Sanche warns: "Ils perdront leurs couleurs, Rosa, si tu les touches." *They will lose their colors, Rosa, if you touch them.* (I.I.v.495) The inclusion of his beloved's name turns the line into a poetic commonplace on the fugacity and fragility of

[4] The butterfly-flower conceit is found in Hugo's poetry as early as *Les Chants du crépuscule* (1835) in "La Pauvre fleur disait au papillon céleste." The poem's *envoi* is particularly anticipatory of *Torquemada*. "Roses et papillons, la tombe nous rassemble/ Tôt ou tard." (*Roses and butterflies, the grave brings us together sooner or later.*) In "Vere novo" (*Les Contemplations*) the poet uses torn-up love letters as a point of departure towards the butterflies.

. . . message d'amour, d'ivresse et de délire
Qu'on reçoit en avril et qu'en mai l'on déchire,
On croit voir s'envoler, au gré du vent joyeux,
Dans les prés, dans les bois, sur les eaux, dans les cieux,
Et rôder en tous lieux, cherchant partout une âme,
Et courir à la fleur en sortant de la femme,
Les petits morceaux blancs, chassés en tourbillons,
De tous les billets doux, devenus papillons.

message of love, of rapture and delirium that one receives in April and tears up in May. At the pleasure of the joyous wind, in the meadows, in the woods, over the waters, in the sky, wandering all over, seeking a soul everywhere, and running to the flower upon emerging from the woman, you imagine that you see flying off the little white bits, swept and swirled up, of all the love notes, turned into butterflies.

Also, see above, pp. 13-18.

beauty. This last aspect is clearly prophetic. But Hugo does not linger on any single notion. He prefers to juxtapose the conventions variously, and if the result sounds like a handbook of renaissance poetic conceits, it is an astonishingly lively one. The butterflies in imminent danger of losing their color are immediately transformed into kisses. "On croit voir des baisers errer, cherchant des bouches." *One imagines kisses wandering in search of mouths.* (I.I.v.496) The flight of the butterflies and the movement of the lovers are inextricably combined, their transformations giving the scene its rapid pulse. Rose, like Doña Sol, enters into the game and participates in the image-making. She brings the kisses-mouth invention of Sanche back to the flowers. "Ils en trouvent. Ce sont les fleurs." *They find them. They are the flowers.* (I.I.v.497) But it is Sanche who closes the cadence with, "Alors, Rosa/ Puisque vous êtes fleur!" *Then, Rosa, since you are a flower!* (I.I.v. 497-98) This is the ply of the young poet in love, creating a metaphor and stealing a kiss at the same time. The flower, the girl, the butterfly and the kiss are united by the theatrical collaboration of two characters. In fact, it is the object of the metaphor, Rose, who makes the links which Sanche embellishes. The similarity of form to the love duets in *Hernani* is obvious. The theatrical metaphor is embodied and sounded, its tension thereby increasing. It is rescued from the commonplace as it fulfills a double function, identifying the characters and heightening the scene's lyricism. In the case of Sanche and Rose, the singing is particularized by the renaissance flower conventions. It places them in the corresponding historical epoch.

The butterfly hunt continues until Sanche elicits an avowal of love and a kiss. In a moment of lyric transport, he knits together all the scene's elements and composes a song to God and Nature.[5]

DON SANCHE.

Oh! la nature immense et douce existe!
Vois-tu, que je t'explique. En hiver, le ciel triste
Laisse tomber sur terre un linceul pâle et froid;
Mais, quand avril revient, la fleur naît, le jour croît;
Alors la terre heureuse au ciel qui la protège
Rend en papillons blancs tous ses flocons de neige,
Le deuil se change en fête, et tout l'espace est bleu,
Et la joie en tremblant s'envole et monte à Dieu.
De là ce tourbillon d'ailes qui sort de l'ombre.
Dieu sous le ciel sans borne ouvre les coeurs sans
    nombre,
Et les emplit d'extase et de rayonnement.
Et rien ne le refuse et rien ne le dément,
Car tout ce qu'il a fait est bon!

DOÑA ROSE.

                              Et bien! je t'aime.

DON SANCHE, éperdument.

Rose!   (I.I.v.507-20)

[5] There is a similar love scene in *La Grand'mère* (1865) in which conjugal love becomes a pretext for a hymn to God's magnificence.

On chante, on rit; on sent que l'âme est à genoux;
Et l'on a sur le front je ne sais quoi de doux,
L'air, le printemps, le ciel, l'amour profond des choses,
Des bénédictions faites avec les roses.
. . . . .
Il me semble que Dieu m'a donné le soleil!
Charles, j'ai le soleil.   (iii)

You sing, you laugh, you feel your soul is on bended knee, and you have something sweet upon your brow, the air, the spring, heaven, the profound love of things, of blessings done with roses. . . . It seems that God has given me the sun! Charles, I have the sun.

DON SANCHE. *Oh, immense and sweet nature exists!*
Let me explain. In winter, the sad sky lets down
upon the earth a pale and cold winding-sheet. But
when April returns, the flowers are born, the day
grows longer. Then the happy earth gives back its
snow flakes to the protecting sky in the form of
white butterflies, mourning becomes a holiday, and
the whole firmament is blue, and trembling joy flies
off and up to God. Because of this a rush of wings
emerges from the darkness. God, beneath the end-
less sky, opens numberless hearts, and fills them
with rapture and light. And nothing refuses him
and nothing denies him, for everything that he
does is good!
DOÑA ROSA. *Oh, I love you.*
DON SANCHE, passionately. *Rose!*

This is an instance of theatrical lyricism where the elements introduced through dramatic exchange are summarized, melded into a poem that exhibits qualities common to the lyric tradition, but pertinent to the situation and the stage. The changing of winter to summer recalls "Le temps a laissié son manteau." It sets off a whole series of metamorphoses, ostensibly proof of God's wondrous powers, and incidentally manifesting those of the poet. The reference to divine goodness is a motif linked to Sanche and Rose, in direct contrast to the hellish references dear to Torquemada. The "linceul pâle et froid" opposed to the glorious spring is yet another expression of the basic conflict between the lovers and the monk. The flowers and butterflies give personality to the standard winter-spring transformation, echoing the scene's beginning. The sequence is effectively concentrated in the butterfly-snow evocation, a double identity suggesting the seasons as well as the kisses.

Rose has little choice but to answer in an affirmation
of her love, responding to the apostrophe in the appropriate voice. "Rose," Sanche's utterance, modulates back
to the name-flower confusion with harmonics apparently
simple, but produced with dexterity in the long series
of changes.

A moment later Hugo uses the same rose imagery to
suggest the danger that threatens the young lovers in
the person of Torquemada.

> Doña Rose. Oh! le méchant rosier qui m'a piqué le
> doigt!
> Don Sanche. Ces roses! cela veut boire du sang des
> anges! (I.I.v.526-27)

> Doña Rose. *Oh! The wicked rose bush has pricked*
> *my finger!*
> Don Sanche. *These roses want to drink the blood*
> *of angels!*

As the flowers turn ominous, Rose and Sanche perceive
the mysterious monk. The extended image of the rose
changes contour through time, adapts itself to a stage
action, characterizes and creates movement. The image
is admittedly simple and conventional, and for these
reasons flexible enough to run through the scene and
give a variety of recognizable clues to the reader. Not
the least of its functions is the partial realization of
Gucho's prophetic, "Là des fleurs, là des feuilles
séchées."[6]

Torquemada's long monologue immediately following the love scene demonstrates the dramatic clash of
image and rhetoric towards which Hugo strives in his
theatre. The poet falls victim to verbosity as he accumu-
lates a seemingly infinite parade of infernal references

---

[6] See above, p. 86.

in these one hundred and twenty-seven lines. The total effect is wearisome, but an interesting set of allusions to Satan is introduced that will later be exploited. The redemption through fire promised by the fanatic is provocatively similar to the fires of Hell. This is punctuated at the end of the speech when Torquemada announces, "Je ferai flamboyer l'autodafé suprême,/ Joyeux, vivant, céleste! —Ô genre humain, je t'aime!" *I will set aflame the supreme auto-da-fé, joyous, living, celestial! O humankind, I love you!* (I.I.vi.655-56) The expression of universal love is an ironic reprise of Sanche's lyric outburst, at once putting these characters into verbal proximity and setting off their antithetical visions. This pattern will be reiterated at the play's conclusion.

The scene of Torquemada's judgment and entombment is particularly effective, making clever use of group movements and antiphonal voices.[7] In a sequence of cadences established at the beginning, Torquemada's prayer issuing from the tomb is interrupted by an exchange between the lovers, a device already exploited with success in *Hernani*.[8]

LA VOIX, *dans le tombeau.*
  Grâce!
DOÑA ROSE.
              Entends-tu des chants?
DON SANCHE.
                  Non. Mais j'entends des cris.
VOIX DES MOINES. *(Elles vont décroissant de plus en plus et s'affaiblissant dans l'éloignement.)*
  Onus grave super caput.

---

[7] Another example of this sort of antiphony occurs in Act III of *Lucrèce Borgia*, when the drinking songs of the party are interrupted by the chanting monks.

[8] See above, pp. 30, 59.

DOÑA ROSE.
Tu vois qu'on chante.
La nuit avec des chants dans l'ombre est plus
touchante.
Un chant, c'est de la joie offerte au ciel sacré.
Tout aime sur la terre. Aimons!   (I.I.viii.758-62)
THE VOICE, in the tomb. *Mercy!*
DOÑA ROSE. *Do you hear songs?*
DON SANCHE. *No. But I hear cries.*
VOICES OF MONKS. (They diminish, growing more
and more feeble in the distance.) *Onus grave super
caput.*
DOÑA ROSE. *You hear them singing. The night, with
songs in the darkness is more touching. A song is
joy offered to the sacred firmament. Everything
loves upon the Earth. Let us love!*

The lovers offer different interpretations regarding the
sound's origin, making a transition to a figurative world
in which the voice of Torquemada becomes the chant of
the priests, and then a night song of love and God. The
metaphysical element was absent in the *Hernani* confusion over the *tocsin* and the horn, but otherwise the
mechanism is exactly the same, exploiting two points of
view to give movement to lyric ecstasy. In *Torquemada*
the ambiguity between the lovers' transport and divine
love is a constant reminder of the distance that separates
Rose-Sanche and the fanatic monk.[9]

[9] This is visualized in the final moment of the play as the lovers,
expecting deliverance, see the banner of the Inquisition appear in
the distance. Jean-Bertrand Barrère, in *La Fantaisie de Victor Hugo,
1852-1885* (Paris, 1960), II, 435, analyzes the love scene of Rose and
Sanche, and the juxtaposition of the Inquisition during the final
scene, "where the beatitude of the lovers is sinisterly accompanied
by the slowly ascending procession of penitents in white and black
cowls."

Aside from the unnecessary development of the Marquis de Fuentel, Sanche's long-lost grandfather (which gives Hugo the excuse to vent his familiar paternity obsession), Act I of the first part is adroitly constructed. The directions are clear, the characters individualized with appropriate rhetorical signals, the imminent conflict is both theatrical and poetic. The working out of the play is faulty however, and the devices repetitive. A meeting between Torquemada and St. Francis de Paul adds little to the basic confrontation of good and evil. St. Francis de Paul reiterates the innocent faith of Rose and Sanche. When this meeting is interrupted by the libertine Pope Alexander VI, the "third priest," the point is made with deafening insistence. Gucho, the dwarf, is the pivot of the dénouement, a role he hardly deserves. Queen Isabella is introduced briefly, but the opportunity for an interesting development is lost. Most damaging of all is the defective portrait of the protagonist. Torquemada's utterances are unvaried, a reflection of his fanaticism, but static and untheatrical nonetheless. There is one moment, however, when Hugo manages to inject movement into this character's infernal rantings. Against the background of an auto-da-fé, Torquemada again refers to Satan.[10]

Nous sommes deux sous l'oeil de Dieu, Satan et moi.
Deux porte-fourches. Lui, moi. Deux maîtres des flammes.
Lui perdant les humains, moi secourant les âmes;

[10] Pierre Albouy, *La Création mythologique*, p. 183, notes the mythological quality of Torquemada's self-description. Paul Zumthor, in *Victor Hugo, poète de Satan* (Paris, 1946), pp. 309-310, relates Torquemada to the important image of Satan in the poet's works.

Tous deux bourreaux, faisant par le même moyen
Lui l'enfer, moi le ciel, lui le mal, moi le bien;
Il est dans le cloaque et je suis dans le temple.
Et le noir tremblement de l'ombre nous contemple.

(II.II.v.1854-60)

Satan and I are both beneath God's eye. Two pitch-fork bearers. He, I. Two masters of the flames. He destroys souls and I succor them; we are both executioners creating through the same means hell and heaven, evil and good. He is in the sewer and I am in the temple. And the black trembling of the darkness contemplates us.

The decor, simply but effectively exploited in plays like *Marie Tudor* and *Angélo, tyran de Padoue,* here offers a congruent frame for the fire imagery, giving it an extra-rhetorical vitality. More significant is the repeated dialectic between Satan and Torquemada, the only character the priest really "talks" to in the play, or more accurately, the only character capable of giving answer. In this passage, the link with Satan is exchanged for a link with God. Torquemada is a pivot between Heaven and Hell, narrowing the distance with troublesome ambiguity, shuttling between the two realms. It is here that Hugo transforms oratory into theatre, leaving intact the character's singularity, but bestowing upon him a life, a vision, and a sound consonant with the stage.

B. THE RANGE OF PARODY

Although written two years before *Torquemada,* *Mangeront-ils?* more faithfully exemplifies the final epoch in Hugo's career as a dramatist. It truly belongs to the *Théâtre en liberté,* reflecting the theatrical freedom of Musset's armchair theatre, and suggesting at the same time that Hugo has finally come to terms with

97

Shakespeare. The tonal ambiguities of *Mangeront-ils?* are closer to the spirit of that romantic ideal than the plays written immediately after the Preface to *Cromwell.* This makes it a particularly apt summa to Hugo's theatre. The official aesthetic and the homage to Shakespeare shared by all the young romantics come to fruition for Hugo forty years later.

The wedding of the lyric and the comic, ingeniously and consistently accomplished by Musset, comes hard to the stentorian Hugo. The buffoons of the early plays do little to vary the prevailing gloom; the Mack Sennett closet exchange in Act I of *Hernani* provides momentary, but unrepeated comic tone; Don César de Bazin enlivens the dramatics of *Ruy Blas,* but aside from his initial encounter with the hero in Act I his participation in the principal action is quite arbitrary. We must await *Mangeront-ils?* before meeting a full-fledged comic hero, and moreover, a comic hero whose presence is congruent with the play's lyric élan. The mercurial Aïrolo represents a variety of mood and texture unequaled in Hugo's theatre. Invective against tyranny, purely romantic love poetry, farce, and gothic legendizing are woven together, played against each other, and even mocked. The title is clearly ironic, a theatrical question resounding through the action, putting the serious gestures in a strained light, giving these gestures a freshness they had long ago lost. An element of self-parody is the play's strength, for it allows Hugo to renew the platitudes through ironic projection. It is the freedom of juxtaposition and the fluidity of tone that give *Mangeront-ils?* a privileged place in Hugo's theatrical canon.

The first clue to Hugo's newly found paradoxality lies in the description of the play's setting. In early plays the poet tended to make a stage metaphor out of the setting. The portrait gallery of *Hernani*, the prison of *Marie Tudor*, and of course the *caveau perdu* of *Les Burgraves* are examples of dramatic tensions represented in plastic configuration. In *Mangeront-ils?* the setting is no less pertinent to the action, but its characteristics are in disorder. Here, a ruined cloister harbors the lovers, is sanctuary and freedom to Aïrolo and Zineb. Outside the surrounding wall lie the forest and the sea and slavery. Thus, we see on the stage two distinct realms, the liberty of the enclosed cloister opposed to the slavery of the open world beyond. This universe is all the more absurd when we learn that the freedom of the cloister is qualified by the fact that all the plants growing there are poisonous. The only nourishment lies outside the wall, the area controlled by the tyrannical king. Hugo equates death with freedom, and life with slavery, a formula whose elements are ripe for reversal. The play's spatial relationships have the potential for dramatic and poetic movement built into them. The system posited at the beginning is intolerable, unseemly, and will ultimately be transformed by the imposition of values consistent with Hugo's universe.

This universe is controlled by a degree of coherence which links lovers with the sun, the moon, and the sometimes benevolence of the Creator. Nature is a great temple which permits sweet confusion between divine and human adoration. There is but one love scene in *Mangeront-ils?* Its first lines, intoned by Lord Slada, offer no surprise. "Viens! vois! Ce bois semble content./ Il chante, et comme nous l'aube heureuse l'embrase." *Come, see! This wood seems contented. It sings, and the happy dawn sets it ablaze like us.* (I.iii.362-63) This pattern is strongly reminiscent of *Hernani* and will be repeated in *Torquemada*. The landscape is turned into a love song, and the love song then becomes the presence of the beloved.

LORD SLADA.

Ma vie est dans l'azur, flottante, épanouie,
Lumineuse, et mon coeur s'ouvre, et je te reçois,
Et je t'aspire, esprit, femme, qui que tu sois!
Car il est impossible enfin que tu contestes
Cet éblouissement de tes regards célestes
Qui te fait souveraine et terrible, et qui rend
Insensé le pauvre homme à tes côtés errant.
Oh! vivre ensemble est doux! Ton front au jour
     ressemble.

LADY JANET, *posant sa tête sur l'épaule de Lord
     Slada.*
Quelque chose est plus doux encor; mourir en-
     semble.   (I.iii.380-88)

LORD SLADA. *My life is in the blue, floating, full-
blown, luminous, and my heart opens up, and I
receive you, and I breathe you, spirit, woman,
whichever you are! For it is impossible that you
dispute the dazzle of your heavenly eyes, which
make you sovereign and terrible, and which drives
mad the poor man wandering at your side. Oh! it
is sweet to live together! Your brow is like the day.*
LADY JANET, putting her head upon Lord Slada's
shoulder. *There is something sweeter still; to die
together.*

These are pale echoes of romanticism's first flush. This pair of lovers is nothing more than a caricature, their voices faint when compared to the passionate outpourings of Hernani and Doña Sol. They do reinforce, however, the major polarity of *Mangeront-ils?*; life in nature versus death in nature. Janet's voice harmonizes with Slada's, blending love, life, and death, hardly a new recipe but one that is about to be freshly spiced by the poet.

The exchange between Janet and Slada is capped by yet another familiar device, the poetic crescendo so fully realized in *Hernani*, and in the love scenes of *Torquemada*. Again, one of the characters sums up and synthesizes the elements previously introduced in tandem.

LORD SLADA.
    Viens! aimons-nous. Le rire et les pleurs apparaissent
    En perles dans ta bouche, en perles dans tes yeux.
    Tu t'es transfigurée en un rayon joyeux.
    Je crois te voir fouler de vagues asphodèles.
    Où donc prends-tu cela que nous n'avons point d'ailes?
    Je sens les miennes, moi. Je suis prêt. Si tu veux
    Dénouer dans l'aurore immense tes cheveux,
    Si tu veux t'envoler, je suis prêt à te suivre,
    Je te verrai planer, je me sentirai vivre,
    Pendant que tu feras derrière toi pleuvoir
    Des étoiles dans l'ombre auguste du ciel noir!
    Si tu savais, je t'aime! Ô Janet, mes paroles,
    Je les prends aux parfums, je les prends aux corolles,
    J'en suis ivre; ces flots, ces rochers, ces forêts,
    Aident mon bégaiement, et sont là tout exprès
    Pour traduire à tes yeux ce que ma voix murmure.
    Et sais-tu ce qui sort de toute la nature,
    Ce qui sort de la terre et du ciel? c'est mon coeur.
    Ce que je dis tout bas, ce bois le chante en choeur.
    Dans l'univers, qu'un songe inexprimable dore,
    Il n'est rien de réel, hors ceci: je t'adore!

Un mot remplit l'abîme. Un mot suffit. Il faut
Pour que le soleil monte à l'horizon, ce mot.
Et ce mot, c'est Amour! L'éternité le sème.
Dieu, quand il fit le monde, a dit au chaos: J'aime!
(Il lui prend la main et la pose sur ses cheveux.)
Met sur mon front ta main. Je suis ton protégé.
Déesse, inonde-moi de ta lumière.   (I.iii.420-46)

LORD SLADA.   *Come! We love each other. Laughter
and tears seem like pearls in your mouth, like pearls
in your eyes. You have been transfigured into a
joyous ray of light. I imagine you treading on hazy
asphodels. Why do you suggest that we lack wings?
I feel mine. I am ready. If you wish to unbind your
hair in the immense dawn, if you wish to fly away,
I am ready to follow you. I see you floating and I
feel myself alive, while you rain down stars in the
majestic shadow of the black sky! If you knew how
I love you! O Janet, I take my words from the
scents, I take them from the corollas, I am drunk
with them. These waves, these rocks, these forests
come to the aid of my stammering, and deliberately
exist to translate for you what my voice murmurs.
And do you know what comes forth from nature,
what comes forth from earth and heaven? It is my
heart. This wood sings in chorus what I whisper. In
the universe, gilded in an inexpressible dream,
there is nothing real beyond this: I adore you! One
word fills the abyss. One word is enough. This
word is necessary if the sun is to rise above the
horizon. And this word is Love! It is sowed by
eternity. When God created the word he said to
the chaos, I love!* (He takes her hand and places it

upon his hair.) *Put your hand on my brow. I am in
your power. Goddess, engulf me with your light.*

This sort of ecstatic transport is a frequent mode of
Hugo's lyricism at this point in his career. The duet of
Emma Gemma and Charles in *La Grand'mère*, and that
of Rose and Sanche in *Torquemada* exhibit similar
transformations, using nature as a keyboard for sounding the strains of love. Slada expresses himself in a
rapid series of metaphors. Laughter and tears become
a double string of pearls, light-reflecting images which
expand to make of Janet "un rayon joyeux." As light,
she flies up, propelled by the creative energy of the
metaphor as well as by its specific luminosity. The poet
who accomplishes the metamorphosis follows her, flying on words. Having achieved flight, the poet addresses
himself to earth, sky, and universe, and hears his love
song amplified in chorus. The song is the word, the only
word, the love that links the poet creator and the divine creator. The ultimate return to earth is in no sense
disappointing for the goddess of light accompanies him.

Slada's outburst is another one of those repertoires of
poetic devices so dear to Hugo.[11] Its length and eloquence are exceptional, especially in contrast to Janet's
immediate reaction. The goddess of light, whose love
is caroled by all of nature, reveals in an aside, "J'ai/ Une
faim." *I am hungry.* (I.iii.446-47) The poet, who has
barely finished his duet with the universe, rejoins with
"Oh! la soif!" *Oh! This thirst!* (I.iii.447) Here lies the
secret of Hugo's conscious self-parody. It requalifies his
lyricism. The love of Janet and Slada interests him
only slightly. The mature Hugo has assimilated the
sentimental lyric vocabulary into his transcendentalism;

[11] See above, p. 47.

now he sings of life rather than death. The comic under-cutting of the love scene does not so much ironize ro-mantic love as put it in a new relief. Janet and Slada function in concert with Aïrolo and Zineb. They repre-sent only a part of the playwright's intention, that of finding a theatrical language to express an old man's wonder at existence. Will they eat? Will they love? Will they live? Hugo's willingness to render comic Slada's hymn is proof of a new flexibility, a rhetoric and a technique capable of serving a variety of aims, and eminently theatrical because of this variety. Hugo is attempting to poeticize, through a succession of voices, the link between man and nature.

The voices of Janet and Slada are rarely heard again. They contribute to the general shape of the poem rather than constitute its center. Zineb is the same type of character. Her woes and wailings offer Hugo another frame for comedy and self-parody. This soul-sister of Guanhumara carries a feather rather than chains; the very day the play takes place is her hundredth birth-day. Whoever has read *Les Burgraves* will recognize the shade of the gloomy wandering hag. The excesses of the former here become a comic grotesquerie, an ab-surd reiteration of an image that even in its first in-carnation bordered on the ludicrous. As a result of her magic feather, her century, this caricature injects yet another brand of comedy into a theatrical poem about life and death. She expresses Hugo's transcendentalism from a viewpoint quite different from that of Slada. The lover predictably uses nature as a vast analogy for his love. This same vastness of nature prompts Zineb to sing of death.

104

Voir se superposer d'inconcevables voûtes,
Dans un tremblement triste et vague être aux écoutes,
Avoir, sans savoir où, ni comment, ni pourquoi,
La dilatation d'une fumée en soi,
C'est là mourir. L'horreur d'expirer vous étonne.
On craint d'être trop près de l'endroit où Dieu tonne.
En même temps on sent de la naissance. On croit,
Pendant qu'on s'amoindrit, comprendre qu'on
    s'accroît.
On distingue, en un lieu sans contour, un mélange
De soir et de matin, de suaire et de lange,
Les roses, ô terreur, qui vous boivent le sang,
Et le ciel qui vous prend votre âme, et l'on se sent
Finir d'une façon et commencer de l'autre.

                         (I.vi.811-23)

*To see unimaginable vaults merging, to be alert while
possessed by a sad and vague trembling, to have inside yourself, without knowing where, nor how, nor
why, the dilation of a puff of smoke—that is dying.
The horror of dying astonishes you. You fear being
too close to where God thunders. At the same time
you feel birth. While you are being diminished you
understand how you are growing. In a shapeless
place, you distinguish a mixture of the evening and
the morning, the shroud and the swaddling-clothes,
the roses, O terror, which drink your blood, and the
heavens which take your soul, and you feel yourself
finishing in one way and beginning in another.*

The contrasts, the movement, and metaphors that characterized Slada's evocation of nature are present here,
linking death and the grand universal plan. The evening, the morning, the shroud, the swaddling-clothes,

and the blood-sucking roses are lumped together by this creature whose breast "fut jadis choisi par les démons/ Pour allaiter des dieux terribles dans les monts!" *was once chosen by the demons to nurse terrible gods in the mountains!* (I.vi.845-46) The resulting mixture is heady indeed and grants the play yet another comic flavor. At the same time, Hugo manages to present a different aspect of the man-nature tension.

C. IRONY: FROM DISCORD TO HARMONY

This tension is maintained by a series of antitheses, polarities produced by shifts of tone and opposing characters. One type of tonal disharmony is demonstrated in the love scene of Janet and Slada, with its unexpected hunger-thirst coda. Another lies in the parodization of Zineb's lofty verse. It is in the conflict of characters, one of the most basic theatrical devices, that Hugo expresses the play's rather obvious message, a bold affirmation of life. Aïrolo, the chameleon-like hero, is thrust into contact with the others, illuminating their poses with the frank light of common sense. His reaction to the lovers is indicative of a consistently ironic attitude.

> Oui, c'est le paradis de s'aimer de la sorte,
> Mais toutefois un peu de nourriture importe;
> Vous êtes, j'en conviens, deux anges, mais aussi
> Deux estomacs; daignez me concéder ceci.
> Paradis, mais terrestre. Adam voudrait, en somme,
> —Pardon! — sa côtelette; Ève voudrait sa pomme.
> (I.iv.451-56)

> *Yes, it's paradise to love each other in that way, but sometimes a little food is a good thing. I agree that you are two angels, but you also have two stomachs.*

*You must concede me that. Paradise, but an earthly
one. In short, Adam would like (Excuse me!) his
cutlet; Eve would like her apple.*

If these lines lack subtlety and wit, their crudity sets
off the precious effusions that preceded. More interesting
is the way in which Aïrolo reduces the drama of the
situation to the basic problem of eating, faithfully
harking back to the play's title. Love, life, and freedom
are consistently framed by the basic existential need to
satisfy hunger pangs. This is both funny and theatrical.
It gives the play a unity of focus, notwithstanding the
variety of character and situation.

Aïrolo's concern for eating is a refrain. It serves to
deflate Zineb's death wish just as it did the love scene.

> ZINEB, *regardant autour d'elle les broussailles.*
> Ce lieu plein de venins me plaît. Port souhaité!
> Toute cette herbe, ami, c'est de l'éternité.
> C'est de l'évasion. Les poisons sont nos frères.
> Ils viennent au secours de nos pâles misères.
> Mange une de ces fleurs tragiques de l'été,
> Tu meurs. Te voilà libre.
> AÏROLO, *à part.*
> Une tasse de thé,
> Sucrée et chaude, avec un nuage de crème,
> Me plairait mieux.   (I.vi.885-92)

> ZINEB, looking at the scrub around her. *I like this
> place full of poisons. O yearned for port! All of
> these herbs, friend, are eternity. They are escape.
> The poisons are my brothers. They come to the aid
> of our pale misfortunes. Eat one of these tragic
> summer flowers and you die. You are free.*
> AÏROLO, to himself. *I would prefer a hot and sugared
> cup of tea with a bit of cream.*

But there is more than contrast in the relationship between Zineb and Aïrolo. They are both children of nature. She seeks death in the forest; he seeks life. The
rather ingenuous A to Z pattern described by their
names is carried out in terms of youth and age, action
and stasis pivoting around a profound and shared
respect for nature. Aïrolo understands his ambivalent
link to the witch. "Quoique de même espèce, elle
m'intimidait./ Elle est démon du bois dont je suis farfadet." *Although like me, she intimidated me. She is
the demon of the forest and I am its elf.* (I.vi. 749-50)
The plot illustrates this pattern. Zineb dies so as to give
life to Aïrolo, grateful because he helps her to die. This
is another interesting reversal since the character who
represents death grants life and vice-versa.

The pattern of links is further complicated by the
King. Through him Hugo fulfills an unusual design. He
creates two opposing doubles for the same character.
Aïrolo functions in a variety of interlocking contexts.
The poem about nature is served by his link to Zineb;
the poem about freedom is structured in terms of an
especially intricate juxtaposition of the King and the
"nature boy." Connecting these seemingly distinct
realms is the bold axis of life and death.

The King is an *opera buffa* tyrant. He pursues vehe-
mently the lovers, the witch, and Aïrolo while handing
out orders of execution with great relish. And yet he too
represents vitality. "Je vis, c'est tout." *I live, that is all.*
(I.ii.203) His hedonism, a hint of the soon-to-be-created
King Ferdinand in *Torquemada*, is a menace to all other
life, but it is an expression of life just the same. This
makes his opposition to Aïrolo less complete than one
would expect. Aïrolo introduces himself with a long
speech of self-identification in which he clearly dis-

tinguishes himself from the King. These apparently antithetical characters will literally and dramatically become one. *Mangeront-ils?* is not as far from *Hernani* as
it would seem. Both plays have motors that consolidate
superficial opposites.

> AïROLO. Mes bons amis, il est deux hommes sur la
> terre;
> Le roi, moi. Moi la tête, et lui le cimeterre.
> Je pense, il frappe. Il règne, on le sert à genoux;
> . . . . .
> Le prince est la médaille, et je suis le revers;
> Et nous sommes tous deux mangés des mêmes vers.
>
> (I.iv.495-506)

> AïROLO. *My good friends, there are two men on the
> earth; the king and I. I am the head, and he is the
> scimitar. I think, he strikes. He rules, he is served
> on bended knee. . . . The prince is heads and I am
> tails; and we are both eaten by the same worms.*

With this schematic type of characterization Hugo
establishes two opposing modes of existence that will
be regularly confused. His freedom is subtly associated
with the King's unquenchable will.

> LE ROI. Lâcher, reprendre, ouvrir, puis refermer la
> pince,
> C'est ma manière. Ainsi je me sens maître et prince.
> Pour jouer de la sorte avec l'espoir, l'effroi,
> La mort, la vie, il faut, vois-tu bien, être roi.
>
> (I.ii.275-78)

> THE KING. *My method is to release, to recapture, to
> open and then close my grip. Thus I am master and*

> *prince. Don't you see that to play in such a way*
> *with hope, fear, life, and death you must be king.*

AÏROLO. Être un bandit céleste errant au firmament,
Un esprit ouragan changeant cent fois de formes,
Faisant en plein azur des sottises énormes!
(I.iv.570-72)

AÏROLO. *To be a heavenly bandit wandering in the*
firmament, a spirit of the hurricane changing shape
a hundred times, doing enormously foolish things
in the big blue sky!

These capacities for change and playfulness are Aïrolo's
most interesting traits, for they describe the play as well
as the character. Aïrolo, more than lover, more than free
spirit, more than happy savage, and more than hungry,
is a singularly apt hero for *Mangeront-ils?* The play
moves and turns in rhythm with his liberating presence.

AÏROLO. Sous mes yeux tout s'épouse, et sans gêne
on s'unit,
On s'accouple, le nid encourage le nid,
Et la fauve forêt manque d'hypocrisie. (I.iv.633-35)

AÏROLO. *Everything is being married before my*
eyes, and without embarrassment all is united,
coupled; one nest encourages another, and the wild
forest contains no hypocrisy.

This is a pertinent description of his influence on the
play's development, the resolution of conflict, the wedding of Janet and Slada, the imposition of the values of
the forest on a hypocritical world. Through him nature,
freedom, and life are made one. But before the wedding
feast can take place there must be space and time for
its preparation. "Dieu, s'il n'était pas Dieu, voudrait

être le Diable. / Je vois l'envers de tout. Que c'est risible, hélas!" *God, if he weren't God, would want to be the Devil. I see the reverse side of everything. How laughable it is, alas!* (I.iv.668-69) By evoking the God-Devil antithesis, and injecting a slightly bitter laugh, Aïrolo winds up an equilibrated machine, but winds it up awry.[12] Thus he establishes a syncopation in the rhythm of episode, character, and diction, giving lightness and verve to the play's rather stodgy symbolism.

The Aïrolo-King doubling is brought to theatrical fruition in Act II when the tyrant's life is made to depend upon that of the slave. Aïrolo's abstract definition of Act I is transformed into an ironic fact. The King, who normally decrees death, is forced to plead for life. The lively "farfadet" threatens his double with suicide.

> LE ROI. Comment nous dépêtrer l'un de l'autre? Il est roi,
> Je suis esclave. Horreur! je cesse d'être moi,
> Je deviens lui. S'il a la jaunisse, le jaune,
> C'est moi. Dans son gibet, je reconnais mon trône.
> (II.iii.1229-32)

> THE KING. *How can we get untangled from each other? He is king, I am a slave. Horrors! I stop being myself, I am becoming him. If he has jaundice, I get yellow. In his gallows I recognize my throne.*

Aïrolo has assumed the identities of the other characters: the forest of Zineb, the love of Janet and Slada, the power of the King. Echoing the voice of the witch, he speaks for death, but turns death into a plea for liberty, and of course, the overthrow of the tyrant King. "Eh bien, je sens un joug. Mais la porte est ouverte. /

---

[12] This is a comic version of the God-Devil axis found in *Torquemada*, see above, p. 97.

La mort calomniée, oui, c'est la liberté!" *Ah well, I feel a yoke. But the door is open. Slandering death is liberty!* (II.iii.1412-13)

During the mock suicide of Aïrolo, Hugo exposes the play's essence, and in doing so has recourse to a technique that served him well in *Hernani* and later. It is the dramatic juxtaposition of two levels of perception, the poetic and the banal interpretation of the fiction's reality. Aïrolo swings in a tree while hanging over a precipice. The King, who thinks he will die the moment Aïrolo does, is afraid that the branch will crack.

> LE ROI.   L'arbre va s'effondrer, ô ciel! pour peu qu'il
>   bouge!
>   Il s'est blessé! Du sang! qu'est-ce qu'il a de rouge?
> AïROLO, *souriant.* Une fleur.   (II.iii.1439-41)

> THE KING.   *Heavens, the tree is going to break if he
>   budges at all! He is wounded! Blood! Does he have
>   something red?*
> AïROLO, smiling. *A flower.*

Hugo evokes a tired image, that of the flower, and restores its color in a theatrical context. The reader instantly recognizes the flower's value, an emblem of life and beauty. The King, whose understanding of life is brutal and degraded, through fear and moral blindness interprets the flower as blood. Aïrolo, who is part of the tree and nature, restores to the flower its true value. Hugo concentrates his voice in a clash of words, in an exchange of gestures and poses. To add to the effectiveness of the image he involves it in yet another ironic reversal. The King, out of fear for his life, turns the flower into death. Play-acting suicide, Aïrolo brings the flower back to the realm of the living.

In his role as poet-creator, master-of-ceremonies, Aïrolo gives the play's title its full metaphoric significance while serving the plot. Driving the King to increasing desperation, he orders a banquet to which he will eventually invite Janet and Slada.

Que le gibier, peuplade vagabonde,
S'abatte tout rôti dans des assiettes d'or!
Donnez tous vos oiseaux, de la grive au condor,
De quoi faire au seigneur Polyphème une tourte,
Bois où j'ai vu courir Diane en jupe courte!
Que les monstres exquis nageant au gouffre amer
Viennent, et pour la sauce abandonnent la mer!
Qu'un vin pur fasse fête aux poulardes friandes!
Et que de cet amas de fricots et de viandes,
Du chaudron qui les bout, du fourneau qui les cuit,
Il sorte une fumée assez épaisse, ô nuit,
Pour aller dans le ciel rougir les yeux des astres!
(II.iii.1504-15)

Let the game, that wandering tribe, crash down all roasted in golden plates! O woods through which I've seen Diana run in a short skirt, give all your birds, from the thrush to the condor, enough to make a pie for Sir Polyphemus! Let exquisite monsters swimming in the bitter gulf come and abandon the sea for our gravy! Let a pure wine celebrate the dainty fowl! And from this collection of stews and meats, from the pot which boils them, from the stove which cooks them, let there rise steam thick enough, O night, to go up to heaven and redden the stars' eyes!

The mixture of tones and dictions expresses the play's variegated texture and its liberty of movement.[13] Aïrolo,

[13] Michael Riffaterre, in his excellent "Un Exemple de comédie symboliste chez Victor Hugo," *L'Esprit Créateur*, III, No. 3, Fall

who up to this point has spoken the voice of common sense, in a suitably common register, here makes the grumbling stomach sing like a poet. The poetic feast is a hymn to nature, the various dishes merge with the universe. Hernani sang of love, Sanche will sing of butterflies, flowers and kisses, Aïrolo sings of food. His lyric transport is achieved on the steam rising from a pot, and he too reaches the sky, even if by doing so the stars' eyes must smart a bit. Of course, a strong element of self-parody runs through this passage. But if the voice of the Castilian lovers has become slightly raucous it nonetheless carries to heaven a message of man's participation in a great and beautiful plan in which a woman's dark eyes, a voice, a sauce, and some steam are modes of flight accomplished by the poet in search of unity, consonance, and harmony.

This feast heralds the wedding of Janet and Slada, freedom, life, and love. Aïrolo presides, and it is through a verbal signal that he bridges the final gap between the various realms of the play.

> AÏROLO.
> Hors moi, tout est mensonge.
> Déjeunons. —Commencez par vous donner un kiss
> Correctement.
> (Les deux amants s'embrassent éperdument.)
> C'est fait. —Mangeons.   (II.iv.1560-62)

(1965), 170, discusses the rhetorical function of Aïrolo. "The stylistic structure of this kind of comedy is simple: Aïrolo constantly leaps from one level of diction to another, from low to high style, from common speech to specialized languages. Nothing more is needed to overthrow the preconceptions, the moral clichés which by themselves maintain verbal habits."

114

AïROLO. *Outside of me, everything is a lie. Let's dine. Begin by kissing in a proper way.* (The two lovers kiss passionately.) *That's done. Let's eat.*

Aïrolo posits his identity as the play's only relevance. His fleetness, his capacity for change, and his values thrust into final coherence the lovers, the witch, and the tyrant. The words "déjeunons" and "mangeons" are resounding answers to the title's question. They frame "un kiss," a precious anglicism which when uttered by the rustic Aïrolo is shaded by irony. Love and eating, mutually exclusive at the play's beginning, now enter into concord. The proper order of things is restored, the universe makes sense, the play ends with the King's abdication and Slada being called to the throne by acclamation. Aïrolo has the last word. "Vous, vous allez régner à votre tour. Enfin,/ Soit. Mais souvenez-vous que vous avez eu faim." *Now it is your turn to rule. All right. So be it. But remember that you were once hungry.* (II.iv.1581-82) Aïrolo and food are the standard for life, the parody of romantic love is resolved in an English kiss, the hunger pangs are satisfied by a romantic banquet. It is Aïrolo's fantasy, his power of transformation, that remind us of Musset's heroes while expressing Hugo's identity as poet-dramatist. The theatre is a place of poetic vision manifested in the constant working out of metamorphoses. The pretexts of love, politics, and melodrama are exchanged for an essentially manneristic exercise in poetic imagination. Hernani, without his Doña Sol, is called Aïrolo or Fantasio.

five

ANALOGY AND SENTIMENT:
La Nuit vénitienne and
André del Sarto

MUSSET'S career as a dramatist is even more unorthodox than Hugo's although for entirely different reasons.
Impertinently dotting "i's" with moons, weeping over
the tomb of la Malibran, and spinning verse tales of
Italy and Spain, Musset is at once an ironic caricature
of the romantic and a singularly pure example of the
species. His theatre manifests this paradox, with attitudes expressive of commitment and sincerity counter-
balanced by shafts of parody and sarcasm. Though he is
the most frequently performed romantic playwright in
France today, only one of his plays was initially destined for the stage.[1] His peculiar brand of "armchair
theatre," designed with freedom, imagination, and disdain for the mechanics of representation, has proved
eminently stageworthy.[2] Many of the exquisite little

---

[1] La Nuit vénitienne (1830).

[2] Léon Lafoscade, in Le Théâtre d'Alfred de Musset (Paris, 1901),
p. 245, aptly characterizes the fine distinctions between stage and
non-stage in Musset's theatre. "Such is plot in Musset's works; in general development, it is not noticeably different from that which we
find in true theatre. In certain ways it recalls melodrama or vaude-

theatrical proverbs which Musset composed from 1835 until shortly before his death in 1855 scrve as curtain-raisers at the Comédie-française. They reveal a sure theatrical sense, a gift for *badinage* and niceties of sentiment which are still fresh. Yet these entertainments are not representative of Musset's dramatic vision, and do not reveal his projection of a poetic mode into a theatrical genre. It is only in the first moments of his creative life, from 1830 to 1835, years marked by an exhilarating variety of manner and culminating in the initiation of the *Nuits* series, that Musset finds in the dialectic of the theatre a degree of tension that allows the voicing of his artistic self-consciousness.

Before conceiving of *Un Spectacle dans un fauteuil* as a collection of prose plays, Musset had attempted to integrate theatrical devices into his poetry. As early as 1829 *Don Paez* and *Les Marrons du feu* show Musset's interest in verse dialogue, or more precisely in dialectic poetry. These poems give Musset ample opportunity to parody the taste for the exotic. *La Coupe et les lèvres* (1832) is a full-fledged Byronian melodrama in verse, replete with romantic hero.[3] Franck, the demon-lover with shades of *Hernani* and *Die Räuber*, is an atypical Musset creation: René's volcanic perch is not one the poet can long endure. The poetry of this period, heavily injected with irony, displays Musset's verbal wizardry, his flexibility of attitude. It projects a series of poses

---

ville, in others the tragedy of passion or the comedy of sentiment. He utilizes techniques common to all dramatic authors, and the results certainly exhibit a great deal of theatricality."

[3] This verse play, along with *À quoi rêvent les jeunes filles* and the poem *Namouna*, comprise the first version of *Spectacle dans un fauteuil* (1832).

that tend to shield his feelings. The range of diction and tone, the sensitivity to contemporary literature are manifested in the poet's early obsession with the purely evocatory power of language, in the pictures and voices of the *Contes d'Espagne et d'Italie.*

Beneath this belles-lettres mannerism we discern his lucidity about the nature of perception, the conditions of a poetic consciousness, the working out of poetry and reality. This set of matrices is resolved in the self-probing *Nuits* cycle, where the poet reduces art to the basic confrontation between expression and inspiration. The poet-muse encounter is preceded however by years of inquiry. It is not surprising that the bald exchanges of the *Nuits* are a concentration of a process that controls almost all of Musset's early theatre, namely the dramatization of the poet's identity.[4]

A. THE PROJECTION OF FORM

La Nuit vénitienne was a fiasco that did much to deter Musset from entrusting any more of his plays to a theatrical troupe. It is admittedly an imperfect play, but its imperfections are revealing, and its positive qualities suggest the direction his theatre will eventually take. An eerie prefiguration of Musset's personal *nuit vénitienne*, and undoubtedly inspired by the ritualistic exoticism of the period, the play is strewn with gondolas and serenades. The suicide-bent lover, the epigraph from Shakespeare's *Othello*,[5] and generally undistinguished prose show the extent to which Musset has yielded to cliché romanticism.

---

[4] Henri Lefebvre, in *Alfred de Musset dramaturge* (Paris, 1955), p. 86, discusses the theatricalization of Musset's poetry, and the period in which he became a dramatic poet.

[5] "Perfide comme l'onde," "She was false as water" (V.ii)

There is, however, one character who throws the play out of its predictable equilibrium: the Prince d'Eysenach, Laurette's husband by proxy. He introduces a tone that is governed by the use of highly inflected prose, and a point of view that is categorically opposed to banality. The tone and point of view are of course related. The rejection of common norms for judging reality is verbalized by the rejection of common speech patterns. The preciosity and the literary inventions of the Prince are part of his search for ideal beauty. He is not interested in Laurette the woman, but rather a presence of femininity, which can be captured only through style and art. He has purposely married Laurette in absentia to preserve the magical integrity he first encountered in a portrait.

The portrait-reality doubling is swiftly acted out as the Prince makes his entrance. Musset's directions leave no doubt of his intention. "Le prince entre par le fond; il a à la main un portrait; il s'avance lentement, en considérant tantôt l'original, tantôt la copie." *The prince enters at the back. He has a portrait in his hand; he advances slowly looking now at the original, now at the copy.* (ii.406)[6] A drastic alteration of point of view is insured by the reversal of elements in the comparison. The original is in effect the portrait. What follows is a rather conventional avowal on the part of the Prince that art is inferior to nature, after all. "La blancheur de cette peau pourrait s'appeler de la pâleur; ici je trouve que les roses étouffent les lis. —Ces yeux sont plus vifs, —ces cheveux plus noirs. —Le plus parfait des tableaux n'est qu'une ombre: tout y est à la surface; l'immobilité

---

[6] The extracts cited from the plays of Musset, unless otherwise indicated, are drawn from the edition of his *Théâtre complet* published by the Bibliothèque de la Pléiade (Paris, 1962).

glace; l'âme y manque totalement; c'est une beauté qui ne passe pas l'épiderme." *The whiteness of that skin might be called pallor; here I find that the roses smother the lilies. Her eyes are brighter, her hair more black. The most perfect of pictures is but a shadow: it is all surface; the immovability freezes; the soul is totally lacking; it is a beauty which does not penetrate beneath the skin.* (ii.406-407) These lines express an impatience with art that is amplified in *Les Caprices de Marianne* and *On ne badine pas avec l'amour. Fantasio*, on the other hand, emphatically posits art as a standard, as a means of possessing the object it represents. Metaphor and style have thus a double edge: they bridge the gap between object and version while drawing attention to the distance between them. In *La Nuit vénitienne* this paradox is translated into dramatic terms through the presence of portrait, object and perceiver. The Prince seizes the extravagance of Laurette's beauty through the fiction, the version he holds in his hand, the shadow which he disdains but which is instrumental in gauging his awareness.[7]

This disdain for art is fake. The Prince can barely speak without borrowing analogies from art, thereby revealing the extent to which his perception is dependent upon it. His description of love is an elaborately engineered musical metaphor, replete with variations, andante, and presto. The finale of this "morceau d'ensemble" is particularly rich, indicating the kind of de-

[7] Herbert S. Gochberg, in *Stage of Dreams, The Dramatic Art of Alfred de Musset (1828-1834)* (Genève, 1967), p. 76, uses the portrait to develop his thesis about dream and reality. "Laurette is real, but her portrait is not. The prince strides in with his portrait, but it does not help him confront and decipher the reality of his situation." It seems that both the Prince and Musset prefer not to decipher this reality, a banal one at best.

velopment Musset is prepared to grant a metaphor. "Ici, sans contredit, commence le chef-d'oeuvre; l'andante, les yeux humides de pleurs, s'avance lentement, les mains s'unissent; c'est le romanesque, les grands serments, les petites promesses, les attendrissements, la mélancolie. —Peu à peu tout s'arrange; l'amant ne doute plus du coeur de sa maîtresse; la joie renaît, le bonheur par conséquent: la bénédiction apostolique et romaine doit trouver ici sa place; car sans cela, le presto survenant . . ." *Here without contradiction commences the chef-d'oeuvre; the andante, the eyes wet with tears, advances slowly with hands clasped; here comes in the romantic, the grand vows, the little promises, the tenderness, the sadness. Little by little all is regulated; the lover no longer doubts the heart of his mistress; joy is born again, and consequently happiness: the apostolic and Romanish benediction here finds its place; for without the following presto . . .* (ii.408) The feelings of the character are controlled by strong doses of imagination and irony. In order to create the distance necessary for perspective, the Prince transfers love into non-verbal domains: painting and music. To the musical analogy yeast is added in the form of "le romanesque," "la bénédiction apostolique et romaine," and the whole series of gestures and attitudes which form a caricature. The Prince's craving for love and beauty is tempered and ironized by this measure of condescension.

In *La Nuit vénitienne* Musset attempts to resolve the dilemma inevitable in a theatre whose aim is essentially the elucidation of feeling rather than the working out of destiny. His interests are sentiment and the media of sentiment. These cannot be served through the traditional apparatus of dramatic encounter. The conflict between characters is bypassed. Musset's preoccupations with art and love, with form and personality are focused in the perception of the Prince d'Eysenach. The matter is imagination rather than incident, and the preservation of imagination's integrity is the playwright's major concern. The theatrical encounter of this play is between Laurette and portrait, love and music, and the resulting tension is sufficiently dramatic to give the impression that an action has transpired. It is, of course, only an impression, for if something had really happened Musset would have violated the framework of his interest. He would have traded his reflective hero for theatrical circumstance.

The play's poetic movement is the discovery of a personal ideal of beauty, and hence the possibility of love. The portrait and the musical analogy are levels of style which lead to the ideal woman. The Prince's vision and his sensitivity to art create the form through which the real Laurette can be possessed. The analysis of this process of idealization is misleading in that it is out of proportion to the play's scope and merits. Only these few speeches of the Prince convince us that Laurette is worth the elaborate machinery contrived by Musset. The play itself is weakened by the parenthetical lover, Razetta. The poet-dramatist has not yet found the technique which will do justice to both poetry and drama, but the Prince d'Eysenach leads us to believe that he will.

B. THE POWER OF REALITY

In addition to exhibiting Musset's undeveloped theatrical technique, *André del Sarto* takes up some of the motifs of *La Nuit vénitienne*. The Italian setting, the triangle and its inevitable jealousy, the linking of love and art are predictable ingredients, and their combination is no more successful here than it was in the earlier play. *André del Sarto* is a step backwards in at least one sense, for it has no character as articulate as the Prince d'Eysenach. The plot is without twist, the diction unambiguous. Musset seems victim of the prototype romantic melodrama, a model inimical to his particular ironic stamp.

The play's defects do not stem entirely from its conventionality. One senses that here Musset is inhibited by the fact that both the play's heroes are artists. In *La Nuit vénitienne, Les Caprices de Marianne, Fantasio, On ne badine pas avec l'amour,* and *Lorenzaccio* the author dramatizes the awakening and sharpening of perception in a variety of manners and contexts. The distinguishing factor between these works and *André del Sarto* is the professional status of the heroes. André and Cordiani do not successfully reveal the soul of the artist precisely because for them it is professional baggage. The evolution, the obliquity, and the revelation of perception in characters like the Prince d'Eysenach, Elsbeth, Lorenzo, and others is denied the painter and sculptor. André and Cordiani are unconvincing because they conform to a preconceived and rigid image of the artist. They do however provide insight into that image.

Musset again seeks to define the relationship between art and reality which he introduced in *La Nuit vénitienne.* Cordiani literally invades nature in an effort to capture his lover: ". . . je cours dans ce jardin depuis hier; je me suis jeté dans les herbes humides; j'ai frappé les statues et les arbres, et j'ai couvert de baisers terribles les gazons qu'elle avait foulés." . . . *I have been pacing this garden since yesterday. I threw myself on the damp grass; I caressed the trees and the statues, and I have covered with my kisses the lawn over which she has walked.* (I.iii.1195)[8] This is an emphatic effort to relate nature, art, and sentiment. The lack of differentiation between the statues and trees effectively relegates them to the same category of metaphor. Such an attitude portrays the search for form, an effort to grant life to the image through poetic objectification.

The cliché poetic stance is maintained and enhanced as Cordiani switches references and imagines himself engaged with words rather than colors and shapes.

Et maintenant qu'assis à ma table je laisse couler comme de douces larmes les vers insensés qui lui parlent de mon amour, et que je crois sentir derrière moi son fantôme charmant s'incliner sur mon épaule pour les lire; maintenant que j'ai un nom sur les lèvres, ô mon ami! quel est l'homme ici-bas qui n'a pas vu apparaître cent fois, mille fois dans ses rêves, un être adoré, fait pour lui, devant vivre pour lui? Eh bien! quand, un seul jour au monde, on devrait rencontrer cet être, le serrer dans ses bras et mourir!
(I.iii.9-10)

And now that she is mine, now that seated at my table I let flow like sweet tears the foolish verses which tell her of my love, and that I seem to feel behind my chair her charming spirit leaning against my shoulder to read them; now that there is a name on my lips, O my friend, where is the man here below who has not in his dreams a hundred times, a thousand times, seen the adored being made for him stand living before him? Well! when one day he encounters this being, he must hold it in his arms even if he die for it!

Musset provides a storehouse of poetic commonplaces:

[8] This was cut from the staged version of 1851.

the use of simile, the reference to verses, the search for the phantom-woman, her possession signaled by her naming, the eternalization of the form in love-death.[9] Again, one is reluctant to grant disproportionate significance to this utterance, since Cordiani is an unrealized character in a minor work. Yet the formality of these gestures will be ripened into dramatic coherence in subsequent plays. It seems pertinent to emphasize the reference to naming the beloved, endowing her with life through a purely verbal act, one in which the poet literally christens the form and thereby fashions its uniqueness. This uniqueness is posited on the fulfillment of possession, and the very instant of the fulfillment. The beloved is named, the sonnet is terminated, and Cordiani says: "Là, dans une chambre fermée à tous les yeux, j'ai taillé dans le marbre le plus pur l'image adorée de ma maîtresse." *There, in a room closed to all, I have fashioned in the purest marble the image of my adored mistress.* (I.iii.11) Once the formal possession is complete and coincidental with the possession of sentiment, love-death freezes the two in beauty, in the purest marble of the sculptor, in the dénouements of Musset's comedies.

After these few moments of reflection, Cordiani is reintegrated into the melodrama, but his artist's consciousness is fittingly passed on to his teacher in art and rival in love, André del Sarto. Musset accomplishes an interesting variation on the love-art theme as André's dominance emerges. The teacher replaces the pupil, the disillusioned professional is substituted for the hopeful apprentice. André characterizes the relationship between love, inspiration, and nature in a way that pre-

[9] Gochberg discusses extended metaphors, pp. 134-35.

figures the complaint of sterility expressed in *La Nuit de mai:*

> . . . le peu de talent qu'on me trouvait fit croire à ma famille que j'étais protégé par une fée, et moi, je regardais dans mes promenades les bois et les ruisseaux, espérant toujours voir ma divine protectrice sortir d'un antre mystérieux. C'est ainsi que la toute-puissante nature m'attirait à elle. Je me fis peintre et lambeau par lambeau le voile des illusions tomba en poussière devant moi. . . . Elle seule! Oui, quand elle parut, je crus que mon rêve se réalisait et que ma Galathée s'animait sous mes mains. Insensé! mon génie mourut dans mon amour. (II.xiv.1230)[10]

> . . . *the small amount of talent which the world has found in me made my family believe that I was protected by a fairy. As for me, during my walks I used to search in the woods and streams, always hoping to perceive my divine protectress appear from some mysterious grotto. It was thus that all-powerful Nature drew me to her. I made myself a painter, and bit by bit the laurels of fame fell in dust at my feet. . . . She alone! Yes, when she appeared I thought that my dream was realized, and that my Galatea breathed beneath my hands. Foolish man, my genius died in my love.*

A struggle develops between the ideal woman, muse, fairy, and the real woman, the unfaithful Lucrèce. Reality is stronger than illusion, the painter can function no more, the poet is silenced.[11] The tenuous link be-

---

[10] This was cut from the 1851 version.

[11] In order to exemplify another of the unrealizable dreams which he finds in Musset's work, Gochberg scores the problem of inspiration. "The parallelism of inspiration and love, seen before in Musset's

tween the artist's craft and his life is here responsible for the passage from love to despair. André recalls the Prince d'Eysenach's imposition of form upon life. Musset perceiver and Musset artist are not always identical. The distance that separates impression and art will be bridged in various ways by the characters in Musset's theatre, but their awareness of the gap is not always a guarantee of success in closing it. Such distinctions account for the most intriguing ambiguities and the dramatic tension of the subsequent plays.

In *André del Sarto* Musset cannot discard the cliché version of the artist or surpass theatrical conventionality. The irrelevant swordplay will be translated into a dialectic of attitude and conflict of perception when Musset finds a framework that can house his own diction and his own free invention. The rhetorical artists, Cordiani and André, will be replaced by the secret, unprofessional poets who make life from verses rather than verses from life. The amateur Prince d'Eysenach is their spiritual master.

---

attitudes toward his work, appears again in André's words. Both quintessences are of divine origin, both are elusive and beyond the mastery of mortals, both are perennial and often unrealizable dreams of those who live and crave love, and of those who create and crave perfection." p. 134.

six

FROM RHETORIC TO POETRY:
Les Caprices de Marianne

PUBLISHED only a month and a half apart in the *Revue des Deux Mondes*, the distance between *André del Sarto* and *Les Caprices de Marianne* is enormous. Musset suddenly finds the means for rendering his most pressing intentions; the characters and the diction take on the sentimental irony that is peculiar to his best work. More significant, and perhaps the key to these changes, the latter play is both theatrical and poetic.

One of the strengths of *Les Caprices de Marianne* is its consistency of tone. The isolated scene of the Prince d'Eysenach and the remarks of Cordiani and André, provocative and anticipatory, suddenly blossom into a play. Acuteness of perception is vested even in minor characters, creating a linguistic system closed to banality. Claudio, Marianne's husband, appears only briefly, yet his diction is as highly inflected as that of the heroes. Despite the fact that he represents conventionality, his speech is figurative, and he enunciates one aspect of the play's dominant motif. "Oui, il y a autour de ma maison une odeur d'amants. Personne ne passe naturellement devant ma porte; il y pleut des guitares et des messages secrets." *Yes, there is an odor of lovers about my house; no one seems to pass my door naturally. There is a rain of guitars and procuresses.* (I.ii.230)[1] The "odeur d'amants" immediately ironizes the amorous activities of Célio, who is inadequate to the demands of the role he is trying to play: Harlequin yearning for Columbine. His love instead is emphatically unconventional, transcending the under-the-balcony mooning of a young Neapolitan swain. Claudio subjects the caricature to a rain of guitars. The play is full of guitars; music is closely allied to the crux of Célio's dilemma: the relationship between love and poetry, love and expression. Claudio is ironic in reducing lovemaking to guitars. For Célio, love is poetry and music, and it is his task to transform the pose into sentiment through the projection of his unique personality.

A. A COUNTERPOINT OF ARTICULATION

Célio's confusion and frustration are clear reminders of the poetic problem encountered in *La Nuit vénitienne* and *André del Sarto*. Ostensibly suffering because he cannot speak of love to Marianne, he is really tormented by an inability to speak of love at all.

Malheur à celui qui se livre à une douce rêverie, avant de savoir où sa chimère le mène, et s'il peut être payé de retour! —Mollement couché dans une barque, il s'éloigne peu à peu de la rive; il aperçoit au loin des plaines enchantées, de vertes prairies, et le mirage léger de son Eldorado. Les flots l'entraînent en silence, et quand la Réalité le réveille il est aussi loin du but où il aspire, que du rivage qu'il a quitté. Il ne peut plus ni poursuivre sa route ni revenir sur ses

[1] In the first version of the play, which appeared in the *Revue des Deux Mondes* (1833), Claudio's remark was more piquant. The "messages secrets" were "entremetteuses."

pas. (*On entend un bruit d'instruments.*) Quelle est
cette mascarade? N'est-ce pas Octave que j'aperçois?
(I.iii.232)

*Unhappy he who gives himself up to a sweet dream
before knowing where his chimera is leading him,
and whether his love be returned! Softly pillowed in
a boat, little by little he leaves the shore; from afar
he perceives enchanted plains, green prairies, and the
light-mirage of his Eldorado. The winds silently bear
him on, and when reality awakens him, he is as far
from the goal he aspires to as he is from the shore
he has left. He can no longer continue on his way, nor
retrace his steps.* (The sound of music is heard.)
What is this masquerade? Is it not Octave I perceive?

Célio is neutralized, caught between reality and vision,
unwilling to participate in the first and unable to reach
the second. Exiled from both realms, he will use the
other characters in an effort to take up the movement
again. His failure marks him as the play's victim. He is
denied the successful resolution of the image-object
identity that is granted to the Prince d'Eysenach. Célio
never finds the language that fixes possession, the magic
word that turns sentiment into art.

Célio's musing is immediately polarized by another
character, thus thrusting his attitude into a dialectic.
The "bruit d'instruments" that announces Octave's arrival is a theatrical rendering of the previous references
to serenades. The musical bridge between the characters is not merely decorative, for it contains the essence of their theatrical and poetic relationship. Octave
and Célio voice a contrapuntal composition, a thorough
working out of one destiny, one personality through the
conjunction of two halves. It is not the reflection of one

or the other, but the juxtaposition of two identities, a dramatic collaboration that gives the play movement. This is a significant advance in technique over *La Nuit vénitienne* and *André del Sarto*. Célio is the poet of vague countries, cut off from life and unable to find an alternate existence either in art or in the realization of his dreams. Octave the rhetorician never lacks the right word, the pertinent image. The whole of life is a well of metaphors; living and talking are acts of boundless energy. During this first meeting the introspection of Célio is played against the activity of Octave. The characters shadow each other. Célio's voyager image is redefined by Octave. We perceive the difference between the two characters in the quality of its elaboration. They share the same self-consciousness, two voices sound their dual presence, and the details of manner reinforce their antiphony.

Figure-toi un danseur de corde, en brodequins d'argent, le balancier au poing, suspendu entre le ciel et la terre; à droite et à gauche, de vieilles petites figures racornies, de maigres et pâles fantômes, des créanciers agiles, des parents et des courtisanes, toute une légion de monstres se suspendent à son manteau et le tiraillent de tous côtés pour lui faire perdre l'équilibre. Des phrases redondantes, de grands mots enchâssés cavalcadent autour de lui; une nuée de prédictions sinistres l'aveugle de ses ailes noires. Il continue sa course légère de l'Orient à l'Occident. S'il regarde en bas, la tête lui tourne; s'il regarde en haut, le pied lui manque. Il va plus vite que le vent, et toutes les mains tendues autour de lui ne lui feront pas renverser une goutte de la coupe joyeuse qu'il porte à la sienne. Voilà ma vie, mon cher ami; c'est ma fidèle image que tu vois. (I.iv.233)

Imagine a rope-dancer, in silver buskins, his balancing pole in his hands, suspended between the heavens and the earth. To right and to left little shriveled old figures, phantoms pale and thin, agile creditors, relatives and prostitutes. A whole legion of monsters cling to his coat and pull him on all sides to make him lose his balance. Redundant phrases, with big words introduced, circle around him; a multitude of sinister predictions blind him with their black wings. He continues his airy course from Orient to Occident. If he looks down, his head swims; if he looks up, he loses his footing. He is fleeter than the winds, and all the outstretched hands around him can not make him spill a drop from the gladsome cup he holds in his own. That is my life, my dear friend; it is a faithful image of myself that you perceive.

Célio lies placidly in a boat, drifting away from the shore of reality, and then motionless. Octave seems to be suspended as well, but this serves only to distinguish him further from Célio. He is upright, dancing in little silver boots, defying earth and heaven with his individuality and unique style. The impersonal "celui" of Célio[2] becomes a tight-rope walker, fully characterized, menaced by recognizable forces. The poet finds equilibrium a prison, the rhetorician proudly sustains it as necessary to his eloquence. The first is doomed to silence, the second is a master of style. Energy is style itself, and replaces sentiment in Octave. The extent to which Octave's existence is defined by expression is revealed in the last line of this passage. For him, the true reality is the metaphor. The personality refined by

[2] See above, p. 129.

allusions and images is the seizable essence.[3] The elaboration of metaphoric personality intensifies the distinction between Célio and Octave. Célio lacks the precise metaphor. At the outset, his inarticulateness is thrust upon Octave's glibness. Both characters are aware of the relationship between image and reality. Célio is a victim of a dichotomy he perceives. Octave refuses to separate the two elements. He cedes to the power of reality, of which he himself is the image.

The first encounter between Célio and Octave is subtly modulated to provide an increasingly complex set of clues. Each enthusiasm of Octave is feebly parried by Célio's pessimism, his self-deprecation. "Quel charme j'éprouve, au lever de la lune, à conduire sous ces petits arbres, au fond de cette place, mon choeur modeste de musiciens, à marquer moi-même la mesure, à les entendre chanter la beauté de Marianne!" *What a charm I feel, as the moon rises, in leading beneath these trees, at the rear of this garden, my modest band of musicians, in leading them myself and hearing them sing the praises of Marianne!* (1.iv.234) His small joys are second-hand. This tender reprise of the guitar motif introduced by Claudio in the first scene follows Octave's tight-rope act, and aptly defines the distinct manners of the two characters. Célio's participation in the serenade is theoretical, abstract. He provides the beat while a modest group of musicians sings the melody. Musset again exploits the rather pathetic frustrations of Célio, the incomplete artist, desirous but incapable of making his own music.

The doubling device seems to prove that Célio and

[3] This is a reversal of the portrait-object notion elaborated in *La Nuit vénitienne*, see above, pp. 119-20.

Octave are but two parts of the same man, the heart
and the brain, or perhaps the soul and the voice.[4]
Célio sighs and Octave sings, one providing the feeling
and the other its expression. Musset is here dramatizing
the symbolic process, but is careful to clothe the allegory with plot, exotica, and recognizably human characters.

> CÉLIO.   Vingt fois j'ai tenté de l'aborder; vingt fois j'ai
> senti mes genoux fléchir en approchant d'elle. Quand
> je la vois, ma gorge se serre et j'étouffe, comme si
> mon coeur se soulevait jusqu'à mes lèvres.
> OCTAVE.   J'ai éprouvé cela. C'est ainsi qu'au fond des
> forêts, lorsqu'une biche avance à petits pas sur les
> feuilles sèches et que le chasseur entend les bruyères
> glisser sur ses flancs inquiets, comme le frôlement
> d'une robe légère, les battements de coeur le pren-
> nent malgré lui; il soulève son arme en silence, sans
> faire un pas, sans respirer.   (I.iv.235)

> CÉLIO.   *Twenty times have I endeavored to accost
> her; twenty times have I felt my knees giving way
> as I approached her. When I see her I am stifled, as
> if my heart rose e'en to my mouth.*
> OCTAVE.   *I have felt the same. It is thus that in the
> depths of the forest, when a deer advances slowly
> over the dry leaves, and the hunter hears the
> heather brushing against its heaving sides, like the
> rustling of a dress, his heart beats in spite of him-
> self. He silently raises his gun, without moving,
> almost without breathing.*

Célio expresses a death-like anguish at the mere thought

---

[4] Gochberg, in *Stage of Dreams*, interprets Célio's dilemma as an
inability to distinguish between reality and fantasy, p. 141.

of approaching Marianne. Musset capitalizes on this conventional attitude. The love-death cliché is the pivot around which the author turns the plot, expressing degrees of perception through nuances of vagueness and precision. Célio trembles and chokes when he thinks of love; Octave constructs elaborate images. He is Célio's metaphor.

The hunter, the doe, and the forest are a romantic reduction of the pastoral.[5] Musset locates love and death in a recognizably literary framework. Here he reveals his taste for the metaphor within the metaphor, linking Célio's Marianne to the doe to the unnamed woman suggested by the "robe légère." This circular scheme is inflected by widening the distance between the object and its referents. The Marianne-*biche* relationship is extended aurally through the sound of little hoofs on dry leaves to the sensual trembling of bushes against the body of the animal. This ambiance is suddenly lifted into another and even more tantalizing sphere, and the whisper of the passing dress truly makes the pulse of both hunters race faster. The initial comparison, a visual and synthetic one, is replaced by provocative noises, very close to silence, and then resolved in the hunters' bated breath. Through his construct Octave changes the essence of the object. The inhibited Célio becomes the pursuing hunter who hesitates not through fear but delicious anticipation. Octave's version turns the victim into the victor. The poet triumphs in the work of art as the hunter aims his rifle. Célio lacks the strength to do either.

Célio however is not a coward. His fault is one of tech-

---

[5] Chateaubriand's *Atala*, a mine of nature imagery and a remarkably complete transposition of the pastoral, consistently qualifies the beloved as a *biche*.

nique. Borrowing Musset's own metaphor, Célio is the hunter who sees the doe but is unable to take aim. The special poignancy of this character comes from his consciousness, his lucidity. Once again he is rooted in immobility by the perception of a far-off beauty.

> Pourquoi ce qui te rendrait joyeux et empressé, ce qui t'attirerait, toi, comme l'aiguille aimantée attire le fer, me rend-il triste et immobile? La réalité n'est qu'une ombre. Appelle imagination ou folie ce qui la divinise. Alors folie est la beauté elle-même. Chaque homme marche enveloppé d'un réseau transparent qui le couvre de la tête aux pieds; il croit voir des bois et des fleuves, des visages divins, et l'universelle nature se teint sous ses regards des nuances infinies du tissu magique. Octave! Octave! viens à mon secours! (I.iv.235)

> *Why does that which would make you happy and ardent, that which would attract you, as the magnetic needle attracts steel, why does it make me sad and motionless? Reality is but a shadow. Call imagination or folly that which defies it. Folly is then beauty itself. Each man walks enveloped in a transparent network that covers him from head to foot. He believes that he sees woods and rivers, divine forms and faces and universal nature, beneath his glance, assuming the infinite hues of the magic web. Octave! Octave! come to my aid!*

This reiteration of the reality-vision conflict is a personal answer to Octave's image-making. Célio accepts and understands the magic of a poetic existence, one in which things are infinitely transformable and therefore infinitely beautiful. He asks only to participate in it, to abandon reality for creativity. Célio seeks help from he who possesses the madness and the word.[6]

B. MEMORY AND INSPIRATION

If Octave represents art in the making, Hermia is art in the remembering. Célio seeks to extract from both relationships a power of evocation he does not himself possess. This verbal pursuit is firmly rooted in areas of affect, friend and mother, giving the search for art a distinctly human rhythm. As the exemplary mother, Hermia shows concern for her son, but their conversation does not dwell on the maternal-filial relationship. Célio projects upon Hermia the visage of the beloved. He sees in her an earlier Marianne, and asks of her the language of love.

> CÉLIO. Ma mère! —Et vous aussi, vous avez été belle; sous ce long voile qui vous entoure, l'oeil reconnaît le port majestueux d'une reine.[7] Ô ma

[6] In the Pléiade edition of Musset's *Théâtre complet*, p. 1329, Maurice Allem signals a similar passage in *Fantasio*. Fantasio is speaking to Elsbeth. "Chacun a ses lunettes; mais personne ne sait au juste de quelle couleur en sont les verres. Qui est-ce qui pourra me dire au juste si je suis heureux ou malheureux, bon ou mauvais, triste ou gai, bête ou spirituel?" *We all have our spectacles, but no one can tell to a shade the color of the glass. Who can tell me to a nicety whether I am happy or unhappy, good or bad, sad or merry, dull or witty?* (II.i.303) In fact, Fantasio performs much the same role for Elsbeth as Octave does for Célio, but aside from the identity confusion, these two passages are quite different. Célio is prompted by longing, Fantasio expresses his own nature; the "réseau transparent" in *Les Caprices de Marianne* is a sure focus into beauty, the "lunettes" in *Fantasio* constitute a kind of mask.

[7] In the play's first edition, which appeared in the *Revue des Deux Mondes* (May 15, 1833), this description was completed by "et les formes gracieuses d'une Diane chasseresse." (*and the graceful shape of a huntress Diana.*) This reference is another reminder of the pastoral tradition referred to above.

mère! vous avez inspiré l'amour! sous vos fenêtres
entr'ouvertes a murmuré le son de la guitare; sur
ces places bruyantes, dans le tourbillon de ces fêtes,
vous avez promené une insouciante et superbe
jeunesse. —Vous n'avez point aimé; un parent de
mon père est mort d'amour pour vous.

HERMIA. Quel souvenir me rappelles-tu?

CÉLIO. Ah! si votre coeur peut en supporter la tristesse, si ce n'est pas vous demander des larmes,
racontez-moi cette aventure, ma mère; faites-m'en
connaître les détails.   (I.xii.246-47)

CÉLIO. *Mother! And you too, you have been beautiful! Beneath those silver locks that shade your
noble forehead, beneath that long cloak that covers
you, the eye recognizes the majestic carriage of a
queen. O my mother! You have inspired love! Beneath your half-open windows the sound of guitars
has been heard; on these noisy squares, in the
whirl of these fêtes, you have paraded a heedless
and superb youth. You have never loved: a relative
of my father died of love of you.*

HERMIA. *What memories are you recalling to my
mind?*

CÉLIO. *Ah! If your heart can bear the sadness of it,
if it will not cost you bitter tears, relate to me that
adventure, mother mine, let me know the details.*

Célio imagines a model for Marianne, replete with
the serenading guitars and the "insouciante et superbe
jeunesse." The duplication is prophetic since Célio too
will die for love of such a woman. He solicits his mother's
love story just as he begs Octave to intercede with
Marianne in his behalf, hoping to grant form to his
own passion.

It gives Célio some measure of satisfaction to hear a version of his own life recounted, especially through the filter of his mother's memory. Musset reserves the fullest exposition of memory's part in love and perception for *On ne badine pas avec l'amour*. In this brief scene he articulates the need to evoke the past, to make it an image useful in the present as both example and style. The death of Hermia's lover elicits the expected reaction in Célio. "Non, ma mère, elle n'est point cruelle, la mort qui vient en aide à l'amour sans espoir. La seule chose dont je le plaigne, c'est qu'il s'est cru trompé par son ami." *No, mother, death which comes to the aid of a desperate love is not cruel. The only thing I find unfortunate is that he believed he was betrayed by his friend.* (I.xii.248) The reply to Hermia brings him closer to a realization of love-death, and in the reference to friendship, links this scene to his previous exchange with Octave. This time it is Hermia who must extend her hand to Célio in an effort to release him from the intolerable neutrality of wordless sentiment. Octave provides precise images, force, vitality. Hermia gives Célio a perspective, a point of reference in the past which impinges on the present. But even this representative of the past is closer to life than Célio, and urges him to cast off despair as did his friend.

Ne songez point à mes chagrins, ce ne sont que des souvenirs. Les vôtres me touchent bien davantage. Si vous refusez de les combattre, ils ont longtemps à vivre dans votre jeune coeur. Je ne vous demande pas de me les dire, mais je les vois; et puisque vous prenez part aux miens, venez, tâchons de nous défendre. Il y a à la maison quelques bons amis, allons essayer de nous distraire. Tâchons de vivre, mon

enfant, et de regarder gaiement ensemble, moi le
passé, vous l'avenir. —Venez, Célio, donnez-moi la
main.   (I.xii.248)

Do not think of my misfortunes, they are only mem-
ories. Yours touch me much more. If you refuse to
struggle against them, they will live for a long time
in your young heart. I do not ask that you tell them
to me, but I see them; and since you share in mine,
come, let us try to have done with it. There are some
good friends at home. Let us try to amuse ourselves.
My child, let us attempt to live and together gaily
look at, for me the past, for you the future. Come,
Célio, give me your hand.

As if to score the importance of its components Musset
ends the act with this scene.[8] Hermia casts her fleeting
but indelible shadow on Célio. Her appearance, brief
and undeveloped as it is, lends another dimension to
Célio's still unformed poetic nature. It is amply justified
by the tonality she provides, and by the grace with
which her presence characterizes Célio's dilemma.

C. POETRY AS MODEL

Musset completes the sketch of Célio's rhetorical education with a poem, concentrating the hero's sentiment,
his mother's experience, and his friends' eloquence in a
finished work of art. As usual, Célio himself outlines the
theory: "L'Amour et la Mort, Octave, se tiennent la
main: celui-là est la source du plus grand bonheur que
l'homme puisse rencontrer ici-bas; celle-ci met un terme

---

[8] This disposition was fixed in the 1853 edition of *Comédies et
Proverbes*. Before then it was I.ii, immediately following Octave's
encounter with Marianne. Thus the act ended with an exchange between Tibia and Claudio.

à toutes les douleurs, à tous les maux." *Love and Death, Octave, hold each other's hand: the former is the source of the greatest happiness that man can find in the world; the latter puts an end to all sorrow, to all pain.* (II.ii. 250) Célio draws this wisdom from a book he is reading. He sees some comfort in the degree of his suffering, and in death a means of giving form to his love, as he recites a French prose version of Leopardi's "Amore e morte."[9]

[9] The following are excerpts from the Leopardi original and Musset's version.

27　Quando novellamente
　　Nasce nel cor profondo
　　Un amoroso affetto,
　　Languido e stanco insiem con esso in petto
　　Un desiderio di morir se sente:
　　Come, non so ma tale
　　D'amor vero e possente è il primo effetto.
　　Forse gli occhi spaura
　　Allor questo deserto: a se la terra
　　Forse il mortale inabitabil fatta
　　Vede omai senza quella
　　Nova, sola, infinita
　　Felicità che il suo pensier figura:
　　. . . . .
62　Fin la negletta plebe,
　　L'uom della villa, ignaro
　　D'ogni virtù che da saper deriva
　　Fin la donzella timidetta e schiva
　　Che già di morte al nome
　　Sentì rizzar le chiome,
　　Osa alla tomba, alle funeree bende,
　　Fermar lo sguardo di costanza pieno,
　　Osa ferro e veleno
　　Meditar lungamente;
　　E nell'indotta mente
　　La gentilezza del morir comprende.

Lorsque le coeur éprouve sincèrement un profond sentiment d'amour, il éprouve aussi comme une fatigue et une langueur qui lui font désirer de mourir. Pourquoi? je ne sais. . . . Peut-être est-ce l'effet d'un premier amour, peut-être que ce vaste désert où nous

Leopardi teaches Célio that love and life are mutually exclusive. The languor of love is an intimation of death. Similarly, Octave, the rhetorical complement to Célio, becomes death's procurer. The play's nucleus, poetic and lyric, is perceived in the literary affectation of Act I and the completeness of the Leopardi reference. This is where sentiment and theatre meet, where the mechanics of coincidence and melodrama give body to the hero's destiny, allow him to relish *amore e morte*.

Octave, Hermia and finally the reading of Leopardi are the stages which lead Célio to the definition of his muteness. "Ah! que j'eusse pu me faire un nom dans les tournois et les batailles! qu'il m'eût été permis de porter les couleurs de Marianne et de les teindre de mon sang!

---

sommes effraye les regards de celui qui aime, peut-être que cette terre ne lui semble plus habitable, s'il n'y peut trouver ce bonheur nouveau, unique, infini, que son coeur lui représente. . . . Le paysan, l'artisan grossier qui ne sait rien, la jeune fille timide, qui frémit d'ordinaire à la seule pensée de la mort, s'enhardit lorsqu'elle aime jusqu'à porter un regard sur un tombeau. (II.ii.251)

When the heart sincerely experiences a deep feeling of love, it also experiences something like a tiredness and a languor which make it desire to die. I do not know why. . . . Perhaps it is caused by a first love, perhaps this vast desert of ours frightens the gaze of he who loves, perhaps this earth no longer seems inhabitable to him if he cannot find on it this new, unique, infinite happiness that his heart depicts for him. . . . The peasant, the common artisan who knows nothing, the timid young girl who usually shivers at the mere thought of death, are filled with courage to look at a grave when they are in love.

Paul de Musset, in *Biographie d'Alfred de Musset, sa vie et ses oeuvres* (Paris, 1877), p. 280, refers to Musset's passionate interest in Leopardi. In 1842 he began a study of the Italian poet; see "Mélanges de littérature et de critique," *Oeuvres complètes en prose*, Bibliothèque de la Pléiade (Paris, 1960), pp. 934-36. In addition, the last four stanzas of "Après une lecture" (*Nouvelles poésies*) constitute a touching homage to Leopardi, and conclude with a reference to "le charme de la mort."

qu'on m'eût donné un rival à combattre, une armée entière à défier! que le sacrifice de ma vie eût pu lui être utile! je sais agir, mais je ne sais pas parler. Ma langue ne sert point mon coeur, et je mourrai sans m'être fait comprendre, comme un muet dans une prison." *Ah! Would that I had been born in the time of tournaments and fights! Would that I had been permitted to wear the colors of Marianne and dye them with my blood! Would that I had been given a rival to fight with, an entire army to defy! Would that the sacrifice of my life had been of service to her! I know how to act, but cannot speak. My tongue does not serve my heart, and I shall die without having made myself understood, like a mute in a prison.* (II.ii.251-52) This poor poet has no words adequate to his vision. Octave must speak his love to Marianne; his mother is a source of memory; Leopardi's poem is another man's song of love and death. The character created by this variety of perspective is complete, thrust into relief by the generosity of others. As the musicians again serenade beneath the window of his lady-love, Célio's silence becomes increasingly resonant. The dilemma of the silent poet, seeking inspiration or death to express his love, delineates theatrically the obsession of all artists.

D.   THE BETRAYAL OF SENTIMENT

Musset does not abandon the structure of a dual hero he initiated in Act I. The voice of Octave is evoked as a response to Célio's silence. Gratuitous flourishes of style define its nature, musical but frivolous, in sharp contrast to Célio's unrelenting gravity. Octave is ever ready to engage in word games. The clever Marianne is a worthy measure of his verbal dexterity. During their first meeting they speak of nothing but love without once uttering its name. The word, unspoken yet the object of a series of metaphors, is the hinge of their imaginative and literary self-consciousness.

> OCTAVE. Un mal le plus cruel de tous, car c'est un mal sans espérance; le plus terrible, car c'est un mal qui se chérit lui-même et repousse la coupe salutaire jusque dans la main de l'amitié; un mal qui fait pâlir les lèvres sous des poisons plus doux que l'ambroisie, et qui fond en une pluie de larmes le coeur le plus dur, comme la perle de Cléopâtre; un mal que tous les aromates, toute la science humaine ne sauraient soulager, et qui se nourrit du vent qui passe, du parfum d'une rose fanée, du refrain d'une chanson, et qui puise l'éternel aliment de ses souffrances dans tout ce qui l'entoure, comme une abeille son miel dans tous les buissons d'un jardin.
>
> MARIANNE. Me direz-vous le nom de ce mal?
>
> OCTAVE. Que celui qui est digne de le prononcer, vous le dise! Que les rêves de vos nuits, que vos orangers verts, que le printemps vous l'apprennent! Que vous puissiez le chercher un beau soir, vous le trouverez sur vos lèvres. Son nom n'existe pas sans lui.
>
> MARIANNE. Est-il si dangereux à dire, si terrible dans sa contagion, qu'il effraye une langue qui plaide en sa faveur?
>
> OCTAVE. Est-il si doux à entendre, cousine, que vous le demandiez? Vous l'avez appris à Célio. (I.v.238)

> OCTAVE. *The most cruel harm of all, for it is a hopeless injury. The most terrible, for it is an injury that nurses itself and repels the salutary cup right into the hands of friendship, an injury that causes*

the lips to turn pale from poisons sweeter far than ambrosia, and that melts to tears the hardest of hearts, like Cleopatra's pearl. An injury that all the aromatics, all the human science can not soothe, fed by the passing winds, by the perfume of a faded rose, by the chorus of a song, and which extracts the eternal nourishment for its sufferings from all that surrounds it, as the bee extracts its honey from all the shrubs in a garden.

MARIANNE. *Are you going to tell me the name of this injury?*

OCTAVE. *Let he who is worthy of pronouncing it tell you. May the dreams of your nights, these green orange trees, the springtime, inform you. May you search for it some fine night and you will find it on your lips; its name does not exist without it.*

MARIANNE. *Is it so dangerous to say, so terrible in its contagion, that it renders fearful a tongue that pleads in its favor?*

OCTAVE. *Is it so sweet to hear, cousin, that you ask for it? You have taught it to Célio.*

It is the presence of Marianne that inspires Octave to accumulate the metaphors in a veritable collection of love's clichés: ambrosia, a sickness, the faded rose, the song's refrain, the bee, the honey, the garden, etc. etc. These accoutrements of love are all the more artificial in that their extravagance is dissonant to the simplicity of the absent lover, Célio. The preciosity of Marianne and Octave sets off Célio's sincerity.

Octave's hollow brilliance is opposed to the scope of true art. Célio's wordless perception and Octave's forensic vapidity meet in the union of their personalities and in the unfolding of the play. In Act I Célio's trembling love provided Octave with a theme to which the hunter-doe variation bore little resemblance.[10] Speaking for Célio, using the very mode at which he is most adept, Octave comes to understand his serious friend. Through style he penetrates love, as demonstrated in the continuation of the badinage. Marianne taunts Octave, and suggests that he has refined taste in wine but not in women. The wine-love metaphor is passed back and forth for several pages until Octave takes hold and firmly applies it to Célio's situation.

> Dieu n'en a pas caché la source au sommet d'un pic inabordable, au fond d'une caverne profonde; il l'a suspendue en grappes dorées sur nos brillants coteaux. Elle est, il est vrai, rare et précieuse, mais elle ne défend pas qu'on l'approche. Elle se laisse voir aux rayons du soleil, et toute une cour d'abeilles et de frelons murmure autour d'elle matin et soir. Le voyageur dévoré de soif peut se reposer sous ses rameaux verts; jamais elle ne l'a laissé languir, jamais elle ne lui a refusé les douces larmes dont son coeur est plein. Ah! Marianne! c'est un don fatal que la beauté. La sagesse dont elle se vante est soeur de l'avarice, et il y a parfois plus de miséricorde pour ses faiblesses que pour sa cruauté. —Bonsoir, cousine, puisse Célio vous oublier! (II.viii.260-61)

> *God has not hidden the source at the summit of an inapproachable crag, or in the depths of a bottomless pit; he has suspended it in golden bunches by the side of our paths. She plays the part of a courtesan; she touches the hand of him who passes by; she displays in the sun her plump throat, and a whole court of bees and hornets murmur around her, morning*

[10] See above, p. 134.

and evening. The traveler, parched with thirst, may rest beneath her green boughs; never has she let him droop, never has she refused him the sweet tears of which her heart is full. Ah! Marianne, beauty is a fatal gift. The wisdom which it boasts of is sister to avarice, and there is more compassion in the heavens for its weakness than for its cruelty. Good night, cousin; may Célio forget you!

In this, the last retort of the scene, Octave no longer parries thrusts from Marianne, but speaks seriously about Célio. The final shift from wine to love to pity is poetic in its rapidity, and reflects Octave's growing awareness of the true nature of sentiment. He is tiring of the game, the caprices that are ostensibly the work of Marianne but in which he has so ably participated.

Before the final scene there is another indication of Octave's transformation. In an oblique reappraisal of his own identity he shows lack of faith in his former style and impatience with his own wit. He tries to plead Célio's cause to Marianne in a serious tone: "Je sais qui je suis; je le sens: un pareil langage dans ma bouche a l'air d'une raillerie. Vous doutez de la sincérité de mes paroles; jamais peut-être je n'ai senti avec plus d'amertume qu'en ce moment le peu de confiance que je puis inspirer." *I know who I am, I feel it; such language from my lips has the appearance of a joke. You doubt the sincerity of my words; never perhaps have I felt with such bitterness as at this moment, at the little confidence I am capable of inspiring.* (II.xi.266) This avowal signals a basic change in his relationship to Célio, first established as antithetical and now resolved into a unison of mind and word. The time for brilliance is past. Octave and Célio, both in full consciousness of their shortcomings and ideals, are ready to collaborate on their version of "Amore e morte."

In the play's final moments the confusion of identity is complete.

> OCTAVE. Célio m'aurait vengé, si j'étais mort pour lui comme il est mort pour moi. Son tombeau m'appartient; c'est moi qu'ils ont étendu dans cette sombre allée; c'est pour moi qu'ils avaient aiguisé leurs épées; c'est moi qu'ils ont tué! . . . Adieu, la gaieté de ma jeunesse, l'insouciante folie, la vie libre et joyeuse au pied de Vésuve! Adieu les bruyants repas, les causeries du soir, les sérénades sous les balcons dorés! Adieu, Naples et ses femmes, les mascarades à la lueur des torches, les longs soupers à l'ombre des forêts! Adieu l'amour et l'amitié! —Ma place est vide sur la terre.
> MARIANNE. En êtes-vous bien sûr, Octave? Pourquoi dites-vous: adieu l'amour?
> OCTAVE. Je ne vous aime pas, Marianne; c'était Célio qui vous aimait. (II.xx.274)

> OCTAVE. *Célio would have avenged me had I died for him, as he died for me. This tomb is mine; it is me they have stretched out beneath this cold stone; it was for me their swords were sharpened; it was me they killed. Farewell, the gaiety of my youth, the careless folly, that free and happy life at the foot of Vesuvius! Farewell the noisy feasts, the evening chats, the serenades beneath the gilded balconies! Farewell to Naples and its women, the torch-lit masquerades, the long suppers in the shadows of the woods! Farewell to love and friendship! My place on earth is empty.*

MARIANNE. *But not in my heart, Octave. Why do you say, "Farewell to love?"*
OCTAVE. *I do not love you, Marianne; it was Célio who loved you.*

The scheme of reciprocity has been further realized. Célio learns something about words by listening to the voice of Octave. Octave gains insight into love by witnessing Célio's torment and accepting his sincerity. Both of them find ultimate satisfaction in death, in its fact and in its poetization. The shared identity is the element which rechristens the love-death commonplace.

Musset's particular irony focuses these concerns through the caprices of Marianne. The poetic stance is set in a small, in fact a diminishing frame. The disproportion between intent and manner gives an unexpected tone to love, death and poetic expression. This play's mixture of stock characters, conventional *peripéties*, literary self-consciousness, sincerity, and paradox is the first example of a formula Musset will use to great advantage in *Fantasio* and *On ne badine pas avec l'amour*. The poets Célio-Octave, Fantasio, and Perdican assume a variety of ironic and often ridiculous poses, but neither they nor Musset can conceal an obsession with the essence of art. The caprice is the spring which holds the poet and the man in theatrical tension.

seven

THE ORDER OF POETRY:

Fantasio

WRITTEN in the same year as *Les Caprices de Marianne*, *Fantasio* is a reinvestiture of Musset's interests, a variation on the unresolved motif of imagination and expression, a new casting of poetry and sentiment. Here Musset uses a scheme even more manneristic and concentrated than that of the preceding play. The title is a clue to his willingness to confront the character of his own artistry and dramatize it with transparent conventions. Musset's creative consciousness lies closer to the surface of *Fantasio* than it does in any of his other plays, making it an exceptionally rich object for inquiry. The notion of armchair theatre has indeed a double sense. Conceived apart from the stage, the armchair provides an infinitely variable proscenium. Yet there is a nuance of introspection and solitude in the term which aptly fits this probing analysis of the roots of the author's fancy.

A. THE PERSONALITY OF IMAGINATION

True to his name, Fantasio is another poet figure, who lives his poetry instead of writing, intoxicated with words and fabulation. The delightful insanity of his

existence is contagious as he projects his artful life on
those he meets. We are immediately reminded of Octave's enthusiasm, the torrent of images, the verbal
thrill. However, the difference between these two characters is more revealing than their similarity. Fantasio
is the spirit of art. He does not need to learn Octave's
lesson for he is the lesson itself, the mechanism of creativity. Predictably, this play has a comic ending. It is
the only one so blessed among the poet's theatrical
works of this period. Art succeeds in *Fantasio*, lifting
the characters into the realm of comic joy. Fantasio
himself is the medium of transformation.

His first appearance unleashes a chain of metaphors.

HARTMAN. Tu as le mois de mai sur les joues.
FANTASIO. C'est vrai; et le mois de janvier dans le
coeur. Ma tête est comme une vieille cheminée
sans feu: il n'y a que du vent et des cendres. Ouf!
(*Il s'assoit.*) Que cela m'ennuie que tout le monde
s'amuse! Je voudrais que ce grand ciel si lourd fût
un immense bonnet de coton, pour envelopper
jusqu'aux oreilles cette sotte ville et ses sots habi-
tants. Allons, voyons! dites-moi, de grâce, un
calembour usé, quelque chose de bien rebattu.

(I.ii.282)

HARTMAN. *You have the month of May on your
cheeks.*
FANTASIO. *That's true; and January in my heart. My
head is like an old grate without fire; nothing but
wind and ashes in it. Ouf!* (Sitting down.) *What a
plague it is that everybody should be amusing
themselves! I would like this great heavy sky to be
a huge cotton night-cap, to cover up this silly town
and its silly inhabitants to the very ears. Come, for*

151

pity's sake let me hear some worn-out pun—something really hackneyed.

Fantasio immediately displays his gift for invention. He takes up the image tendered by Hartman and constructs a bigger and better one. The season-temper linkage is only a point of departure, affording Fantasio a passage to the more unusual fireless hearth, an image obliquely inspired, and suggestive of a different state of being. Fantasio lacks sources of inspiration. This is his first, and as we will see, practically his only concern. Indirect association is the path his imagination most readily follows, up the flue to the sky as it were, then back to his head with "un immense bonnet de coton," ending in a turn which associates the local dullards to his own feeling of spiritlessness. This winding route through connective imagery deviates from standard patterns of comparison, freely juggling the human and natural elements. The intricacy of the development qualifies precisely the ennui and staleness which are intolerable to Fantasio, indicating at once the reasons for his need to escape and his capacity to do so. Throughout the play he shows displeasure with reality and succeeds in changing it. Even a too-familiar pun is better than the ordinary rhythm of existence. The reference to the pun is fleeting here, but later it will be at the center of one of Fantasio's most important inventions.

This hero's impatience with the habitual and the common extends beyond the poor pleasures of his fellow burghers to the contour of nature itself. "Comme ce soleil couchant est manqué! La nature est pitoyable ce soir. Regarde-moi un peu cette vallée là-bas, ces quatre ou cinq méchants nuages qui grimpent sur cette montagne. Je faisais des paysages comme celui-là quand j'avais douze ans, sur la couverture de mes livres de classe." *How miserably that sunset is done! Nature is wretched this evening. Just look at the valley down there and these four or five sorry clouds climbing up the mountain. I used to do landscapes like that when I was twelve years old, on the back of my school copybooks.* (I.ii.283) With this statement, Fantasio affirms his mastery over nature, a mastery guaranteed by aesthetic perception and executed in style. Through puns and plotting the hero will rearrange the *paysage*, the destiny of Princess Elsbeth, so as to make it pleasing, fitting, and above all beautiful. Her intended husband, the Prince of Mantua, is analogous to the poor clouds on the mountain. Fantasio can alter reality by rearranging the clouds or disposing of a prince.

Fantasio has the passion of imagination. He speaks of boredom like a man who has never known it, so readily is it transformed into a fascinating object. Boredom permits that imaginative leap to art, provides a gulf to be breached, gives the poet the impression of real movement through an act of creation. Fantasio describes his boredom at walking through the streets of Munich day after day:

Eh bien donc! où veux-tu que j'aille? Regarde cette vieille ville enfumée; il n'y a pas de places, de rues, de ruelles où je n'aie rôdé trente fois; il n'y a pas de pavés où je n'aie traîné ces talons usés, pas de maisons où je ne sache quelle est la fille ou la vieille femme dont la tête stupide se dessine éternellement à la fenêtre; je ne saurais faire un pas sans marcher sur mes pas d'hier; eh bien, mon cher ami, cette ville n'est rien auprès de ma cervelle. Tous les recoins m'en sont cent fois plus connus; toutes les rues, tous

153

les trous de mon imagination sont cent fois plus
fatigués; je m'y suis promené en cent fois plus de sens,
dans cette cervelle délabrée, moi son seul habitant!
je m'y suis grisé dans tous les cabarets; je m'y suis
roulé comme un roi absolu dans un carrosse doré; j'y
ai trotté en bon bourgeois sur une mule pacifique, et
je n'ose seulement pas maintenant y entrer comme un
voleur, une lanterne sourde à la main.   (I.ii.286)

*Well then? Where would you have me go? Look at
this dingy old town; there is not a square, a street,
an alley, I have not prowled over thirty times; there
is not a pavement I have not dragged my worn-out
heels across, not a house where I don't know who is
the girl or the old woman whose stupid head is eternally in relief at the window; I can't take a step without walking on yesterday's trail. Well, my dear friend,
this town is nothing to my brain. All its nooks are a
hundred times more familiar; all the streets and all
the holes of my imagination a hundred times more
worn out; I have strolled through that dilapidated
brain, its sole inhabitant, in a hundred times more
directions; I have fuddled myself in all its publics; I
have rolled through it like an absolute monarch in a
gilded chariot; I have ambled through it like an hon-
est burgher on a quiet mule, and now I do not so
much as dare enter there burglar-wise, with a dark
lantern in my hand.*

This is the second time Fantasio draws the city into his
own feeling of emptiness, the second time he centers
attention on the state of his "cervelle." This wonderful
place, an imaginary city of various satisfactions, seems
closed to him now. Again, the absence of light serves
him well, first the fireless hearth and now the hooded

lantern. Fantasio's problem is loneliness. His art is in danger of self-extinction because he cannot escape from the confines of self-awareness. He is a tired poet, still functioning on a reservoir of rhetoric but in want of significant inspiration. The reprise of the "cheminée sans feu" passage reveals both his power of improvisation and the limitations of the subject. The self is diminishing, cut off from sources of stimulation and renewal.

Spark's reaction to this explicitly reveals the extent of Fantasio's self-absorption. "Je ne comprends rien à ce travail perpétuel sur toi-même." *I can not understand this perpetual study of yourself.* (I.ii.286) Fantasio's identity has become a machine of fancy. It is time for a transformation. Octave and Célio lurk nearby, urging Fantasio on to self-realization. The change that occurs is markedly different however from the modulated duet of *Les Caprices de Marianne.* Fantasio, through his profound understanding of art, the rules that govern it, and the anguish that makes it necessary, immediately finds the means of escape. It is death, of course, here a figurative one befitting someone named Fantasio. The death of his depleted self is preceded by a cogent appraisal of the uses and scope of art.

> FANTASIO. Oh! s'il y avait un diable dans le ciel! s'il y avait un enfer, comme je me brûlerais la cervelle pour aller voir tout ça! Quelle misérable chose que l'homme! ne pas pouvoir seulement sauter par sa fenêtre sans se casser les jambes! être obligé de jouer du violon dix ans pour devenir un musicien passable! Apprendre pour être peintre, pour être palefrenier! Apprendre pour faire une omelette! Tiens, Spark, il me prend des envies de

m'asseoir sur un parapet, de regarder couler la rivière, et de me mettre à compter un, deux, trois, quatre, cinq, six, sept, et ainsi de suite jusqu'au jour de ma mort.

SPARK. Ce que tu dis là ferait rire bien des gens; moi, cela me fait frémir: c'est l'histoire du siècle entier. L'éternité est une grande aire, d'où tous les siècles, comme de jeunes aiglons, se sont envolés tour à tour pour traverser le ciel et disparaître; le nôtre est arrivé à son tour au bord du nid; mais on lui a coupé les ailes, et il attend la mort en regardant l'espace dans lequel il ne peut s'élancer.

FANTASIO, *chantant.*

Tu m'appelles ta vie, appelle-moi ton âme,

Car l'âme est immortelle et la vie est un jour . . .

Connais-tu une plus divine romance que celle-là, Spark? C'est une romance portugaise. Elle ne m'est jamais venue à l'esprit sans me donner envie d'aimer quelqu'un.   (I.ii.289)

FANTASIO. *Oh! if only there were a devil in heaven: if there were a hell, how gladly I would blow out my brains to go and see it all. What a wretched thing man is! Not to be sufficiently able to jump through a window without breaking his legs! To be obliged to play the violin ten years to become a decent musician! To learn in order to be a painter or a groom! To learn before he can make an omelette! Look, Spark, fancies come on me to sit down on a parapet and watch the river flowing, and fall to counting one, two, three, four, five, six, seven, and so on to the day of my death.*

SPARK. *This talk of yours would make many a man laugh; it makes me shudder; it is the history of the*

whole century. Eternity is a great aerie whence all
the ages like young eaglets have in their turn taken
wing to cross heaven and vanish. Ours has in its
turn reached the nest's edge; but its pinions have
been clipped, and it waits for death, looking out
upon the space into which it cannot wing its way.
FANTASIO, singing.
Life of my life, say you: nay, soul, say, of my soul,
For soul it hath no ending, and life is but a day.
Do you know a diviner song than that, Spark? It is
Portuguese. That song never came into my head
without making me want to love some one.

Musset introduced one aspect of time, the use of
memory, in the scene between Célio and Hermia.[1]
Memory is the poetic time of the past, a facet of time
elapsed that is seizable in art. What of future time and
the poet? Just as he shapes the past through memory
he gives form to the future by embracing the fact of
death. In both cases the present is only an accident of
status, ripe for substitution. Poetry is style for living
out of time, or more exactly, out of the time that passes.
Fantasio's initial remarks on boredom, on the endless
repetition of existence, take on special significance in
light of this sphere of time.[2] Fantasio walks the streets
of Munich like a dying man who accepts the passing of
the minutes, the victim of an inexorable calender and

[1] See above, pp. 137-40.
[2] Georges Poulet, in "La Distance intérieure," *Études sur le temps
humain* (Paris, 1952), II, 237-44, comments on monotony and empty
time in Musset, characterizing them as a source of anguish. In
Fantasio however it is apparent that this anguish is not genuine. It
is almost immediately by-passed in the creative élan to joy. The happy
solution of *Fantasio* is admittedly an isolated case, and Poulet's remarks certainly describe the state of Perdican in *On ne badine pas
avec l'amour.*

clock. Brief flights of fancy only intermittently divert
his attention. He is ripe for a drastic encounter with
death which will liberate him through the completeness
of its art. His craving for novelty makes him curious of
heaven and hell, but they are only hypothetical goals,
traditional terms of death that are ultimately unsatis-
factory to his starved imagination. He must make death
his own poem. Straining in a man's poor body, he com-
plains of physical and chronological contingency. Playing a violin and making an omelette, two worthy modes,
ought to be free from the strictures of time and human
inadequacy. Fantasio's first reaction to these terrible
realizations is to imitate the beat of time. If the world
ticks away, he might as well count the ticks.

Here the presence of Spark, the vital other voice,
effects the first intimation that such an uncompromising
pose is not the only one available to Fantasio. Through
Spark Fantasio will accomplish a miraculous passage
from the time of prose to the time of poetry, from a
chronological conception of existence to one which
abolishes time altogether in a kind of fabulous eternity.
Spark tries to explain Fantasio's trouble, much like a
critic explaining the text of a poet. He makes the usual
critical gestures, relating Fantasio to the grand context of time, the whole of tradition. In this case, he reduces Fantasio's malaise to the unending cycle of history. Without knowing it, Spark restates the essence of
Fantasio's perception while misinterpreting it. It is
seemingly inappropriate to include the example of so
singular a man in the sweep of historical time, but that
very sweep is precisely what torments him. Spark has
simply enlarged the frame. The banality of Munich's
streets is replaced by the banality of passing centuries.
Fantasio is shocked by the enormity of Spark's refer-

ence. He has suddenly seen a blow-up of his own ennui, and through the grossness of Spark's perception is able to pass out of time altogether. What better way to signal this than with a song, a song about man's link to eternity. The key to the song's meaning is only revealed as Fantasio resolves the passage in love. Célio recites "Amore e morte," Fantasio sings of love and eternity, and both of them find release from an inimical reality. Fantasio however sings of love without being its victim.

This exchange with Spark is typical of the liberty Musset takes with the traditional canon of prose exposition. By reserving the mention of love until the end of the series he has denied the reader the central link between the elements. Love is the catalyst which transforms body into soul, clock time into eternity. The relationship between Fantasio's expression of boredom and his song is vague indeed until he introduces love. Only in this coda do the themes merge, the point of juncture effortlessly disappearing because Musset avoids a logical progression of elements. This is symptomatic of a fundamentally poetic outlook, one which seeks to transcend the boundaries of logic in order to verbally reorganize existence. The principal mode is metaphorical, but even Fantasio's avoidance of normal transitions is an act of poetic reorganization. The song and its sense proclaim a new rhythm, defiantly opposing the implacable beat of 1, 2, 3, 4, 5, 6, 7, eternity. This is the primary goal of Musset's theatre, concentrated in the person and style of Fantasio.

B. THE PERCEPTION OF PATTERN

Fantasio has died to the world. By imposing his new order he has effectively destroyed the tired streets and the tired brain. Musset marks the birth of the new character in the most obvious way possible. Fantasio assumes the identity of a dead man, playfully transcending death as a poet should. The young man, dying as the minutes are counted, passes into timelessness through the medium of an old clown's death. Saint-Jean the buffoon cannot die twice. Fantasio's new body is impervious to time.

In addition to being already dead, Saint-Jean has a particular professional appeal for Fantasio. This is expressed clearly by Princess Elsbeth.

> Cela est singulier; son esprit m'attachait à lui avec des fils imperceptibles qui semblaient venir de mon coeur; sa perpétuelle moquerie de mes idées romanesques me plaisait à l'excès, tandis que je ne puis supporter qu'avec peine bien des gens qui abondent dans mon sens; je ne sais ce qu'il y avait autour de lui, dans ses yeux, dans ses gestes, dans la manière dont il prenait son tabac. C'était un homme bizarre; tandis qu'il me parlait, il me passait devant les yeux des tableaux délicieux; sa parole donnait la vie, comme par enchantement, aux choses les plus étranges.
>
> (II.i.298)

> *It is odd; his wit bound me to him with imperceptible threads that seemed to come from my heart; his perpetual mockery of my romantic ideas delighted me beyond measure. Whilst I can scarcely tolerate many a person who is just of my own way of thinking, I do not know what it was about him; something in his eyes, in his motions, in the way he took his snuff. He was a strange man; as he spoke to me delicious pictures passed before my eyes; his speech gave life, as if by enchantment, to the unlikeliest things.*

Elsbeth's words are prompted by sincere sorrow over the clown's death. Musset's Saint-Jean represents the joy of poetic transformation, a process defined by one who loved him.[3] As we have come to expect, the order of elements is particularly revealing. Elsbeth first refers to a charm, a sympathy of feeling that linked her to the clown. The reasons for this must remain imperceptible. It is the unarticulated wonder evoked by beauty, like that of a reader who initially surrenders his imagination to a work of art because it is engaging. The clown is here a metaphor for art, the particular art of Musset. Something in Saint-Jean's aspect made Elsbeth want to be with him. She then begins to analyze the roots of her attachment, and in doing so shows Musset's acute self-awareness as an artist. The clown turns to irony "idées romanesques," the poet desentimentalizes the excesses of romanticism through caricature and parody. The sentiment of Musset's own theatre remains attractive to modern audiences because he consistently punctures it with shafts of self-denigrating sarcasm, and assumes a pitiless attitude towards his most graceful and languid poses. This will be keenly felt in *On ne badine pas avec l'amour*. Elsbeth cherished the tone of Saint-Jean which served as a stylistic balance for her girlish sighs. She then notices that the ensemble of the buffoon's personality pleased her because of many small details, wit and grace constituted in trivia, in the complicated pattern of words and gestures that through their repetition became dear to her. She loved his style, an amalgam of affect, contrast, irony, and harmony which, through a varying prism, colors life and extracts from it "tableaux délicieux." This style restores to ob-

---

[3] Hugo's clowns in *Cromwell* and *Le Roi s'amuse* are quite dissimilar; they are sources of bitter irony.

jects their true life, puts them in the meaningful and related order denied by banality. The enchantment effected through the word of the poet releases Elsbeth just as Fantasio is released by the song in Act I. Their ability to articulate the function of style reveals Musset's own deepening understanding of himself as an artist.

The ensuing meeting of Elsbeth and Fantasio exemplifies the concentrative and suggestive power of Musset's style, the provocative grouping of familiar elements. "Il me semble qu'il y a quelqu'un derrière ces bosquets. Est-ce le fantôme de mon pauvre bouffon que j'aperçois dans ces bluets, assis sur la prairie? Répondez-moi; qui êtes-vous? que faites-vous là, à cueillir ces fleurs?" *It seems to me there is someone behind those shrubs. Is it the ghost of my poor jester that I see sitting in the meadow among the cornflowers? Answer me; who are you? What are you about there pulling those flowers?* (II.i.299) Musset again offers us a germ of his theatrical technique; harmony emerges from a seemingly frivolous pattern. A mourning princess discovers a handsome young man, disguised as an old, hunchbacked clown, surrounded by cornflowers. The garden cliché has been radically challenged by the weight of details pertinent to *Fantasio*.[4] Expectation is thwarted in every way. The young man and the young woman, ripe for love, so much alike in spirit, are not and will not fall in love during the course of this play. The image of fresh flowers, suggestive of youth, is associated with a misshapen old man. All these factors are qualified by a recent death. Such a combination will

[4] David Sices, in "Musset's *Fantasio*: The Paradise of Chance," *Romanic Review*, LVIII (Feb. 1967), 23-37, discusses the significance of the garden. Hugo extends this conceit to its extreme in the Sanche-Rose love scene of *Torquemada*, see above, pp. 88-93.

prove instructive to Elsbeth, teaching her to accept Fantasio's order. It is an additional example of ironizing her "idées romanesques."

This same flower garden provides the source for another lesson in perception.

FANTASIO. Je ne dispute pas; je vous dis que cette tulipe est une tulipe rouge, et cependant je conviens qu'elle est bleue.

ELSBETH. Comment arranges-tu cela?

FANTASIO. Comme votre contrat de mariage. Qui peut savoir sous le soleil s'il est né bleu ou rouge? Les tulipes elles-mêmes n'en savent rien. Les jardiniers et les notaires font des greffes si extraordinaires, que les pommes deviennent des citrouilles, et que les chardons sortent de la mâchoire de l'âne pour s'inonder de sauce dans le plat d'argent d'un évêque. Cette tulipe que voilà s'attendait bien à être rouge, mais on l'a mariée; elle est tout étonnée d'être bleue: c'est ainsi que le monde entier se métamorphose sous les mains de l'homme; et la pauvre dame nature doit se rire parfois au nez de bon coeur, quand elle mire dans ses lacs et dans ses mers son éternelle mascarade. Croyez-vous que ça sentît la rose dans le paradis de Moïse? ça ne sentait que le foin vert. La rose est fille de la civilisation; c'est une marquise comme vous et moi.

ELSBETH. La pâle fleur de l'aubépine peut devenir une rose, et un chardon peut devenir un artichaut; mais une fleur ne peut en devenir une autre: ainsi qu'importe à la nature? on ne la change pas, on l'embellit ou on la tue. La plus chétive violette mourrait plutôt que de céder, si l'on voulait, par des moyens artificiels, altérer sa forme d'une étamine.

163

FANTASIO. C'est pourquoi je fais plus de cas d'une violette que d'une fille de roi.   (II.i.301-302)

FANTASIO. *I am not disputing: I tell you this tulip is a red tulip, and yet I allow it is blue.*

ELSBETH. *How do you settle that?*

FANTASIO. *Like your marriage. What man under the sun can say whether he was born blue or red: the very tulips know nothing of it: gardeners and lawyers make such extraordinary grafts that apples turn pumpkins, and that thistles leave the ass's mouth to be drowned in sauce on a bishop's silver plate. This tulip you see no doubt expected to be red; but it was married; it is quite surprised at being blue; this is how the whole world is metamorphosed under the hands of man; and my poor lady nature must laugh in her own face heartily from time to time when she surveys in her lakes and her seas this eternal masquerade of hers. Do you believe that was how the rose smelt in Moses's paradise? It only smelt of green hay. The rose is a daughter of civilization; a marchioness just like you or I.*

ELSBETH. *The hawthorn's pale flower may turn to a rose, and a thistle to an artichoke; but one flower cannot be made into another: so what matter to nature? You cannot change her; you beautify her or you kill. The meanest violet would die rather than yield if someone wanted, through artificial means, to alter its form by one stamen.*

FANTASIO. *That is why I think more of a violet than of a king's daughter.*

Through the reference to flowers the new Saint-Jean shows his skill at metamorphosis, turning an old philosophical game into an excuse for shaking Elsbeth's faith in appearance. Fantasio must bring her back to the world of Saint-Jean, where royal rank has little power, where the red tulip is turned blue by the poet-gardener, and a princess has the right to love because a clown tells her so. It must be noted that Fantasio's explanation of this miraculous color change far surpasses in degree the needs of his argument. The examples of metamorphosis are designed to please as well as to convince, recalling Elsbeth's initial description of Saint-Jean's talent. The bishop's silver plate is absurdly gratuitous, and hence appropriate as the engaging factor, grasped and retained beyond the structure of Fantasio's discourse. He has ostensibly employed a floral analogy to explain the uselessness of Elsbeth's marriage, but it becomes clear that the marriage is a pretext for the analogy. Having just changed his own destiny, he has full power to change that of others. The averted marriage of Elsbeth is the theatrical event that makes *Fantasio* a play; the violet helps make it a poem. Fantasio's reply to Elsbeth's doubt is prophetic, and it will not be fully explained until the garden engulfs all else in the play's final moments. Elsbeth does not believe that flowers are basically alterable. Fantasio admits the difficulty, but as a poet, is capable of accomplishing the impossible.

For the moment, Elsbeth continues in her obstinacy, refusing to speak the language of Fantasio.

FANTASIO. Vous vous trompez de sens; il y a une erreur de sens dans vos paroles.

ELSBETH. Ne me fais pas de calembour, si tu veux gagner ton argent! et ne me compare pas à des tulipes, si tu ne veux gagner autre chose.

FANTASIO. Qui sait? Un calembour console de bien des chagrins; et jouer avec les mots est un moyen comme un autre de jouer avec les pensées, les actions et les êtres. Tout est calembour ici-bas, et il est aussi difficile de comprendre le regard d'un enfant de quatre ans, que le galimatias de trois drames modernes. (II.i.302-303)

FANTASIO. *You miss the sense; your words have the wrong sense.*
ELSBETH. *Pun me no puns, if you would earn your money, and avoid comparing me to tulips if you don't want to earn something else.*
FANTASIO. *Who knows? A pun consoles many griefs, and playing with words is as good a way as any other to play with thoughts, actions, and creatures. All in this world below is one great joke, and it is as hard to read the looks of a child of four years old as to construe the rubbish of three modern melodramas.*

The princess rejects the style of puns; the clown finds in it the key to existence. Puns are of course his stock in trade, but here Musset raises the intensity of the reference, going beyond the realm of the clown in order to use the pun as a generic example of the artist's language. Through it he juxtaposes the meaning of this particular scene and the basic premise of Fantasio's mode of life. By imposing his order of play, reality is stripped of its anguish and words become a new reality that need not be understood or penetrated. Structures complete unto themselves, the pun, the looks of a four-year-old, and the nonsense of the *drame romantique* are certainly more efficient ways of dealing with an unwanted marriage than the logic of this unhappy maiden. According to Fantasio, even the enigmatic four-year-old knows that.

Fantasio's understanding of his poem is profound. While creating he makes a glose that reveals the most personal devices of Musset's art.

N'est-ce pas la princesse que j'aperçois dans la chambre voisine, à travers cette glace? Elle rajuste son voile de noces; deux longues larmes coulent sur ses joues; en voilà une qui se détache comme une perle et qui tombe sur sa poitrine. Pauvre petite! j'ai entendu ce matin sa conversation avec sa gouvernante; en vérité, c'était par hasard; j'étais assis sur le gazon sans autre dessein que celui de dormir. Maintenant la voilà qui pleure et qui ne se doute guère que je la vois encore. Ah! si j'étais un écolier de rhétorique, comme je réfléchirais profondément sur cette misère couronnée, sur cette pauvre brebis à qui on met un ruban rose au cou pour la mener à la boucherie! Cette petite fille est sans doute romanesque; il lui est cruel d'épouser un homme qu'elle ne connaît pas. Cependant elle se sacrifie en silence. Que le hasard est capricieux! Il faut que je me grise, que je rencontre l'enterrement de Saint-Jean, que je prenne son costume et sa place, que je fasse enfin la plus grande folie de la terre, pour venir voir tomber, à travers cette glace, les deux seules larmes que cette enfant versera peut-être sur son triste voile de fiancée;

(II.iii.306-307)

Is not that the Princess I see through this glass in the next room? She is putting a few touches to her wedding veil; two long tears are trickling down her cheeks; look, there is one detaching itself and falling on her breast like a pearl. Poor child: I overheard her talk with the governess this morning; on my faith it was by accident; I was sitting on the turf without any purpose but to sleep. Now there she is crying, and never suspecting that I see her again. Ah! were I a student of rhetoric, how profound would be my reflections on this crowned misery, this poor ewe lamb, round whose neck they are tying a pink ribbon to lead her to the slaughter-house! That little girl is romantic, no doubt: it is a cruel trial to her to wed a man she does not know. Yet she sacrifices herself in silence. How capricious fortune is! needs must I get drunk, meet Saint-Jean's funeral, assume his garb and his place, play in short the maddest trick that ever was played, just to come and, through this glass, see falling the only two tears perhaps that the child will shed on her unhappy wedding veil!

He first perceives the presence of a frame, effectively separating Elsbeth from distracting elements, allowing his gaze to concentrate on her alone. He has begun to give her form. At the center of the picture are the two tears, introduced and quickly transformed in a cliché metaphor. The primary function of the pearl is to reflect back on the tears.[5] Musset wisely avoids a more original comparison. The tear must remain the focus of attention

---

[5] The tear-pearl metaphor is the final element in a poem which constitutes a brief *art poétique* for Musset, "Impromptu, en répose à cette question: Qu'est-ce que la poésie?"

D'un sourire, d'un mot, d'un soupir, d'un regard
Faire un travail exquis, plein de crainte et de charme,
Faire une perle d'une larme:

(*From a smile, from a word, from a sigh, from a glance to make an exquisite work, full of fear and charm, to make a pearl from a tear.*)

in this passage, for it is the ultimate object in Fantasio's fabulation. He then exploits another purely formal technique, that of résumé, which puts Elsbeth's tears in a perspective interior to the play, and exhibits Fantasio's wish to tell their story. The first is necessary to the play's hermetic nature. It will become increasingly clear that Musset's interest lies in the harmonious grouping of elements rather than in the oft-preached sermon about marrying for love. On its most satisfying level, *Fantasio* is closed to itself, using the state marriage as a convention for giving dramatic substance to Elsbeth's tears. Fantasio's account of the circumstances of his meeting with Elsbeth shows his need to make it a fiction, imposing himself on factors that the reader has already perceived, and thus reappropriating them for integration into his own design.

The hero then introduces a notion not yet articulated in Musset's theatre—the value of chance. At last we can fully appreciate his taste for odd groupings, unorthodox tonalities, seemingly dissonant patterns of diction and objects. Elsbeth defined this in her eulogy of Saint-Jean.[6] The unpredictable, by definition detached from the stultifying rhythm of the ordinary, is posited upon a chance combination of factors which are linked for no other reason than their contiguity. The combination is therefore unique, exhilarating and pleasurable in its newness. It gives the impression of discovery, thus extracting from beauty its accident and its miracle. A statement of the wonder of chance is the axis for the continuing résumé which comes to a close in a reprise of the tears. Now the object is restored to itself and enhanced by the weight of its accoutrements, drawing together the admittedly disparate elements of the play,

[6] See above, p. 160.

from Fantasio's fake hump to the cornflowers. The tears of course manifest the character's sadness but so do practically all tears. These particular tears illuminate *Fantasio*. Each stage of his absurdly involved plot is necessary to the general improbability relished by the hero. The retelling at this point in the play's development amplifies its mad pattern. All the elements are related like the images in a poem, echoing each other, contained in a tightly woven fabric, put in relief by the dominant motif, the tracing of two tears.

C. THE PRIORITY OF STYLE

The lesson continues, and it is a basic one. A superb teacher, Fantasio finds the root of Elsbeth's problem. She does not understand his language. The tulip episode revealed her defective perception. It is now time to continue her exercises, and Fantasio seasons them with a healthy dose of sarcasm, an oft-used pedagogical device.

FANTASIO. Je fais la conversation avec les petits chiens et les marmitons. Il y a un roquet pas plus haut que cela dans la cuisine, qui m'a dit des choses charmantes.

ELSBETH. En quel langage?

FANTASIO. Dans le style le plus pur. Il ne ferait pas une seule faute de grammaire dans l'espace d'une année.

ELSBETH. Pourrai-je entendre quelques mots de ce style?

FANTASIO. En vérité, je ne le voudrais pas; c'est une langue qui est particulière. Il n'y a pas que les roquets qui la parlent; les arbres et les grains de blé eux-mêmes la savent aussi; mais les filles de roi ne la savent pas. À quand votre noce? (II.v.310)

FANTASIO. *I hold conversation with the puppies and the scullions. There is a cur only so high in the kitchen who said charming things to me.*
ELSBETH. *In what language?*
FANTASIO. *In the purest style. He would not make a single mistake in grammar in the space of a year.*
ELSBETH. *Could I hear a few words in this style?*
FANTASIO. *By my word, I would not have you to; it is a tongue that is peculiar to him. It is only curs that speak it; the trees and the very ears of wheat know it too; but kings' daughters do not know it. When is your wedding to be?*

Musset reduces the play's matter to a question of style. One must penetrate this style in order to understand life. Musset describes the poet's traditional role in the process. Interpreter of nature's secrets, possessing a song with which to answer the birds, Fantasio translates the undecipherable for the vulgar ear. He bridges the gap with the simplest of devices, the metaphor, essentially a link between two apparently separate realms. In this passage the terms are purposely simplistic, fitting the scope of a lesson in rudiments. Elsbeth shows here an eagerness to learn that was absent during their first meeting. Fantasio devalues "les filles de roi," and by doing so reaffirms the priority of a poet's concerns.

The force of reiteration has its effect, and Elsbeth begins to perceive through Fantasio. The insistence of the teacher has proved successful. Through his recurring allusions to formal elements Elsbeth can now distinguish pattern. Fantasio immediately thrusts the tears into a form; Elsbeth's ability to imitate the process is embryonic. Her first success is achieved through the most accessible means, Fantasio himself. "Tu me parles sous la forme d'un homme que j'ai aimé, voilà pourquoi je t'écoute malgré moi. Mes yeux croient voir Saint-Jean; mais peut-être n'es-tu qu'un espion?" *You speak to me in the guise of a man I loved. That is why I listen to you in my own despite. My eyes think they see Saint-Jean; but perhaps you are only a spy?* (II.v.312) The suspicion is misleading, for she now truly believes in all that Fantasio represents. The strength of her belief is cemented by the purely formal link between her and Fantasio. It is true that she loved Saint-Jean, but the real buffoon would have been incapable of imparting the truths unearthed by the imposter. The best explanation of style is its example, the best way to understand metaphor is to witness metamorphosis. Fantasio, by assuming the form of Saint-Jean, represents style and metamorphosis. He is removed from himself through imitation; he has made the gesture of becoming something else. But he is not Saint-Jean, and this is the clue to his ability to express the essence of the clown. Suggesting rather than being, he enjoys a vantage point in the scheme of all these elements. It is the priority supplied by style, a distance that creates perspective and the poetic movement of metaphor. Fantasio owes his special power of revelation to the fact that he is a metaphor for a man whose word gave life.[7]

Fantasio makes a final résumé of the play's improbable plot after he has been put in prison for accomplishing the most absurd and yet most meaningful gesture of all—removing the wig of the fake prince. Completing the play's pattern with his wig-fishing, Fantasio comments on the totality. "S'il n'y a pas là le sujet d'un poème épique en douze chants, je ne m'y connais pas.

[7] See above, p. 160.

Pope et Boileau ont fait des vers admirables sur des sujets bien moins importants. Ah! si j'étais poète, comme je peindrais la scène de cette perruque voltigeant dans les airs! Mais celui qui est capable de faire de pareilles choses dédaigne de les écrire. Ainsi la postérité s'en passera." *If there is not in that the subject for an epic poem in twelve cantos, I am no judge. Pope and Boileau have written admirable verses on subjects far less important. Oh, were I a poet! How I would paint the scene of that wig fluttering in the wind! But the man who is capable of such exploits disdains to write of them. So posterity must do without it.* (II.vii.318) The grade of Musset's irony can be perceived in this observation. Fantasio correctly links this play to the tradition of the mock-heroic. War has actually been declared because of the snatched wig. It is an irresistible chain of cause and effect for a poet with a taste for the ridiculous. This literary consciousness is colored by a corresponding awareness of frivolity, as if the poem in question were a hypothetical one, censored even before it is passed to the first reader. Musset's ambiguity is self-saving. He unmistakably signals that the play is not to be taken too seriously yet makes it the vehicle of a most explicit inquiry into the workings of his imagination. We are reminded of his half-playful attitude toward the characteristics of his own romanticism. The poet of "La Nuit de mai" is also the poet of "Dupont et Durand." There are three artists at work in *Fantasio*: Saint-Jean the example, Fantasio the spirit in action, and Musset, that rarest of poets who deigns to set it all down. Posterity will not do without this bauble whose center is thick with aesthetics.[8]

[8] Another interesting statement of Musset's aesthetics is found in *Carmosine* (1850). It falls to Minuccio, the troubador, to define

Fantasio has a comic climax. In the face of war, Elsbeth accepts the fullness of Fantasio's vision, his mercurial changes, his laughing dismissal of contingency. In fact, it is she who perpetuates the hero. Along with money to pay his debts, she gives him the key to her garden. "Eh bien! je te les donne; mais prends la clef de mon jardin: le jour où tu t'ennuieras d'être poursuivi par tes créanciers, viens te cacher dans les bluets où je t'ai trouvé ce matin; aie soin de prendre ta perruque et ton habit bariolé; ne parais pas devant moi sans cette taille contrefaite et ces grelots d'argent; car c'est ainsi que tu m'as plu: tu redeviendras mon bouffon pour le temps qu'il te plaira de l'être, et puis tu iras à tes affaires. Maintenant tu peux t'en aller, la porte est ouverte." *Very well, you shall have them; but take the keys of my garden. The day you are weary of being hunted by your creditors, come and hide among the cornflowers, where I found you this morning. Be careful to bring your wig and your motley coat. Never appear before me without this counterfeit figure and these silver bells, for it was so you won my favor. You shall turn into my jester again for such time as shall please you, and then you shall go about your business. Now you may be off; the door is open.* (II.vii.323) The image of their meeting is consecrated, each detail an integral part of a poem that Elsbeth can now understand. She hears the rhythm of flowers, disguise, youth and death, and cherishes the

---

beauty. "La beauté. Dieu l'a mise au monde dans trois excellentes intentions: premièrement, pour nous réjouir, en second lieu, pour nous consoler, et, enfin, pour être heureuse elle-même." *Beauty. God put it in the world for three excellent reasons; first, to make us happy, in second place, to console us, and finally, so that it be happy itself.* (I.viii.796) There is a further link between Minuccio and Fantasio. The troubador makes a song out of the story of Perillo and Carmosine just as Fantasio makes a play out of Elsbeth's predicament.

fixed form of the garden which allows her to reevoke it all. Her last words guarantee the freedom of imagination, the freedom of change. They guarantee the fluidity of poetic invention, whose power must be untrammeled if it is to be exerted at all. The key to Elsbeth's garden opens existence to an infinity of transformation.

Fantasio is the clearest theatrical statement of Musset's aesthetics, and thus even more striking is the omission of the poet's dearest theme—love. Aside from Fantasio's amorous reaction to his own song,[9] and Elsbeth's repeated avowal of affection for Saint-Jean, the play avoids reference to love. The hero and the heroine do not fall in love.[10] The exchanges between Elsbeth and Fantasio contain all the elements of a lyric poem except its subject. The potentiality of a sentimental attachment is never realized. Musset's particular logic would permit the princess to fall in love with the imposter-clown, and yet this does not happen. The play's mannerism remains exactly that, the plot's artificiality is never modulated into a semblance of reality. The mechanism of style retains its purest state in a metaphorical garden presided over by a poet who never sighs for his princess.

[9] See above, p. 157.

[10] Octave, in *Les Caprices de Marianne*, is perhaps another loveless hero, but seen as a complement to Célio he too is an aspect of love for Marianne.

eight

TIME AND IDENTITY:
On ne badine pas avec l'amour

ON *ne badine pas avec l'amour* marks the end of a
series comprising *Les Caprices de Marianne* and *Fantasio*, products of the years 1833-34. The poet's obsessive inquiry into modes of perception comes to an
abrupt and stunning close in this bitter proverb.[1] But
here the references to inspiration, imagination, and invention are carefully hidden. The Prince d'Eysenach,
Cordiani, André del Sarto, Célio, Octave, and Fantasio
are allegorized to varying degrees, as Musset attempts
to articulate through them a common artistic consciousness. Perdican is shaped by the same mannerism that
surfaces with insistence in the preceding plays. In this
case however the manneristic elements are filtered
through his secret yearnings, his actions rather than his
intelligence. The relationship between Perdican, Camille, and Rosette is controlled by the matrices of art,
but their understanding of it is fatally grounded in the
vagaries of their intuition.

[1] *On ne badine pas avec l'amour* is a subtly tooled variation of this
genre made popular by Carmontelle, and which Musset will continue
to exploit in the future.

176

A. CONFLICT THROUGH DICTION

The play's first lines are spoken by the Chorus, a convention Musset has not utilized before. "Doucement bercé sur sa mule fringante, messer Blazius s'avance dans les bluets fleuris, vêtu de neuf, l'écritoire au côté. Comme un poupon sur l'oreiller, il se ballotte sur son ventre rebondi, et les yeux à demi fermés, il marmotte un *Pater noster* dans son triple menton. Salut, maître Blazius; vous arrivez au temps de la vendange, pareil à une amphore antique." *Gently rocked on his prancing mule, Master Blazius advances through the blossoming cornflowers; his clothes are new, his writing-case hangs by his side. Like a chubby baby on a pillow, he rolls about on top of his protuberant belly, and with his eyes half closed mumbles a paternoster into his double chin. Welcome, Master Blazius; you come for the vintage-time in the semblance of an ancient amphora.* (I.i.327) The voice of the Chorus could hardly be more literary. It speaks with the most highly inflected diction of the play. Musset makes no attempt to reproduce a recognizable pattern of speech. Aside from the salutation, this passage is descriptive, and reveals nothing of the speaker except his resources of observation and eloquence. As a result, the quality of the Chorus' voice is in direct opposition to what it represents: the simple life, nostalgia for childhood, homely virtue. This tonal imbalance is but one of the styles of the play.[2] Musset achieves in *On ne badine pas avec l'amour* the Shakespearian effect so desperately sought by Hugo, and so rarely realized— the mixture of voices. Maître Blazius, Maître Bridaine,

[2] This imbalance between station and diction is reminiscent of the pastoral tradition, a pertinent echo considering the forests and fountains of *On ne badine pas avec l'amour*.

the Baron and Dame Pluche speak through comic masks; Rosette is the voice of innocence; Camille and Perdican work out the poetic and sentimental dilemma as a passionate dialectic. These three areas of diction are never invaded by the Chorus, which stands apart, comments, and through its hybrid nature thrusts the others into relief.

The measure of the Chorus' importance can be gauged by its strategic introductory position, and by the way it announces the play's poetic intent. In the first few minutes a semi-anonymous voice describes a minor character by projecting him through two metaphors and qualifying him in nine or ten different ways.[3] In *On ne badine pas avec l'amour* Blazius is essential but secondary to Musset's center of interest. The initial description is quite obviously a pretext to create a multi-dimensional image, one of the poet's most engaging tics. But even more significantly, the Chorus reveals its own

---

[3] Musset began to write *On ne badine pas avec l'amour* in verse, but after the first exchanges between Blazius and the Chorus decided that prose would be more appropriate. It is interesting to note that the transformation into prose does not alter the intensity of the rhetoric. In fact, the use of such rhetoric in prose serves Musset's manneristic purpose even better than poetry. Paul de Musset, in *Oeuvres complètes d'Alfred de Musset*, édition dédiée aux Amis du Poète (Paris, 1865-66), IX, 391-92, ascribes the harmony and rhythm of the prose version to its poetic source, a rather short-sighted interpretation considering the usual quality of Musset's prose. For purposes of comparison we reproduce the first lines of the rhymed version.

> Sur son mulet fringant doucement ballotté,
> Dans les bluets en fleur, messer Blazius s'avance,
> Gras et vêtu de neuf, l'écritoire au côté.
> Son ventre rebondi le soutient en cadence.
> Dévotement bercé sur ce vaste édredon,
> Il marmotte un Ave dans son triple menton.
> Salut! maître Blazius; comme une amphore antique,
> Au temps de la vendange on vous voit arriver. (1377-1378)

manner of observation, its imaginative power, its liberty of association.

The mixture of Perdican's freshly doctored pedantry and Blazius' stupidity is dear to Musset, and its resulting ambiguities help fix the play's direction. This is clear in the old man's first exchanges with the Chorus. "Il revient aujourd'hui même au château, la bouche toute pleine de façons de parler si belles et si fleuries, qu'on ne sait que lui répondre les trois quarts du temps. Toute sa gracieuse personne est un livre d'or; il ne voit pas un brin d'herbe à terre, qu'il ne vous dise comment cela s'appelle en latin; et quand il fait du vent ou qu'il pleut, il vous dit tout clairement pourquoi." *This very day he comes home to the château with his mouth full of such fine flowery phrases, that three-quarters of the time you do not know how to answer him. His charming person is just all one golden book; he cannot see a blade of grass on the ground without giving you the Latin name for it; and when it blows or when it rains he tells you plainly the reason why.* (I.i.327-28) Blazius is officially describing a learned young man; without knowing it he describes a poet as well. The tutor refers specifically to the jargon of the student. Perdican has in fact developed a florid style, one that is difficult to penetrate. The desire to explain the blade of grass, the wind and the rain can of course be attributed to erudition, but it is also a function of the poet, the interpreter of nature. Blazius invests Perdican with beauty and grace, expressing the young man's search for these qualities in nature and people. He notices both simplicity and complexity in Perdican's style. This antithesis of manner will be translated into theatrical conflict through the presence of the double heroine, Rosette-Camille.

179

Blazius' inadvertently precise appraisal of Perdican's nature is followed by a remark of the Chorus which consciously labels the nostalgic quality of the young man's yearnings. "Puissions-nous retrouver l'enfant dans le coeur de l'homme!" *May we find the child in the grown man's heart.* (I.i.328) Through this remodelled convention of the Chorus, Musset introduces, with stunning concision, the play's dominant movement. Their wish prefigures Perdican's own fruitless efforts to reach back to a past self, to find the innocence he has irretrievably lost. The exclamation of the Chorus brings to Musset's theatre a commonplace of lyric poetry rarely encountered on the stage. This nostalgia for past happiness, for the comfort of a recent memory is a perspective cherished by lovers from Petrarch to Lamartine. Musset is about to elaborate the sweet remembrance in a theatrical frame, strictly timed and rooted to the present.

Maintaining the rhythm of contrasts established by the alternation of the Chorus and Maître Blazius, Musset now sets the Baron's voice against that of Perdican. He creates a clash between the chronometer of the Baron and the nostalgia of the Chorus and Perdican. "Maître Bridaine, vous êtes mon ami; je vous représente maître Blazius, gouverneur de mon fils. Mon fils a eu hier matin, à midi huit minutes, vingt et un ans comptés; il est docteur à quatre boules blanches." *Master Bridaine, you are my friend: let me introduce Master Blazius, my son's tutor. My son yesterday, at eight minutes past twelve, noon, was exactly twenty-one years old. He has taken his degree, and passed in four subjects.* (I.ii.330) The Baron's only means of identifying people is the official standard.[4] His perception is reduced to machine

[4] In *On ne saurait penser à tout* (1849) another baron will express himself in precisely the same manner. "Partant à trois heures de

language. Personalities are abstracted into the unrelated and inhuman signs of days and "boules blanches"; the counting process is extended to all realms of existence, from the joy attendant upon his son's academic success to the anticipation of Perdican's marriage to Camille. "J'ai formé le dessein de marier mon fils avec ma nièce; c'est un couple assorti: leur éducation me coûte six mille écus." *I have formed the project of marrying my son to my niece. They are a couple made for one another. Their education has stood me in six thousand crowns.* (I.ii.331) The voice of the Baron literally ticks off minutes and coins, while Perdican speaks the harmonies of poetry. But Musset is quick to avoid an overly pat opposition, a dialectic that smacks of traditional logic. Perdican, the poet out of time, the disinterested lover, is subject to the very personification of a clock, and yet it does not make a bit of difference. Musset discards the obvious clash of will between father and son for the more important one that consists of their diverging conceptions of time. Perdican voluntarily submits to his father because he is in love with Camille; the arranged marriage is precisely what the hero desires. An old theatrical ply is thereby given a delightful turn. The poet's love is guaranteed by the will of the tax collector.

Montgeron, je devais par conséquent être au tourne-bride positivement à quatre heures un quart. J'avais une visite à faire à M. Duplessis, qui devait durer tout au plus un quart d'heure. Donc, avec le temps de venir ensuite ici, cela ne pouvait me mener plus tard que cinq heures. Je lui avais mandé tout cela avec la plus grande exactitude. Or, il est cinq heures précisément, et quelques minutes maintenant. Mon calcul n'est-il pas exact?" (i, 728)

Setting out from Montgeron at three, I ought to reach the tavern at quarter past four. I called on M. Duplessis, which took me perhaps fifteen minutes. Then allowing sufficient time to make the distance, I should reach this place by five o'clock. Then it must be just five now. Is my calculation correct?

It is precisely the apoetic Baron who makes the next reference to words. In a play where semantic values are crucial to life and death, the words of the poet Perdican are the most important, and it is these which his father wishes to elicit. As was the case with Blazius, the character of the poet is misinterpreted. "Je serais bien aise de vous voir entreprendre ce garçon, —discrètement, s'entend, —devant sa cousine; cela ne peut produire qu'un bon effet; —faites-le parler un peu latin, —non pas précisément pendant le dîner, cela deviendrait fastidieux, et quant à moi, je n'y comprends rien; —mais au dessert, —entendez-vous?" *I should be very pleased to see you put the lad through his paces—discreetly of course—before his cousin: that cannot fail to produce a good effect. Make him speak a little Latin; not exactly during dinner, that would spoil our appetites, and as for me, I do not understand a word of it: but at dessert, do you see?* (I.ii.333) The inability of the comic masks to understand Perdican is reiterated, the value of his words is again reduced to the cabalistic mumblings of a learned young man performing before an ignorant public. A few minutes of Latin will go well with dessert.

B. The Definition of Nostalgia

This play is a semantic progression, an evolution of meaning and words linked in improbable pairs, rearranged, and finally put into the unalterable focus of truth. The clashes already discussed hover over the play. The tension created by the divergent points of view of the Chorus and Blazius, of the Baron and Perdican, prepare an atmosphere of conflict for the crucial verbal duel between Perdican and Camille. The lines of communication between the hero and heroine are those essential to the play, and they are, of course, tangled.

Musset creates a system in which the reader's receptivity to modulation of tone is acute, and which insures the impact of the lovers' first words.

> PERDICAN. Bonjour, mon père, ma soeur bien-aimée! Quel bonheur! que je suis heureux!
> CAMILLE. Mon père et mon cousin, je vous salue.
> (I.ii.333)

> PERDICAN. *Good day, father, and you, my darling cousin. How delightful; how happy I am!*
> CAMILLE. *How do you do, uncle? and you, cousin?*

The affective quality of utterance is carefully measured to reveal the initial sentimental distance between them. Perdican's enthusiasm is parried by Camille's cold and rigid greeting. Thus Musset establishes a distance to be bridged by words. The protagonists strive for common meanings. Through the convention of salutation Musset makes a clear distinction between excesses of cordiality and standoffishness, both extreme attitudes and ripe for modification. Camille and Perdican are inspired by a priori assumptions that cannot withstand the theatrical present.

Perdican seeks to appropriate his fiancée into the time of a poetic universe. His conception of time is exposed as he responds to his father's question.

> LE BARON. Quand as-tu quitté Paris, Perdican?
> PERDICAN. Mercredi, je crois, ou mardi. Comme te voilà métamorphosée en femme! Je suis donc un homme, moi! Il me semble que c'est hier que je t'ai vue pas plus haute que cela.   (I.ii.334)

> BARON. *When did you leave Paris, Perdican?*
> PERDICAN. *Wednesday, I think—or Tuesday. Why, you are transformed into a woman! So I am a man,*

> *am I? It seems only yesterday I saw you only so high.*

Perdican rejects his father's calendar in confusion, and erects another temporal standard, the span of nostalgia which colors the present with tenderness by grafting on to it a dimly remembered past. Perdican is confident because this past seems vivid, but it will prove to be faithless. He attempts to transform Camille into the little girl he thinks she once was. Nostalgia is a vehicle for metaphorical movement, and it is this possibility of metaphor which fascinates Perdican. The poet seeks to turn the present into a reflection of a past his memory controls.

Perdican celebrates reminiscence, relishing all the clichés of childhood evoked: the birthplace, the playground of first impressions, and first love. In Act II, as the hero's words change value, his sincerity and innocence will be harshly questioned. But here Musset painstakingly depicts that part of poetic consciousness which is the yearning for the lost innocence of childhood. He seizes in the child's perception, or more exactly in the memory of the child's perception, the wonder that changed the world into a place of beauty. Camille refuses to share Perdican's nostalgia for their lost childhood. He seeks to escape the present by substituting a version of the past; her means of escape is the cloister. Both methods will prove faulty. In Act I it is Camille's rebuttal of sentiment which seems reprehensible. She rejects all that is dear to them both, a costly betrayal of identity which provokes the play's badinage. This first betrayal initiates a series of gestures that tie the lovers in a guilt which bears out the title's warning.

PERDICAN. Cela ne te ferait pas plaisir de revoir la prairie? Te souviens-tu de nos parties sur le bateau? Viens, nous descendrons jusqu'aux moulins; je tiendrai les rames, et toi le gouvernail.

CAMILLE. Je n'en ai aucune envie.

PERDICAN. Tu me fends l'âme. Quoi! pas un souvenir, Camille? pas un battement de coeur pour notre enfance, pour tout ce pauvre temps passé, si bon, si doux, si plein de niaiseries délicieuses? Tu ne veux pas venir voir le sentier par où nous allions à la ferme?

CAMILLE. Non, pas ce soir.

PERDICAN. Pas ce soir! et quand donc? Toute notre vie est là. (I.iii.338)

PERDICAN. *Would it not please you to see the meadow again? Do you remember our boating excursions? Come, we will go down as far as the mill; I will take the oars, and you the tiller.*

CAMILLE. *I do not feel the least inclined for it.*

PERDICAN. *You cut me to the heart. What! not one remembrance, Camille? Not a heart-throb for our childhood, for all those kind, sweet past days, so full of delightful sillinesses? You will not come and see the path we used to go by to the farm?*

CAMILLE. *No, not this evening.*

PERDICAN. *Not this evening! But when? Our whole life lies there.*

Perdican gives her the choice of three trips quite literally down memory lane—the field, the boat and the path itself. Camille remains locked in her convent, unwilling to follow Perdican's lead, to hear the resonance of the commonplaces. Perdican's final words in this ex-

change are a distillation of his version of the past. He
denies the present for this dream-like childhood. It is
of course impossible for Camille and Perdican to recapture the innocence and rapture of their first love
after the experiences of convent and university. The old
garden path leads to a much changed meadow. If all of
life lies in the past there is no hope in the present.
Camille stays aloof for the wrong reason, but her refusal is just, even on poetic grounds. Perdican the poet
tries to forget the man in his search for the child. The
present, the sophistication of his life, and his art always
catch up with him.

The hero's attempt to play the child is momentarily
successful. Camille turns away, but the Chorus, that
anonymous manifestation of literary self-consciousness,
echoes his feelings.

> PERDICAN. Bonjour, amis. Me reconnaissez-vous?
> LE CHOEUR. Seigneur, vous ressemblez à un enfant
> que nous avons beaucoup aimé.   (I.iv.340)

> PERDICAN. *Good day, friends; do you know me?*
> CHORUS. *My lord, you are like a child we loved
> dearly.*

The Chorus answers with effusion, with the affect that
was absent from Camille, yet there is a difference of register between Perdican's question and the response. He
is not perfectly recognizable because he has grown
older. There is a resemblance, duly noted by the Chorus,
a likeness which correctly preserves the span of elapsed
time. In the eyes of the Chorus, the measure of two
Perdicans is retained, the child is a shadow remembered
with love which projects itself back upon the man. The

Chorus expands upon the mechanics of resemblance and makes it the basis of acute perception. "Votre retour est un jour plus heureux que votre naissance. Il est plus doux de retrouver ce qu'on aime, que d'embrasser un nouveau-né." *Your return is a happier day than your birth. It is sweeter to recover what we love than to embrace a new-born babe.* (I.iv.341) It accepts neither the Baron's inexorable timetable nor Perdican's faulty version of the past. Instead, time is given depth and shape, releasing it from the ungraspable fleeting minute and the false grip of a forever dead past. The Chorus dresses Perdican in his shadow, a true refrain, and through consciousness of repetition puts him into the context of a familiar rhyme.

Perdican is deaf to the song of the Chorus. He persists in seeking a renewal of his childish delights by passing in review the mise-en-scène of romantic poetry, the clichés of innocence: his valley, his trees, his green paths, his little fountain. But the mystery of dreams cannot survive childhood revisited. The distance between his memory and reality is unbreachable.

> LE CHOEUR.   Il s'est fait plus d'un changement pendant votre absence. Il y a des filles mariées et des garçons partis pour l'armée.
>
> PERDICAN.   Vous me conterez tout cela. Je m'attends bien à du nouveau; mais en vérité je n'en veux pas encore. Comme ce lavoir est petit! autrefois il me paraissait immense; j'avais emporté dans ma tête un océan et des forêts, et je retrouve une goutte d'eau et des brins d'herbe. Quelle est donc cette jeune fille qui chante à sa croisée derrière ces arbres?   (I.iv.341)

187

> CHORUS. *There has been many a change during your absence. Girls are married, boys are gone to the army.*
>
> PERDICAN. *You shall tell me all about it. I expect a deal of news; but to tell the truth, I do not care to hear it yet. How small this pool is; formerly it seemed immense. I had carried away an ocean and forests in my mind: I come back to find a drop of water and blades of grass. But who can that girl be, singing at her lattice behind those trees?*

The rapidity of Perdican's disenchantment is shocking, and suggests a degree of ruthlessness that becomes more and more apparent as the play progresses.

The hero's fickle nature is exhibited as he abandons the drop of water for the simple peasant girl singing at the window. She offers him a new means of reestablishing the poetry of innocence. The girl is Rosette, the *soeur de lait* of Camille. She is an ideal metaphor, transforming Camille into an accessible rustic lover with a ready song on her lips and the simplicity of ignorance. Yet there are two parts to Perdican's poem. One is the yearning for the lost vision of the child; the other is the sophisticated inventiveness of the mannered young man. The complexity and interest of this character are produced by the unsettling mixture of two opposing attitudes. His dalliance with Rosette is provoked by the first; his pursuit of Camille is a realization of the second. The childish infatuation and the great love both belong to the sentiment of the poet.

Rosette is unable to speak to Perdican. Time and education have drastically separated them. She is a silent object, a rich source of inspiration. She is given a voice by Perdican, something he could not do if she were able to express herself. Her passivity, shaded by innocence, provides a field for the wonder he sought at the play's beginning.

ROSETTE. Vous respectez mon sourire, mais vous ne respectez guère mes lèvres, à ce qu'il me semble. Regardez donc; voilà une goutte de pluie qui me tombe sur la main, et cependant le ciel est pur.
PERDICAN. Pardonne-moi.
ROSETTE. Que vous ai-je fait, pour que vous pleu-riez? (II.iii.350)

ROSETTE. *You respect my smile, but you do not spare my lips much, it seems to me. Why, do look; there is a drop of rain fallen on my hand, and yet the sky is clear.*
PERDICAN. *Forgive me.*
ROSETTE. *What have I done to make you weep?*

This exchange is a successful example of theatrical lyricism. Musset extracts from carefully prepared elements a sincere reaction from Perdican, refined through the filter of Rosette's candor. The facile seduction of the country lass awakens in the hero an unarticulated feeling of remorse. The kiss he forces on Rosette is a betrayal of Camille, and the tear an admission that an ideal of innocence has failed. Guilt and regret are reflected in this tear that is mistaken for a drop of rain. Such a confusion is appropriate to Rosette's perception. It is Perdican's turn to remain silent. His silence is yet another reproach to the incessantly vocal and aggressive seducer. This irony does not prevent Musset from turning the poet into the object of poetry, the stage of transfer, the crux of image.

C. Reflections: Past and Present

Camille eventually yields to Perdican's love, and signals this by accepting his conventions. She appropriately leans over a reflection of her past in the little fountain once so dear to both of them. She passes through a natural looking-glass into the childhood evoked by the hero.

> PERDICAN. Est-ce possible? Est-ce toi, Camille, que je vois dans cette fontaine, assise sur les marguerites, comme aux jours d'autrefois?
> CAMILLE. Oui, Perdican, c'est moi. Je viens revivre un quart d'heure de la vie passée. (II.v.354-55)

> PERDICAN. *Is it possible? Is it you, Camille, that I see reflected in this fountain, sitting on the daisies, as in the old days?*
> CAMILLE. *Yes, Perdican, it is I. I have come to live over again one half-hour of the past life.*

The scene is complete, Laura has returned to the "chiare, fresche e dolci acque" of her fountain. Camille joins in Musset's theatrical game. She plays at being in the past in order to communicate with Perdican.

Once the bond has been made the author indulges in another of his ironic reversals. Camille and Perdican switch attitudes. She represents the niceties of sentiment which he now chooses to ignore. She asks him how many women he has loved, and which one he loved most. "Ma foi, je ne m'en souviens pas." *On my honor, I do not remember.* (II.v.356) This callous avowal of lapse of memory in the realm of sentiment puts his sincerity and his capacity for love into serious doubt. Camille points up Perdican's lack of sensitivity through the very perspective of remembrance he so consistently adopted during his passionate entreaties. The recipe for nostalgia is not infallible proof of a poetic sensibility or of a clean conscience. Camille's accusation helps demolish the caricature of a personality Perdican has built for himself. The inconsistencies of his character, first marked by his prompt disappointment with the dimensions of nostalgia, are now rooted in egotism. Then, shorn of his trappings, Perdican reacts with violence, taking up the duel with Camille. This time his weapons are real, and he uses life rather than memory to counter her wish to return to the cloister. This love is not learned from a faded album but from the flux of existence. "On est souvent trompé en amour, souvent blessé et souvent malheureux; mais on aime, et quand on est sur le bord de sa tombe, on se retourne pour regarder en arrière; et on se dit: J'ai souffert souvent, je me suis trompé quelquefois, mais j'ai aimé. C'est moi qui ai vécu, et non pas un être factice créé par mon orgueil et mon ennui." *One is often deceived in love, often wounded, often unhappy; but one loves, and on the brink of the grave one turns to look back and says: I have suffered often, sometimes I have been mistaken, but I have loved. It is I who have lived, and not a spurious being bred of my pride and my sorrow.* (II.v.364-65) The mutual applicability of the last sentence is not accidental. The frigid silence and the nostalgic sighs were both provoked by *orgueil* and *ennui*. The lovers are shocked back into life by their confrontation, but in the meantime a third person has come between them and the badinage has begun. Camille and Perdican, so alike in their sensitivity, their pride, and their refusal of life, will now claim a sacrifice in their doomed effort to love.

Rosette's identity is the field of action. She is endowed with poetry by Perdican, she is a version of Camille, she is the agent through which the lovers meet and separate. The dramatic movement of *On ne badine pas avec l'amour* is conceived as a series of poetic doubles. Perdican sought his former self at the play's outset. Rosette is a child-like projection of Camille. The hero's revenge is worked out to exploit the scheme of doubles. Two identities, two images are juxtaposed, but they are not congruent. This is the secret brought to surface by the plot. Perdican's imagination cannot turn Camille into Rosette, nor can it do the reverse. The young ladies are complementary aspects of a single woman, a double personality which is reminiscent of the Octave-Célio relationship in *Les Caprices de Marianne*. They are related, but they cannot merge. Perdican plays upon the distinction of character in his mean game of jealousy. "J'ai demandé un nouveau rendez-vous à Camille, et je suis sûr qu'elle y viendra; mais par le ciel, elle n'y trouvera pas ce qu'elle y comptera trouver. Je veux faire la cour à Rosette devant Camille elle-même." *I have asked Camille for another rendezvous, and I am sure she will come; but, by Heaven, she will not find what she expects there. I mean to make love to Rosette before Camille herself.* (III.ii.371) Rosette allows Perdican to include Camille in his poem of nostalgia, this time ironically. The words take on a new value, addressed to the innocent girl and overheard by her sophisticated counterpart. "Je t'aime, Rosette! toi seule au monde tu n'as rien oublié de nos beaux jours passés; toi seule tu te souviens de la vie qui n'est plus." *I love you, Rosette. You alone, out of all the world, have forgotten nothing of our good days that are past. You are the only one who remembers the life that is no more.* (III.iii.372) This is a variation on the words unheeded by Camille in Act I.[5] Camille now hears Perdican because he is speaking to her through Rosette, her model, style itself. As a further complication, Perdican's statement is proved false. Rosette remembers nothing at all, remaining true to her established passivity. None of Perdican's meaning escapes Camille, and it is perhaps because of the artifice and the sarcasm that her love for him finally becomes manifest. The combination of elements, the irony of repetition, the presence of Rosette and the mechanism of eavesdropping are infinitely more engaging than Perdican's gushingly adolescent declaration of love. There is one more lesson to be drawn from Perdican's evocation of the past. "Toute notre vie est là." *Our whole life lies there.* (I.iii.338) is replaced by "la vie qui n'est plus." *the life that is no more.* (III.iii. 372) He accepts the distance he had tried to obliterate at first. He accepts the present because his effort to recapture the past has failed.

The relationship of Camille, Rosette, and Perdican, based on image reflection and temporal perspective, is distilled in the hero's sturdiest verbal structure.

Regarde à présent cette bague. Lève-toi, et approchons-nous de cette fontaine. Nous vois-tu tous les deux, dans la source, appuyés l'un sur l'autre? Vois-tu tes beaux yeux près des miens, ta main dans la mienne? Regarde tout cela s'effacer. (*Il jette sa bague dans l'eau.*) Regarde comme notre image a disparu; la voilà qui revient peu à peu; l'eau qui s'était troublée reprend son équilibre; elle tremble encore; de grands cercles noirs courent à sa surface;

[5] See above, p. 185.

patience, nous reparaissons; déjà je distingue de nouveau tes bras enlacés dans les miens; encore une minute, et il n'y aura plus une ride sur ton joli visage; regarde! c'était une bague que m'avait donnée Camille. (III.iii.372-73)

Now look at this ring. Stand up and let us come near the fountain. Do you see us both in the spring leaning on each other? Do you see your lovely eyes near mine, your hand in mine? Watch how all that is blotted out. (Throwing his ring into the water.) *Look how our image has disappeared. There it is coming back little by little. The troubled water regains its tranquility. It trembles still. Great black rings float over its surface. Patience. We are reappearing. Already I can make out again your arms entwined in mine. One minute more and there will not be a wrinkle left in your pretty face. Look! It was a ring that Camille gave me.*

This is the same fountain which witnessed Camille's first concession to Perdican's manner in Act II. It is the fountain he urged her to rediscover in Act I. Its capacity for reflection has been proved and tested, and now it brings the characters back to a theatrical present by giving their image a substance distinct from the past. Perdican sees himself in the fountain with Rosette. He throws in Camille's ring and erases the image of his false love for the *soeur de lait* with a token received from the woman he truly loves. The great black circles announce doom. Just as Camille's ring effaces Rosette's image, the reality of her presence will destroy Rosette herself. Musset seizes the ring and the fountain in order to fuse the play's elements in an increasingly solid tension of reflection, where the linearity of theatrical development is always at the service of an essentially metaphorical arrangement.

Ever aware of Camille's presence, Perdican makes a final evocation of Rosette's poetic simplicity. His first projection of her capacity to represent childish innocence was merely caricatural. The dénouement of the play turns into hollow disappointment, that simplistic product of his imagination, and is an indictment of his faulty humanity as well. "... tu ne sais rien; tu ne lirais pas dans un livre la prière que ta mère t'apprend, comme elle l'a apprise de sa mère; tu ne comprends même pas le sens des paroles que tu répètes, quand tu t'agenouilles au pied de ton lit; mais tu comprends bien que tu pries, et c'est tout ce qu'il faut à Dieu." *... you know nothing; you could not read in a book the prayer that your mother taught you as she learned it from her mother. You do not even understand the sense of the words you repeat when you kneel at your bedside; but you understand that you are praying, and that is all God wants.* (III.iii.373) Illiteracy and piety may have their own wordless poetry, but they are certainly inappropriate to a spirit like Perdican's. Rosette's reaction makes audible the semantic gap between them. "Comme vous me parlez, monseigneur!" *How speak you, my lord!* (III.iii. 373) That is exactly what he does in excess, paying no heed to the fact that he cannot reenter the world which Rosette represents. There is here a variation on the first linguistic clash between Perdican and Camille. In both cases the poet's effusions are set against quasi-muteness, the first caused by reticence, the second by ignorance. Having sung the praises of rote prayers, Perdican goes on to glorify Rosette's illiteracy: "Tu ne sais pas lire; mais tu sais ce que disent ces bois et ces prairies, ces tièdes rivières, ces beaux champs couverts de moissons, toute cette nature splendide de jeunesse. Tu reconnais tous ces milliers de frères, et moi pour l'un d'eux; lève-toi, tu seras ma femme, et nous prendrons racine ensemble dans la sève du monde tout-puissant." *You cannot read; but you can tell what these woods and meadows say, their warm rivers and fair harvest-covered fields, and all this nature radiant with youth. You recognize all these thousands of brothers and me as one of them. Rise up; you shall be my wife, and together we shall strike root into the vital currents of the almighty world.* (III.iii.373-74) Rosette's answer is the predictable silence. Grandiloquently praising the child of nature and her gift for interpreting the woods and the fields, Perdican bares the flaw of his innocence, first through the disproportionate tone, and then through the ruthless exploitation of Rosette to wound Camille. He crushes the wordless Rosette with words.

D. The Failure of Time

The play's final moments display the coming together of its poetic as well as its theatrical premises. At last Perdican is able to state his nostalgia in a way meaningful both to him and Camille. Love's young dream transcends its conventional weight through its contact with guilt, its inclusion in a poem of various tonalities. Perdican accepts the present, and the sense of irrecoverable loss that it implies.

> Le vert sentier qui nous amenait l'un vers l'autre avait une pente si douce, il était entouré de buissons si fleuris, il se perdait dans un si tranquille horizon! Il a bien fallu que la vanité, le bavardage et la colère vinssent jeter leurs rochers informes sur cette route céleste, qui nous aurait conduits à toi dans un baiser!

Il a bien fallu que nous nous fissions du mal, car nous sommes des hommes. Ô insensés! nous nous aimons. (III.viii.386-87)

The green path that led us toward each other sloped so gently, such flowery shrubs surrounded it, it merged in so calm a horizon—and vanity, light talking, and anger must cast their shapeless rocks on this celestial way, which would have brought us to thee in a kiss. We must do wrong, for we are of mankind. O blind fools! We love each other.

The present tense of the verb *aimer* is significant. Perdican and Camille have grown up, and their love is suited to their age. Pain and intrigue bring them into a contact posited on the present. Obstacles must line the green path before they can tread upon it. The lovers have acquired their own style, a mixture of sentiment, cruelty, and badinage.

The poem is almost complete. What it lacks is the unhappy ending that makes art out of a poet's love. As Camille and Perdican declare their passion they hear a cry from behind the altar. Camille exclaims, "C'est la voix de ma soeur de lait." *It is my foster-sister's voice.* (III.viii.387) It is also an overtone of her own voice, the voice of the innocent girl who exists no more. That part of Camille which once lived in wondrous communion with the trees and the fields has been heartlessly destroyed by words too loud and too clever. We suddenly realize that Camille is incomplete without her past. The significance of nostalgia, parodied, ironized, and rejected, takes on its fullness in absence. It was impossible to love Camille, figment of the past. It is impossible to love Camille trapped in the present, and she is the first to know it. "Elle est morte. Adieu, Perdi-

can!" *She is dead. Farewell, Perdican!* (III.viii.388) This
curtain line, a sure coup de théâtre, is an echo of Camille's initial style. It is prompted by guilt, of course,
but also by the need to complete the play's pattern.
The metaphorical Rosette, her factor of style, brought
the lovers together. Their conception of each other is
locked in the sum of temporal and personal reflections
concentrated in her voiceless identity. Her disappear-
ance must separate them forever.

nine

HEROISM AND ART:
Lorenzaccio

THE manner of *Lorenzaccio* emerges without warning into Musset's tonal spectrum. Critics have cited an array of influences for Musset's change of voice.[1] George Sand's *Une Conspiration en 1537*, other *scènes historiques* written by romantic playwrights such as Vitet and Loève-Veimars, and the ever important Schiller left Musset with more than enough models. The desire to try something of Shakespearian scope and variety was widespread, witness the efforts of Vigny and Hugo. The Italy Musset so cleverly parodied in his first collections of verse, and which reappears in *La Nuit vénitienne* and *Les Caprices de Marianne* was perhaps due for serious treatment. It would be incorrect to speak of development in Musset's theatre, for Perdican and Lorenzo spring from the poet's imagination at practically the same time. The distinctions are thus all the more striking. Almost contemporaneous with the theatrical proverb, this historical play discards the never-never land of serenades, court jesters, and sylvan fountains, the space of precious metaphor, and the time of harmonious duets.

[1] Paul Dimoff, in *La Genèse de Lorenzaccio* (Paris, 1936), fully treats the question of Musset's sources.

The plays manifest no parallels in regard to plot, structure, and diction. The concentration of the quasi-fantasies gives way to a multitude of characters and episodes, bewildering in their organization. A deceptively rosy hue is replaced by harshness, physical cruelty, and realpolitik.

Lorenzaccio does exhibit the same submersion of mannerism that characterizes *On ne badine pas avec l'amour*. The sorrow of Camille and Perdican seems to indicate that Musset has become more interested in the poem itself than in its composition. Men are engaged in existence through their imagination; they transform reality into art. In this way *Lorenzaccio* and *On ne badine pas avec l'amour* are central to Musset's *oeuvre*. Despite differences of technique, they exemplify the poet's search to fix the hero's destiny in form.

A. THE FRAGMENTED IMAGE

Lorenzaccio exhibits an even freer use of the theatrical genre than the other plays. Musset submits to the chronology about which Fantasio and Perdican had so loudly complained, and treats history seriously, yet this does not prevent him from establishing a rhythm more syncopated and erratic than ever before. If the characters in New Arcadia are submissive to poetic clichés, those in sixteenth-century Italy are completely controlled by an image. This image remains the same at the play's climax, unaffected by the action exerted upon it. Florence is the image, and Musset reveals its priority in many ways. Shakespeare's historical plays are about people who are also kings and courtiers; *Lorenzaccio* ruthlessly exploits people to express the city. The characters and the plot are means of focusing upon this image for the span of time it takes to read the play.

The hero's dominating presence puts Florence into high relief. The self is freed from introspection and projected into the organism of a collectivity, an agglomeration. Lorenzaccio's plan to assassinate Alexandre de Médicis, the despot of Florence, is indistinguishable from Musset's variegated presentation of the city. The private anguish of Lorenzaccio is regularly interwoven with an anonymous urban complaint in a fugal pattern of restatement and counterpoint which shapes the theme in time without altering its integrity.[2] The arrangement of scenes diverts our gaze from the singularity of the hero's endeavor to the multiplicity of the general movement. The play is divided into five acts and thirty-eight scenes. Each scene represents a change of locale, of character, formally supporting the sense of fragmentation, literally showing the city bit by bit.[3] In Act I, for example, the first scene presents Alexandre and Lorenzo, *scene ii* shows the public at large and frames Salviati's insult to Louise Strozzi, *scene iii* deals with the Cibo family, *scene iv* dramatizes Lorenzo's fake cowardice, *scene v* is another public encounter, and *scene vi* oddly joins Lorenzo's mother and aunt with the departure of the exiles. Musset deliberately avoids the linking of scenes. Only three times in the play is an action carried through in successive scenes.[4] The play's

[2] The technique is akin to the choral treatment used by Hugo in the *récit* of *Les Burgraves*, see above, pp. 76-80. In both cases the goal is not the theatrical presentation of encounter and conflict, but rather the duration of a theme or image: the stage becomes a platform for many voices.

[3] Hassan El Nouty, in "Théâtre et anti-théâtre au dix-neuvième siècle," *PMLA*, LXXIX (Dec. 1964), 606, states: "Due to this mobility and this scenic rhythm, we finally achieve that ubiquity through which History can be restored to its living plenitude. We have precisely defined what Musset accomplishes in *Lorenzaccio*."

[4] III.ii-iii; III.v-vi; IV.ix-x-xi. Steen Jansen, in "L'Unité d'action

central gesture, the murder of Alexandre, takes place in three rapid scenes that end Act IV. The action of the hero finds its true coherence in an exhilarating series of cinematic shots, a montage whose dynamics depends on the shuffling and interlocking of related but distinct elements. Without softening the focus of the various perspectives, Lorenzo locates them in the acuteness of his own imagination. Characters like Marquise Cibo, Philippe Strozzi, and even the Goldsmith have lives of their own, independent from that of the titular hero. The image of Florence is projected on the disengaged and philosophical merchant, the outraged father, the patriotic adulterous wife, the wailing exile, and the poet of violence.

The initial scene of the play, an exemplary procurement and seduction accomplished by the cousins Lorenzo and Alexandre, is followed by the first of three scenes in Act I devoted to the populace of Florence. A collection of merchants, students, and townspeople tell the story of the city, the hegemony of the Médicis family, the debauchery of Alexandre and Lorenzo. In their quality as citizens they represent the city as a whole. They act not as supernumeraries, but as distinct characters endowed with intelligence and corresponding verbal freedom and responsibility. To the Goldsmith falls the task of explaining the liberty that reigned under the Florentine oligarchy before the interference of pope and emperor. In a later scene, set before the church of San Miniato al monte, Musset further displays his method of diffusion. The Second Bourgeois uses

---

dans *Lorenzaccio,*" *Revue Romane,* III (1968), 116-35, demonstrates how Musset abandons the classical notion of unity of action by the rearrangement of scenes and dramatic conflict.

scandal as an element of diction to define tyranny and disorder. The amorous activities of the Médicis provide a source of imagery appropriate to Florence's political dilemma.

Voilà des malheurs inévitables. Que voulez-vous que fasse la jeunesse sous un gouvernement comme le nôtre? On vient crier à son de trompe que César est à Bologne, et les badauds répètent: "César est à Bologne," en clignant des yeux d'un air d'importance, sans réfléchir à ce qu'on y fait. Le jour suivant, ils sont plus heureux encore d'apprendre et de répéter: "Le pape est à Bologne avec César." Que s'ensuit-il? Une réjouissance publique. Ils n'en voient pas davantage; et puis un beau matin ils se réveillent tout endormis des fumées du vin impérial, et ils voient une figure sinistre à la grande fenêtre du palais des Pazzi. Ils demandent quel est ce personnage, et on leur répond que c'est leur roi. Le pape et l'empereur sont accouchés d'un bâtard qui a droit de vie et de mort sur nos enfants, et qui ne pourrait pas nommer sa mère. (I.v.75)[5]

These are inevitable misfortunes. What would you have the youth of a government like ours do? Somebody announces with the sound of a trumpet that Caesar is at Bologna, and the idlers repeat, "Caesar is at Bologna!" and wink with an air of importance, without reflecting what they are doing. The next day they are happier still to learn and to repeat, "The Pope is at Bologna with Caesar!" What follows? A public rejoicing—they see nothing more in it; and

[5] Jean Pommier, in *Variétés sur Alfred de Musset et son théâtre* (Paris, n.d.), p. 136, compares this to the first Philippic of Demosthenes.

then some fine morning they awaken all stupefied with the fumes of imperial wine, and they see a sinister face at the great window of the Pazzi palace. They demand who the personage is; they are told it is the King. The Pope and the Emperor are delivered of a bastard who has the right of life and death over our children, and who can not call his own mother by name.

The city sounds quite different depending on what category of voice evokes her. Emblematic citizens use history to allegorize Florence; the poet will clothe her with metaphors of love and art.

The end of Act I sounds another register of the public voice. Its strategic position, closing the play's first major division, emphasizes once again Musset's desire to spread the burden of statement between the largest constituency he can accommodate in the work's confines. Enough information has been exposed in Act I to pile guilt upon Alexandre and to vilify the Florence he has created. Nameless men take the road of exile and bitterly salute the city that rejects them.

> LE PREMIER. Adieu, Florence, peste de l'Italie; adieu, mère stérile, qui n'a plus de lait pour tes enfants.
>
> LE SECOND. Adieu, Florence la bâtarde, spectre hideux de l'antique Florence; adieu, fange sans nom.
>
> TOUS LES BANNIS. Adieu, Florence! maudites soient les mamelles de tes femmes! maudits soient tes sanglots! maudites les prières de tes églises, le pain de tes blés, l'air de tes rues! Malédiction sur la dernière goutte de ton sang corrompu. (I.vi.84)

FIRST CITIZEN. *Farewell, Florence, pest of Italy!*
Farewell, sterile mother who no longer has milk for
her children!
SECOND CITIZEN. *Farewell, Florence, vile city,*
hideous specter of your former greatness!
ALL THE EXILES. *Farewell, Florence! Cursed be the*
breasts of your women! Cursed be your sobs!
Cursed be the prayers of your churches, the bread
of your harvests, the air of your streets! A curse
upon the last drop of your corrupted blood.

This is a particularly vivid example of the choral effect
which gives the play its amplitude. The reiteration of
"adieu" and the accumulation of invective constitute a
crescendo. The distinct value of the words is muffled
by the increasing pitch, a reminder that even armchair
theatre aspires to be heard.

B. THE FRAGMENTED HERO

Character doubling is a constant ingredient in Musset's plays. The relationship between Laurette and her
portrait, Octave and Célio, Fantasio and Saint-Jean, and
Rosette and Camille are basic to the poet's conception
of character. It is not surprising to find the double
figure in *Lorenzaccio*. Lorenzo never meets his counterpart, Marquise Cibo. They function in an almost complete identity of manner, and a theatrical encounter
between them is therefore unnecessary. These characters prostitute themselves to Alexandre for love of
Florence. In both cases the love of city is expressed as
love for the corrupt Duke. Lorenzo is his pimp; the
Marquise becomes his mistress. They are functions of
the insatiable lust which has invaded the city. The sexual nature of Alexandre's dominion over Florence is

defined by the Marquise: "Que tu es belle, Florence, mais que tu es triste![6] Il y a là plus d'une maison où Alexandre est entré la nuit, couvert de son manteau; c'est un libertin, je le sais. —Et pourquoi est-ce que tu te mêles à tout cela, toi, Florence? Qui est-ce donc que j'aime? Est-ce toi? Est-ce lui?" *How beautiful you are, Florence, but how sad! There is more than one house down there that Alexander has entered clandestinely by night. He is a libertine, I know. And why do you mingle with all this, Florence? Whom do I love? Is it you, or he?* (II.iii.99-100) Lorenzo was once a paragon of diligence and chastity; in her first scene Marquise Cibo is depicted as a model of wifely virtue. They both sacrifice purity and innocence in their love-hate of Alexandre. The parallel continues in their idyllic expression of peace and harmony following encounters with corruption. The Marquise, revolted by her degradation, imagines her beloved husband at his country estate. "Autour de toi paissent tes génisses grasses; tes garçons de ferme dînent à l'ombre. La pelouse soulève son manteau blanchâtre aux rayons du soleil; les arbres, entretenus par tes soins, murmurent religieusement sur la tête blanche de leur vieux maître, tandis que l'écho de nos longues arcades répète avec respect le bruit de

---

[6] Maurice Allem, in the Pléiade edition of the *Théâtre complet*, pp. 1277-78, cites another reference to Florence's sadness in *La Confession d'un enfant du siècle.* (V, 1) "Florence est triste; c'est le moyen-âge encore vivant au milieu de nous. Comment souffrir ces fenêtres grillées et cette affreuse couleur dont les maisons sont toutes salies?" *Florence is sad; it is the middle ages still living in our midst. How can we tolerate these barred windows and this frightful color with which the houses are all dirtied?* This, and an extract from "À mon frère, revenant d'Italie" also quoted by Allem, seem different in connotation from the sadness evoked by the Marquise. She is not depressed by the physical sadness of the city, but rather by its sense of moral hopelessness.

ton pas tranquille." *Your sleek heifers are grazing
around you; your farm-hands are eating their dinner
in the shade; the lawn spreads its pale mantle to the
rays of the sun; the trees, preserved by your care, are
murmuring religiously above the head of their old
master, while the echo of our long piazzas respectfully
repeat the sound of your light footsteps.* (III.vi.149)
Lorenzo commits murder and is invaded by a wave of
peace at its accomplishment.

The Marquis Cibo is the most obvious referent for his
wife's idealism. Lorenzaccio's corresponding standards
are his mother and aunt, Marie Soderini and Catherine
Ginori. It is through them that Musset extracts the first
traces of the hero's true poetic identity. They voice
concern about Lorenzo in the framework of a beautiful
evening on the banks of the Arno. Catherine notices a
strange harmony, produced by the juxtaposition of
country murmurs and city noises. "Le soleil commence
à baisser. De larges bandes de pourpre traversent le
feuillage, et la grenouille fait sonner sous les roseaux sa
petite cloche de cristal. C'est une singulière chose que
toutes les harmonies du soir avec le bruit lointain de
cette ville." *The sun is setting. Large bands of purple
strike athwart the foliage, and the frog is ringing his
little crystal bell beneath the rushes. A singular thing
is this harmony of evening with the distant sound of
that city.* (I.vi.79) This is an explicit version of the
play's strain of paradox, present in the duplicity of the
city, of Marquise Cibo, and of Lorenzaccio. The core
of a quiet night, along a river so peaceful that frogs are
endowed with crystal bells, withstands the urban chaos.
The antithetical linkage seems to stress the beauty of
those crystal bells. Such is the character of Lorenzaccio,

lodging the purest of motives in acts of degradation. His intransigence survives self-indulgence; the beauty of Florence survives tyranny and oppression.

Lorenzo does not appear in this scene. At this point in the play we only know him from the first seduction, his fainting at the sight of a sword, and uncomplimentary hearsay. His mother's memory and the prelude of a peaceful night are effective changes of key which indicate the complexity of his character. "Tant de facilité, un si doux amour de la solitude! Ce ne sera jamais un guerrier que mon Renzo, disais-je en le voyant rentrer de son collège, avec ses gros livres sous le bras; mais un saint amour de la vérité brillait sur ses lèvres et dans ses yeux noirs; il lui fallait s'inquiéter de tout, dire sans cesse: 'Celui-là est pauvre, celui-là est ruiné; comment faire?' Et cette admiration pour les grands hommes de son Plutarque! Catherine, Catherine, que de fois je l'ai baisé au front en pensant au père de la patrie!" *Such a facility of conception, such a sweet love for solitude! He will never be a warrior, my Renzo, I used to say to myself on seeing him come in from school, dripping with perspiration, with his books under his arm; and such a holy love of truth burned upon his lips and in his black eyes! He was so solicitous about everybody, constantly saying, "So-and-so is poor," or "So-and-so is ruined; what can we do for them? And that admiration for the great men of his Plutarch! Catherine, Catherine, how often I used to kiss his brow in thinking of the father of the country!* (I.vi.80-81) Marie's yearning for her supposedly lost son is remarkable in the number of clues it furnishes about the new, corrupt version of Lorenzo. The hero will cite his love for solitude as a determining factor in the decision to kill Alexandre. His present cowardice is merely a mask for daring and courage. Love for truth hides behind another mask. However concern for others has given way to bitter cynicism and mistrust. He will not lead men, for he has no faith in them. This is an additional affirmation of his solitary nature. The sense of history he often expresses is contained in the references to Plutarch and Côme de Médicis. Without a conception of "the great man" his plan would have no formal basis. The play therefore is a realization of Lorenzo's true identity, the one lamented by his mother. It will emerge through demonstrations of his treachery, his commitment, and his vision.

In a later scene (II.iv) Marie tells Lorenzo of a dream in which he appeared to her as his former self. He reacts by asking Catherine to read the story of Brutus from Plutarch, and then announces to his mother that the phantom she dreamt will perhaps return. The acceptance of his own double nature prefigures the theatrical encounter in "La Nuit de décembre" of poet and shadow. Allowing for the differences of personality between the overtly autobiographical poet of "La Nuit," and the assassin of this play, there is a chilling glose of *Lorenzaccio* in the poem's final lines.[7] The personification of solitude in the double further illuminates the distance that separates the real Lorenzo and the debauched courtier. Marie is forced

---

[7] The poet is addressed by his double.

Le ciel m'a confié ton coeur.
Quand tu seras dans la douleur,
Viens à moi sans inquiétude.
Je te suivrai sur le chemin;
Mais je ne puis toucher ta main,
Ami, je suis la Solitude.

Heaven has entrusted your heart to me. When you are plunged in sadness, come to me without misgivings. I will follow you along your way; but I cannot touch your hand. Friend, I am solitude.

209

to accept the impostor. The solitary, bookish, and frail young man expresses himself through the city's confusion and energy. As she observes the leavetaking of the banished patriots, Marie accepts the burden of guilt, her part in the destiny of Florence. "Ah! ne puis-je voir une fille sans pudeur, un malheureux privé de sa famille, sans que tout cela ne me crie: Tu es la mère de nos malheurs!" *Ah, can I not see a shameless girl, an unfortunate deprived of his family, without they cry to me, 'You are the mother of our misfortunes!'* (I.vi.82) Her anguish is mingled with the general lament, and through her Lorenzo is integrated into yet another panel of the fresco.

The protean Lorenzaccio, impostor, creator, and philosopher, is of course the character most consistently placed under scrutiny by both the author and the other characters. He contains in his own being the essence of the city, and it is through him that its perception is clearest. The first significant description of Lorenzaccio is made by Alexandre. It reveals a tension of identity familiar in Musset's works. The disguises, the role-playing, and the ironies of Fantasio and Perdican lie easily on this committed poet. "Renzo, un homme à craindre! le plus fieffé poltron! une femmelette, l'ombre d'un ruffian énervé! un rêveur qui marche nuit et jour sans épée, de peur d'en apercevoir l'ombre à son côté! d'ailleurs un philosophe, un gratteur de papier, un méchant poète qui ne sait seulement pas faire un sonnet!" *Renzo, a man to fear! The most arrant coward! An effeminate man, the shadow of a nerveless ruffian! A dreamer who never carries a sword for fear of seeing its shadow at his side! In addition to which, a philosopher, a scribbler, a bad poet who can not even compose a sonnet!* (I.iv.70) The interest of this passage lies deeper than the traditional dramatic irony of the victim's refusal to recognize his executioner. Lorenzaccio will of course express himself most fully with the sword before which he shams fear, the dreamer will sum up his being in the violence of an action. It is the reference to the poet which radically bares Lorenzaccio's purpose.[8] He is most definitely a poet unable to make a sonnet. He has ambitions to write a poem of much grander dimensions, one that has a complexity of structure that spills beyond the microcosmic fourteen lines into a rendition of the city itself. The refrain is the murder of Alexandre, planned, recurring, and finally executed. Through the artifice of his degradation Lorenzo draws a new identity and realizes his conception.

Alexandre repeatedly defines his "entremetteur," establishing a point of departure for the gradual revelation of character. "Regardez-moi ce petit corps maigre, ce lendemain d'orgie ambulant. Regardez-moi ces yeux plombés, ces mains fluettes et maladives, à peine assez fermes pour soutenir un éventail, ce visage morne, qui sourit quelquefois, mais qui n'a pas la force de rire. C'est là un homme à craindre?" *Look at that slender frame this day after a strolling orgy. Look at those heavy eyes, those skinny hands, scarce strong enough to wield a fan; that dull face, which sometimes smiles, but has not the force to laugh. Is that a man to fear?* (I.iv.70) Pardoning Musset the rather facile reprise of "un homme à craindre," this continuing portrait repre-

---

[8] Robert T. Denommé, in "The Motif of the 'poète maudit' in Musset's *Lorenzaccio*," *L'Esprit Créateur*, III, No. 3, Fall (1965), 141, signals the poetic nature of Lorenzo. "Musset deliberately transforms Lorenzo's character in order to endow him with the kind of poetic sensitivity that the historical Lorenzo does not possess."

sents a useful cliché for the sensitive young romantic. Sexual ambiguity is common baggage for the poetic soul. A slim physique, a sickly mien, and an enigmatic expression are full of ironic potential, and will be transformed when Lorenzaccio becomes the decisive avenger.

The hero's function as artist, negatively alluded to by the Duke, is related to the play's idealists, his mother, his aunt, the painter Tebaldeo. The man who desecrated Rome's statues in a mass decapitation, attempts to restore to Florence its pristine beauty by eliminating the blight, Alexandre. The city's beauty is guaranteed by the manner of execution, its art, its metaphorical power. Tebaldeo has a special place in the scheme because of his professional status, and it is in his conversation with Lorenzaccio that Musset most obviously expresses his notions about the city and art. A discarded opening scene shows Benvenuto Cellini insisting to leave Florence after casting a medal that bears the likeness of Alexandre. The Duke reluctantly permits the departure. In the final version Musset transfers the task of dramatizing artistic freedom from the renowned goldsmith to the humble Tebaldeo, and reduces Cellini to a remark made by *Un Autre Cavalier.*[9] Tebaldeo is an effective foil, opposing candor to Lorenzaccio's cynicism. He refuses to do a portrait of la Mazzafirra in the nude, contending that Art demands more respect. Describing how he would paint Florence, Tebaldeo opts for an orthodox and facile view and thus robs it of its complexity. "Je me placerais à l'orient, sur la rive gauche de l'Arno. C'est de cet endroit que la perspective est la plus large et la plus agréable." *From the east side of the city, on the left bank of the Arno. It is from that*

9 See I.v.75.

212

point that the perspective is broadest and most pleasing.
(II.ii.90) This is the attitude of a hack that neither
Lorenzaccio nor Musset can tolerate, and furnishes a
point of departure for a discussion of the morality of
art and the morality of the city.

LORENZO. Tu peindrais Florence, les places, les
maisons et les rues?
TEBALDEO. Oui, monseigneur.
LORENZO. Pourquoi donc ne peux-tu peindre une
courtisane, si tu peux peindre un mauvais lieu?
TEBALDEO. On ne m'a point encore appris à parler
ainsi de ma mère.
LORENZO. Qu'appeles-tu ta mère?
TEBALDEO. Florence, seigneur.
LORENZO. Alors, tu n'es qu'un bâtard, car ta mère
n'est qu'une catin. (II.ii.91)

LORENZO. *You would paint Florence, the squares,
the building, and the streets?*
TEBALDEO. *Yes, my Lord.*
LORENZO. *Now why would you not paint a courte-
san, if you would paint a bad place?*
TEBALDEO. *I have not yet been taught to speak
thus of my mother.*
LORENZO. *Who do you call your mother?*
TEBALDEO. *Florence, my Lord.*
LORENZO. *Then you are a bastard, for your mother
is nothing but a harlot.*

The symbolic mother, revered and insulted, is given
theatrical shape by a conflict of interpretation between
two characters.[10] Tebaldeo and Lorenzo both consider

[10] The comparison of a city to a mother is not original, but it is
constant in *Lorenzaccio*. The image of the mother makes Florence's
betrayal of her sons that much more poignant. This cliché helps

Florence a source of art, and art itself. A moment later the positions are altered. Ambiguity and paradox, the very qualities which fascinate the author and his hero, are described by the simple, mediocre painter. "Une blessure sanglante peut engendrer la corruption dans le corps le plus sain. Mais des gouttes précieuses du sang de ma mère sort une plante odorante qui guérit tous les maux. L'art, cette fleur divine, a quelquefois besoin du fumier pour engraisser le sol et le féconder." *A bleeding wound may breed corruption in the healthiest body; but the precious drops of my mother's blood flow from a sweet-smelling plant which heals all ills. Art, that divine flower, has sometimes need of a fertilizer to enrich the soil that bears it.* (II.ii.91) Musset enjoys ironizing his characters, forcing the idealistic Tebaldeo to justify evil while the sceptical courtier spouts pious sarcasms. "C'est-à-dire qu'un peuple malheureux fait les grands artistes. Je me ferais volontiers l'alchimiste de ton alambic; les larmes des peuples y retombent en perles. Par la mort du diable! tu me plais. Les familles peuvent se désoler, les nations mourir de misère, cela échauffe la cervelle de monsieur." *That is to say that an unhappy people begets great artists. I*

---

keep the person of Florence in focus, and reminds us that the play's central character is the city. Philippe Strozzi, the outraged father, and the fulcrum of insurrectionary activity due to the suffering of family, addresses the city in the same tone used by the group of exiles. "Eh bien, Florence, apprends-la donc à tes pavés, la couleur de mon noble sang! il y a quarante de tes fils qui l'ont dans les veines." *Well, Florence, teach thus to thy pavements the color of my noble blood. It flows in the veins of forty of your sons.* (II.v.110) The banality of the rhetoric is relieved by the insistence on maternity, and the fact that it is uttered by the play's father figure. Herbert S. Gochberg, in *Stage of Dreams*, p. 180, discusses the maternity motif.

would like to be the alchemist of your alembic; the tears of the people would there be distilled into pearls. By the death of Satan! you please me. Families may mourn, nations die of misery, all that for the amusement of kings! (II.ii.91-92) We could just as well be listening to Rameau's nephew coercing the apparently virtuous *Lui* to distinguish between art and morality. A dialectic, with a constantly shifting axis, appeals to Musset precisely because of this kind of inversion. Tebaldeo's sacred calling, his wonder before the works of Michelangelo and Raffaello, and his church solo are threatened by contact with Lorenzaccio. The painter grandiloquently talks of the angel's harp and its silver chord. "C'est la plus belle et la plus noble; et cependant le toucher d'une rude main lui est favorable." *It is the most beautiful and the noblest; and yet the touch of a rude hand is favorable to it.* (II.ii.91) He is describing the art of Lorenzaccio, the manner of violence. Tebaldeo's paintings ostensibly illustrate the harmony of nature, but he describes instead an artist for whom inspiration and style are derived from suffering and brutality. The combination of the city's lamentation and the hero's dagger thrust is thus a source of beauty. The *sang* and the *fumier* dispel the "vapeur légère" *light vapor* (II.ii. 88) Tebaldeo discovered in the canvases of the masters.

Musset exploits the scene for an additional irony. At its conclusion Lorenzo invites Tebaldeo to his palace. "Viens demain à mon palais, je veux te faire faire un tableau d'importance pour le jour de mes noces." *Come to my palace tomorrow. I wish to order an important picture from you for my wedding-day.* (II.ii.93) The painter accepts the commission, and thus unwittingly collaborates in the murder of Alexandre. The reference to "le jour de mes noces" is the introduction of the murder's dominant image. It is during one of the sittings that Lorenzo steals the victim's protective coat of mail. But Tebaldeo participates in the murder metaphorically as well as theatrically. He depicts the corrupt Alexandre, who is the sum of Florence; Lorenzo captures the city in the person of Alexandre, and in the style of the murder. Tebaldeo refuses to do the portrait of la Mazzafirra; he paints instead the infinitely more licentious Alexandre.

Musset permits his hero moments of introspection, but they have cryptic elements which require the play's subsequent action for their solution. Again, contact with idealism, as in the scene with his mother,[11] brings forth Lorenzo's most explicit self-consciousness. In a conversation with Philippe Strozzi, Lorenzo attempts to expose the reasons which prompted him to plan the murder of Alexandre. This is the play's longest scene; its position is central. Lorenzo partially unmasks and allows his true voice to be heard. But the promise of revelation is not fully kept, and this sincere appraisal of his character retains a measure of enigma.

Ma jeunesse a été pure comme l'or. Pendant vingt ans de silence la foudre s'est amoncelée dans ma poitrine; et il faut que je sois réellement une étincelle du tonnerre, car tout à coup, une certaine nuit que j'étais assis dans les ruines du Colisée antique, je ne sais pourquoi je me levai; je tendis vers le ciel mes bras trempés de rosée, et je jurai qu'un des tyrans de ma patrie mourrait de ma main. J'étais un étudiant paisible, et je ne m'occupais alors que des arts et des sciences, et il m'est impossible de dire comment cet

[11] See above, p. 207-209.

étrange serment s'est fait en moi. Peut-être est-ce là
ce qu'on éprouve quand on devient amoureux.

(III.iii.133)

*My youth was as pure as gold. During twenty years
of silence the thunderbolt was gathering in my breast;
and I must be in reality the spark of a thunderbolt,
for suddenly, a certain night as I was sitting in the
ruins of the Colosseum, I know not why, I arose; I
stretched my young arms to heaven, and I swore that
one of the tyrants of my country should die by my
hand. I was a peaceful student, and at that time I was
occupied only with art and science, and it is impossible for me to say how that strange oath developed
in me. Perhaps that is what a man feels when he
falls in love.*

Marie Soderini's sketch of the studious young man is
repeated by the subject himself, and then animated by
the proverbial thunderbolt. Something about the ruins
of Rome, history made into art, the presence of time,
and an ultimately indefinable sentiment, set off the reaction of transformation. Lorenzo's book is changed into
a weapon, his purity is hidden beneath the countenance
of perversity. Can hatred of tyranny be the single source
of his passion? By admitting his inability to understand
the reasons for such a drastic upheaval of character
Lorenzo preserves its violent and arcane source.

The amalgam of elements, the twenty years of virtue
and study, the Colosseum, the particular night, constitute inspiration—that convergence of unexpected factors which produces a work of art.[12] The feeling of excitement, akin to love, or love itself, is a lyric élan. It

[12] A more complete analysis of this creative process can be found
in Fantasio's description of Elsbeth's tears, see above, p. 167.

217

is expressed in the sense of miraculous linkage and the creation of a self-contained system of elements. The modes of disguise and action bring Lorenzo out of himself, into a new relationship with existence. He will create a pattern by donning the costume of his particular Saint-Jean. "Une statue qui descendrait de son piédestal pour marcher parmi les hommes sur la place publique, serait peut-être semblable à ce que j'ai été, le jour où j'ai commencé à vivre avec cette idée: il faut que je sois un Brutus." *A statue which should descend from its pedestal to walk in public places among men would perhaps be comparable to what I was the day I began to live with this idea: I must be a Brutus.* (III.iii. 134) The image of the statue successfully renders the historical, temporal, and artistic aspects of Lorenzo's new identity. The statue leaves a double imprint in the public square, for it represents a double Brutus, the assassins of Caesar and Tarquinius. Lorenzo is well furnished with shadows, his own spectre,[13] and two historical identities. This role-playing must be distinguished from that of *Fantasio*. Here it is not an example of substitution, but a restatement of personality through a new set of frames. The models are liberating agents, and reaffirm Lorenzo's solitude in a positive key.

Je voulais agir seul, sans le secours d'aucun homme. Je travaillais pour l'humanité; mais mon orgueil restait solitaire au milieu de tous mes rêves philanthropiques. Il fallait donc entamer par la ruse un combat singulier avec mon ennemi. Je ne voulais pas soulever les masses, ni conquérir la gloire bavarde d'un paralytique comme Cicéron. Je voulais arriver à l'homme, me prendre corps à corps avec la tyrannie vivante,

---

[13] See above, p. 209.

218

la tuer, porter mon épée sanglante sur la tribune, et laisser la fumée du sang d'Alexandre monter au nez des harangueurs, pour réchauffer leur cervelle ampoulée. (III.iii.134)

I wished to act alone, without the aid of any man. I was working for humanity; but my pride mingled with all my philanthropic dreams. It was necessary then to begin by stratagem a single combat with my enemy. I did not wish to arouse the masses, nor to conquer the garrulous glory of a paralytic like Cicero; I wished the man himself, to grapple hand to hand with living tyranny, to kill it, and afterward to carry my bloody sword to the rostrum and let the fumes of Alexandre's blood mount to the nostrils of the haranguers, to revive the ardor of their sluggish brains.

This singular combat, in its loneliness, in the completeness of its detail, in its necessity, is a poetic gesture whose realization is accompanied by feelings of exhilaration and transport.[14]

Not long before the murder Lorenzo is granted a soliloquy, another opportunity to examine the still hidden motives of his actions. He loses himself in a series of conjectures that set off two new metaphorical identities. "Le spectre de mon père me conduisait-il, comme Oreste, vers un nouvel Égiste? M'avait-il offensé alors? . . . Ah! pourquoi cette idée me vient-elle si souvent depuis quelques temps? —Suis-je le bras de Dieu? Y a-t-il une nuée au-dessus de ma tête? Quand j'entrerai dans cette chambre, et que je voudrai tirer mon épée du fourreau, j'ai peur de tirer l'épée flamboyante de

---

[14] Léon Lafoscade, in *Le Théâtre d'Alfred de Musset,* pp. 80-81, describes the hallucinatory quality of Lorenzo's attitude.

l'archange, et de tomber en cendres sur ma proie." *Did
the specter of my father lead me, like Orestes, toward
a new Aegisthus? Has he then offended me? . . . Ah,
why does this idea come to me so often of late—"Am I
following the will of God?" Is there a cloud over my
head? When I enter into that chamber, and wish to
draw my sword from its scabbard, I am afraid of drawing the flaming sword of the archangel, and then of
falling in ashes upon my prey.* (IV.iii.160) The political
revenge of the two Brutuses is modulated into the pri-
mordial murder committed by Orestes. The victim
named here is Aegisthus. Klytemnestra goes unmen-
tioned but not unforgotten in a play where mother-city
has already been described as a prostitute and adulter-
ess. Lorenzo has passed from an historical to a mythic
plane, and following the logical progression, concludes
in apocalypse. This is prophetic of the play's outcome
and symptomatic of the poet's mobility within his design.

C. ACTION AS ART

The most highly poetic diction in the play is associated with Lorenzo's work of art, the murder of Alexandre. Consistent with the theatrical genre, and in an
effort to provide an extra perspective, Musset first presents a dress rehearsal. Lorenzo and his manservant,
Scoronconcolo, duel and shout in order to accustom the
neighbors to the sound of violence. Lorenzo achieves a
kind of hysteria which far surpasses the required subter-
fuge, and indicates the urgency of his need to act. It is
a torrent of images, a concentrated version of the play's
totality. "Ô jour de sang, jour de mes noces! Ô soleil!
soleil! il y a assez longtemps que tu es sec comme le
plomb; tu te meurs de soif, soleil! son sang t'enivrera.
Ô ma vengeance! qu'il y a longtemps que tes ongles pous-

sent! Ô dents d'Ugolin! il vous faut le crâne, le crâne!" *Oh, day of blood! Oh, nuptial day! Oh, sun, sun! you have been dry long enough; you are dying of thirst, sun! His blood will intoxicate you. Oh, my vengeance! How long your nails are in sprouting! Oh, teeth of Ugolino; you need the skull, the skull!* (III.i.119) The various elements of this passage are thrust into the simultaneous identity of vengeance. The *jour de noces* was already introduced by Lorenzo into his scene with Tebaldeo.[15] Now its meaning becomes fuller as it is qualified by the explicit *jour de sang*. The ambiguity of blood, its life-giving and life-sapping capacities, juxtaposes the wedding, the vengeance and the sun. Through the sacrifice of blood the sun will be made drunk, its color and brilliance restored. Lorenzo refers to the sun's lost vitality with mention of dryness and thirst, thus giving Alexandre's presence cosmic scope, and furnishing his own will another range of metaphor. It becomes apparent after the murder that Lorenzo seeks to reestablish the order of nature itself. The image of the sun is not further qualified by the hero, and its only other significant evocation is made by Marquise Cibo as she seeks to explain the character of Alexandre. "Ce que tu as fait de mal, c'est ta jeunesse, c'est ta tête—que sais-je, moi? c'est le sang qui coule violemment dans ces veines brûlantes, c'est ce soleil étouffant qui nous pèse." *Whatever wrong you have done has been due to your youth, your head; what do I know about it? It is the blood which courses madly in your burning veins, the suffocating sun which weighs upon us.* (III.vi.147) She too links the sun and blood in a fatal relationship, creating evil and confusion. Lorenzo's revenge goes far beyond political expediency and helps explain the elation

[15] See above, p. 215.

and wonder he experienced that night in the ruins of the Colosseum. The poem, his wedding with Alexandre, dissipates the chaos with its new harmony. The evocation of the Count Ugolino increases the resonance. The retributive Hell of Dante is a place of both political and moral revenge. Ugolino eternally gnawing at the skull of Ruggieri provides a literary reference pertinent to the play's Tuscan setting, and a degree of allegory consistent with the previous vision of the flaming archangel.

Just before the murder Lorenzo reiterates the sexual motif of the wedding night. "Eh, mignon, eh, mignon! mettez vos gants neufs, un plus bel habit que cela, tra la la! faites-vous beau, la mariée est belle. Mais, je vous le dis à l'oreille, prenez garde à son petit couteau." *Ah, my favorite! put on your new gloves and a finer costume than that; tra-la-la! make yourself handsome, the bride is beautiful. But, I tell you this in a whisper, look out for her little knife.* (IV.ix.176-77) Throughout the play Alexandre and Lorenzo have called each other "mignon." Alexandre describes Lorenzo as a "femelette"[16] and Lorenzo complained to Philippe Strozzi that "il fallait baiser sur ses lèvres épaisses tous les restes de ses orgies." *I had to kiss the remains of his orgies on his thick lips.* (III.iii.135) The victim and assassin are brought together in a horrible intimacy, suggesting love and hate.[17] Lorenzo's assumption of the bride's role is

[16] See above, p. 210.

[17] Herbert S. Gochberg, pp. 182 ff., provides an extended analysis of the sexual aspects of the murder, which he characterizes as "an act of love and a work of art." This is also noted by A. Callen, in "The Place of *Lorenzaccio* in Musset's Theatre," *Forum for Modern Language Studies*, v (July 1969), 225-31, which contains as well an excellent discussion of the relationships between *Lorenzaccio* and the other major plays.

related to his original effeminate pose, but then resolved in an expression of his masculinity with the warning about the "petit couteau." The hero's double nature is expressed as a pseudo-mythical bisexuality. This corresponds to his anagogical purpose. The avenging archangel restores the balance of the universe.[18] The wedding-night murder in Lorenzo's bed-chamber is practically wordless. The hero is liberated by his act, and does not allude to the murder at all.

LORENZO, *s'asseyant sur le bord de la fênetre.* Que la nuit est belle! Que l'air est pur! Respire, respire, coeur navré de joie!

SCORONCONCOLO. Viens, Maître, nous en avons trop fait; sauvons-nous.

LORENZO. Que le vent du soir est doux et embaumé! Comme les fleurs des prairies s'entr'ouvrent! Ô nature magnifique, ô éternel repos!

SCORONCONCOLO. Le vent va glacer sur votre visage la sueur qui en découle. Venez, Seigneur.

LORENZO. Ah! Dieu de bonté! quel moment!

(IV.xi.180-81)

LORENZO, seating himself at the window. *What a beautiful night! How pure the air of heaven is! Breathe, breathe, heart broken with joy!*

SCORONCONCOLO. *Come, master, we have done too much! let us fly.*

LORENZO. *How soft and balmy the evening air is! How the flowers of the fields are bursting their buds! O magnificent nature! O eternal repose!*

SCORONCONCOLO. *The wind will freeze the sweat which is trickling down your face. Come, my Lord.*

LORENZO. *Ah, God of love! what a moment!*

[18] See above, pp. 219-20.

This is a moment of pure lyric transport, reminiscent of the élan that accompanied the project's conception, but even sweeter in its realization. Lorenzo has passed through his identities into the eternity of art and the full embrace of nature. The political air of Florence is not cleansed by the elimination of Alexandre. Lorenzo foresees this before carrying out his plan, and Act V of the play justifies his cynicism. He breathes instead the pure air of artistic order, the night and the river that so inspired his mother and Catherine.[19] Lorenzo's epiphany emanates from many sources: Marie Soderini's anguish over her lost son, Catherine Ginori's innocence endangered by Alexandre's lust, the death of Louise Strozzi and the patriotism of her father, Philippe, the love-hate of Marquise Cibo. These faces of love are worn by Lorenzo as he stabs his victim. The play fills him with the energy required to strike, and he is properly left with a sign of the consumated marriage. Alexandre bites his finger and imprints the mark of a ring.

Musset is not content with the hero's triumph. The painstakingly articulated voice of the city at large, first heard in Act I, is reintroduced in Act V. Lorenzo's voice again becomes one of many. That aspect of Florence personified by Alexandre is gone, and therefore the hero's part in the general design is now over. Lorenzo has composed his version of Florence, and it is time for the power of the city to be reasserted in all its registers. The Merchant, the Goldsmith again have their say, the Strozzi and Salviati children bicker, Lorenzo is thrown into a Venetian canal with astounding rapidity, and another Médicis is invested with power. *Lorenzaccio* is at once a choral work giving full vent to mass effects,

[19] See above, p. 207.

antiphony, a fugal structure, and an effort to contain the voice of the chorus in one throat. Lorenzo's rendition of Florence is compelling, and courageous in its attempt to include a heavy thematic burden. Through its accessibility, concentration, and contrasts of pitch we are able to perceive and grasp the dimensions of the public Florence, the infinitely variable image of the city.

ten

CONCLUSION

HUGO and Musset do not provide for other playwrights a set of formulas or a procedural code that, when followed, would facilitate the union of the two realms—poem and stage. Their successes are distinct from each other, from their contemporaries, and from the subsequent developments of the genre. There are, of course, traces of influence in Rostand, the symbolist theatre, and Claudel, for example. The problem of verse drama has been faced by American poets such as Eliot, MacLeish, and Jeffers, and Maxwell Anderson achieved considerable success with his popular brand of theatrical poetry. Yet these works owe much more to classical models, Shakespeare, and the Bible than they do to Hugo and Musset. Romantic theatre succeeded in liberating a tradition-bound dramaturgy, but it did so without imposing new rules of its own. The individuality of Hugo and Musset is posited upon a freedom of form and a search for an ever-expanding theatrical vocabulary that preclude a clear definition of the genre's limits. Romantic drama, which seemed to be the strongest weapon in the armory of the romantic revolutionaries, turns out to be aberrant, eluding the grasp of an audience reluctant to accept its challenge. It is precisely because the formal struggle was so intense that the results make such heavy demands upon the public. The responses habitually dictated by the genre are jarred by the harmonics of *Hernani*, the time scale of *Les Burgraves*, the introspection of Musset's *oeuvre*.

Despite obvious differences of scope, detail, subject matter, and diction, Hugo and Musset are linked by the same need to refashion a language suited to their theatre. Hugo's best work is neither tragic, in the classical sense, nor dramatic, according to his own definition. The basic elements of dramatic encounter are rearranged in a pattern by turns lyric and epic. The theatre of Musset consistently dramatizes the individual's search to perceive existence, a process of reflection and contemplation whose interiority is threatened by normal modes of conflict. In both cases, language functions autocratically within the poetic experience. The degree of stylization calls attention to itself, thus intensifying the spectator's awareness to essentially non-theatrical configurations: the fullness of song, the sweep of the epic, a teleology of imagination. In this way, Hugo and Musset set themselves apart from the theatrical tradition. Hugo adored Corneille, and Musset celebrated Molière. Yet Hernani and Fantasio are closer in nature to each other than to seventeenth-century counterparts, Rodrigue and Scapin for example. This is not explicable in purely chronological terms. It would seem that Hernani has more in common with a Castilian nobleman who speaks in rhymed couplets than a Bavarian clown who speaks in prose. Yet Hernani and Fantasio are intimately tied. They both trumpet the poet's identity, transcending politics, plot, and even dramatic characterization. Their words are progressively detached from systems other than those contained in their own self-consciousness.

The history of the romantic theatre is brief, its critical stock irregular, its promises perhaps unrealized. Works written for the stage languish on bookshelves; the "armchair theatre" is miraculously transplanted to the proscenium and thrives. Yet through prose, poetry, and a bewildering variety of presentations, the romantic theatre provides a platform which permits us to grasp and retain the sonority of the poet's voice. Shocked by contact with this genre, the poem is liberated from the page. In an unfamiliar ambiance, its redefinition becomes necessary, convenient, and appropriate. The stage restores the poem to the oral tradition.

Appendix

Hernani

Aст I. *Le Roi.* Carlos, King of Spain, while hiding in a closet, overhears avowals of love exchanged by Hernani, the bandit, and Doña Sol, ward and betrothed of the aged Silva. The lovers are discovered by Carlos and Silva.

Aст II. *Le Bandit.* Carlos tries to abduct Doña Sol but is foiled by Hernani. The King refuses to fight the outlaw. The lovers again declare their passion and are separated by the warning bell.

Aст III. *Le Vieillard.* Silva impatiently anticipates his marriage to Doña Sol, and welcomes Hernani who is disguised as a pilgrim. In a jealous rage Hernani unmasks, and mistakenly accuses Sol of infidelity. Silva surprises the lovers but hides Hernani behind a portrait upon the arrival of Don Carlos. Ruled by a point of Castilian honor, Silva lets Doña Sol be abducted rather than betray Hernani's hiding place. The bandit promises his life to Silva whenever the old man sounds his horn. In exchange he asks to be permitted vengeance upon Carlos.

Aст IV. *Le Tombeau.* At Aix-la-Chapelle Carlos awaits the news of the election of a new emperor. He enters into the tomb of Charlemagne. Conspirators plot Carlos' death, and

229

Hernani wins the honor of striking the first blow. Carlos is elected emperor, grants pardon to all, restores to Hernani his titles and true name, and blesses the marriage of his former rival to Doña Sol.

ACT V. *La Noce.* The wedding guests notice a death-like figure cloaked in a domino. Hernani and Doña Sol speak of their love and happiness. The horn is sounded, and Silva appears to exact Hernani's death. The lovers take poison.

Les Burgraves

PART I. *L'Aïeul.* The scene is a portrait gallery through whose windows one sees the *burg.* The hag Guanhumara crosses the stage. Slaves enter and engage in a long discussion of present and past events, covering a span of one hundred years: the magic powers of Guanhumara; the four generations inhabiting the *burg;* a secret room and a wall stained with blood; the supposed death in battle of the Emperor Barberousse; the old story of Fosco's vengeance upon his half-brother Donato, and his lover Ginevra; the wars of the burgraves and the wounding of Barberousse by Job; the present situation in the *burg* complicated by the love of Otbert, Job's young protégé, for Régina, the betrothed of Hatto, Job's grandson. Régina is dying. Guanhumara promises to save Régina if Otbert agrees to do her bidding. The reveling burgraves enter, but are interrupted by the aged Job, and his son Magnus. They disapprove of the indecorous merry-making, and are enraged when Hatto tries to turn away an old beggar. Job asserts himself, and has the beggar brought in with a show of great hospitality.

PART II. *Le Mendiant.* A hall in the *burg.* Régina has been cured by Guanhumara's magic. In return, Otbert has promised to kill someone in the dungeon that night. Job, rejoicing at Régina's recovery, and delighted with her love for Otbert, his favorite, declares that they should marry. As the young couple prepare to leave the *burg*, Guanhumara reveals their plan to Hatto. Otbert challenges Hatto, who cowardly refuses to fight a foundling. Then, the beggar reveals himself to be Barberousse and offers to fight. Magnus wants to hang the Emperor, but Job realizes that only Barberousse can save Germany, and he offers fealty to his old enemy (and still unrecognized half-brother, Donato).

PART III. *Le Caveau perdu*. A dungeon. Job has come to speak to his past and repent for his crimes. A voice calls him Cain. Guanhumara, the Ginevra so sorely treated by Job-Fosco many years before, reveals herself and tells him of the awful vengeance she has planned. Otbert, in reality his lost son George, will kill him. She agrees that Otbert should not know the true identity of his victim. In the ensuing scene, Otbert senses the truth, but Job denies it. Just as the son is about to strike he is stopped by Barberousse. Guanhumara poisons herself, the Emperor pardons his brother and announces his retirement.

Torquemada

PART I, ACT I. *L'In Pace*. A convent cemetery. The Prior encounters a mysterious man who threateningly asks for information, and finally reveals himself to be King Ferdinand. Ferdinand and his confidant, the Marquis de Fuentel, discuss the expansion of the Empire and the King's ambitions. It is hinted that Fuentel sired a son to the former Queen of Spain. Ferdinand notices a young man and woman, Sanche, Prince of Spain, and Rose, Infanta, daughter of the King's rival. They are betrothed. Fuentel learns that he is Sanche's grandfather and resolves to help the young lovers. Torquemada declaims his fiery visions, is judged by the Bishop, refuses to recant, and is sent to be buried alive. Rose and Sanche hear his voice, and release him using a cross as a lever on the stone covering the tomb.

ACT II. *Les Trois Prêtres.* Italy. This is a chance confrontation between the fanatic Torquemada, the peace-loving Francis de Paul, and the libertine pope, Alexander VI.

PART II. ACT I. *Torquemada.* Burgos, the royal patio. Ferdinand tells Fuentel that he has taken a fancy to Rose and wishes to kill Sanche. Fuentel convinces Ferdinand to put Sanche in a monastery.

ACT II. Seville. A room in the old moorish palace. The rabbi offers money in exchange for the lives of the Jews. The King is ready to acquiesce, and persuades Queen Isabella in turn by appealing to her avaricious nature. Torquemada denounces the royal couple and reveals the auto-da-fé already in progress.

ACT III. Seville. The King's secret park. Rose and Sanche await while Fuentel engineers their escape. Torquemada recognizes them as his liberators, promises his aid, yet leaves precipitously when he learns a cross was sacrilegiously used to free him. The lovers are horrified to perceive the skull and crossbones banner of the Inquisition signaling their doom.

Mangeront-ils?

The scene is a ruined cloister on the Isle of Man.

ACT I. *La Sorcière.* Zineb, a hundred-year-old witch, feels death approaching. She rescues a wounded carrier pigeon and reads the attached note warning that if the King touches a church his throne will be endangered. The King is pursuing his cousin Slada, who has eloped with Janet, his fiancée. Aïrolo, a "nature boy," takes refuge in the sanctuary, and quickly learns its principal inconvenience: all the plants growing there are poisonous. He helps Zineb who is being chased by the King's soldiers. She gives him a talisman, a flamingo feather, which guarantees its bearer one hundred years of life.

Act II. *Le Talisman.* Aïrolo is captured and about to be hung. Zineb is made to tell the King's fortune. She predicts that he will live as long as the next man who passes him with his hands tied behind his back. This is, of course, Aïrolo, on the way to his execution. The King immediately grants his pardon and tries to satisfy his every wish. The young man taunts the despot with suicide. A great table is set and the King is further insulted when Aïrolo invites Slada and Janet to dine. In desperation, the King abdicates. Slada is proclaimed successor, and Aïrolo reminds him that he was once hungry.

La Nuit vénitienne

Laurette has been married by proxy to the Prince d'Eysenach. Threatening suicide, her lover, Razetta, entreats her to flee with him. He is asked to join revelers in a passing gondola, and refuses. The Prince charms Laurette, who decides not to elope with Razetta. The unhappy swain again plans suicide and/or murder, but finally accepts the invitation of his friends to join in the festivities.

André del Sarto

Act I. The painter Cordiani is surprised by Grémio while leaving the room of his mistress, Lucrèce, wife of his teacher, André del Sarto. André laments his squandered talent and money. He encounters Cordiani and realizes that his pupil has just murdered Grémio.

Act II. André orders Cordiani to leave Florence. The young painter hides in Lucrèce's room. He is discovered and wounded in the ensuing duel. Lucrèce flees with her lover; André bewails the loss of all that was dear to him and commits suicide.

233

APPENDIX

Les Caprices de Marianne

ACT I. Célio sighs in vain for the love of Marianne, married to the judge Claudio. He relates this to Octave, Claudio's cousin. Octave speaks to Marianne on Célio's behalf, to no avail. Célio confides his chagrin to his mother, Hermia.

ACT II. Octave again confronts Marianne, and she shows obvious interest in him. Claudio defies his wife, who, out of spite, promises to meet Octave. Octave sends Célio in his stead. In the meantime, Marianne has heard her husband plotting with assassins to kill her lover. Célio arrives, and Marianne, assuming it is Octave, warns him to go away. Célio, thinking himself betrayed by his friend, runs to his sure death. Upon learning what has happened, Octave refuses the love of Marianne.

Fantasio

ACT I. The King of Bavaria discusses the coming marriage of his daughter Elsbeth to the Prince of Mantua. Young people of the city welcome Fantasio. The funeral procession of the King's jester, Saint-Jean, passes by, and Fantasio, to escape paying a debt, decides to apply for the vacated job. The Prince of Mantua disguises himself as his own aide-de-camp in order to discover the true nature of the King's daughter.

ACT II. Elsbeth meets Fantasio, disguised as the jester. The foolish (disguised) Prince is dismissed by Elsbeth. Fantasio notices her sadness over the coming marriage. In order to prevent it he de-wigs the real aide-de-camp who is disguised as the Prince. War is declared, Fantasio put in prison, and Elsbeth discovers his true identity. The war notwithstanding, she is grateful for her happiness and grants him liberty, allowing him to return to her garden whenever he wishes to resume his disguise as the jester.

234

On ne badine pas avec l'amour

Act I. The return of Perdican from the university and Camille from a convent is announced by their comic companions, Maître Blazius and Dame Pluche. The young people are destined to be married by the Baron, father of Perdican and guardian of Camille, but their first meeting is a fiasco. In a conversation with peasants, Perdican tries to evoke his past and notices Rosette, Camille's *soeur de lait*.

Act II. Camille tells Perdican that she has decided to enter the convent. Perdican begins to seduce Rosette with an eye to making Camille jealous. Their comings and goings are punctuated by scenes involving the comic characters, the Baron, Maître Bridaine, Maître Blazius, and Dame Pluche. Perdican and Camille continue their debate on love and sincerity.

Act III. Perdican intercepts a letter of Camille's, which he finds insulting. Wishing to take revenge, he invites Camille to a rendez-vous, and makes sure she overhears him speaking of love to Rosette. She retaliates by forcing Perdican to reveal his true feelings while Rosette is hiding behind a curtain. When Perdican learns the ruse he defiantly decides to marry Rosette. A final avowal of love between Perdican and Camille is also overheard by Rosette, who dies as a result. The lovers part.

Lorenzaccio

Act I. *scene i.* Lorenzo and Alexandre, Duke of Florence, abduct a young girl. *scene ii.* Salviati insults Louise Strozzi. *scene iii.* Marquis Cibo takes leave of his adoring wife. Her brother-in-law intercepts a love letter sent to her by Alexandre. *scene iv.* Lorenzo faints at the sight of a sword. *scene v.* Salviati again insults Louise Strozzi, this time in her brother's presence. *scene vi.* Marie and Catherine, Lorenzo's mother and aunt, deplore his debauchery and witness the departure of exiles.

ACT II. *scene i.* Philippe Strozzi learns of Salviati's insult. His eldest son swears vengeance. *scene ii.* Lorenzo makes fun of the idealistic painter Tebaldeo, but asks him to paint Alexandre's portrait. *scene iii.* Marquise Cibo makes confession to her brother-in-law, the Cardinal. She refuses to exploit Alexandre's love for political purposes. *scene iv.* Alexandre tells Lorenzo of his conquest of Marquise Cibo, but asks for a tryst with Lorenzo's aunt, Catherine, *scene v.* Lorenzo congratulates the Strozzis for their attack on Salviati. *scene vi.* While Alexandre is posing for the portrait, Lorenzo steals his protective coat of mail. *scene vii.* The wounded Salviati cries for vengeance upon the Strozzi family.

ACT III. *scene i.* Lorenzo rehearses his murder of Alexandre. *scene ii.* Philippe Strozzi joins the conspiracy against Alexandre. *scene iii.* The Strozzi sons are arrested. *scene iv.* Catherine receives a love letter from the Duke. *scene v.* Alexandre and the Marquise are surprised by the Cardinal. *scene vi.* Alexandre is bored by the Marquise's mixture of love and idealism. *scene vii.* Louise Strozzi is poisoned.

ACT IV. *scene i.* Lorenzo promises Alexandre a tryst with Catherine is his own room. *scene ii.* The Strozzi sons learn of the death of their sister. *scene iii.* In a long monologue Lorenzo reveals his exultation at the imminent murder. *scene iv.* The Cardinal attempts to blackmail Marquise Cibo, but she reveals the truth of her relationship with Alexandre to her husband. *scene v.* Lorenzo makes his final preparations for the murder. *scene vi.* The funeral of Louise Strozzi. *scene vii.* Lorenzo announces his project to disbelieving republicans. *scene viii.* The exilees refuse to act unless Philippe Strozzi leads them. *scene ix.* Lorenzo again rehearses the murder. *scene x.* Alexandre refuses to heed the warning given him by the Cardinal. *scene xi.* Lorenzo murders Alexandre.

ACT V. *scene i.* Côme de Médicis is proposed as successor to Alexandre. *scene ii.* Lorenzo, in Venice with Philippe Strozzi, hears that a price has been put on his head. *scene iii.* The Cibos are reconciled. *scene iv.* Philippe Strozzi laments the loss of his own revenge on Alexandre. *scene v.* The Florentines accept their unchanging political destiny. *scene vi.* A student dies for freedom. *scene vii.* Lorenzo is murdered in Venice. *scene viii.* Côme is proclaimed Duke.

A Selected Bibliography

Albouy, Pierre, *La Création mythologique chez Victor Hugo*, Paris, 1963.

Barrère, Jean-Bertrand, *La Fantaisie de Victor Hugo, 1802-1851*, Paris, 1949.

———, *La Fantaisie de Victor Hugo, 1852-1885*, Paris, 1960.

Brombert, Victor, "Victor Hugo, la prison et l'espace," *Revue des Sciences Humaines*, cxvii (Jan.-Mar. 1965), 59-79.

Butor, Michel, "Le Théâtre de Victor Hugo," *La Nouvelle Revue française*, xii (Nov. 1964), 862-78 (Dec. 1964), 1073-81; xiii (Jan. 1965), 105-113.

Callen, A., "The Place of *Lorenzaccio* in Musset's Theatre," *Forum for Modern Language Studies*, v (July 1969), 225-31.

Champigny, Robert, *Le Genre dramatique*, Monte Carlo, 1965.

Constant, Benjamin, *Oeuvres*, ed. Alfred Roulin, Bibliothèque de la Pléiade, Paris, 1957.

Denommé, Robert T., "The Motif of the 'Poète maudit' in Musset's *Lorenzaccio*," *L'Esprit Créateur*, iii, No. 3, Fall (1965), 138-46.

Descotes, Maurice, *Le Drame romantique et ses grands créateurs*, Paris, 1955.

———, *Le Public de théâtre et son histoire*, Paris, 1964.

Dimoff, Paul, *La Genèse de Lorenzaccio*, Paris, 1936.

BIBLIOGRAPHY

Draper, F.W.M., *The Rise and Fall of the French Romantic Drama, with special reference to the influence of Shakespeare, Scott and Byron,* New York, n.d.

Dumas, Alexandre, *Antony, Nineteenth Century French Plays,* ed. Joseph L. Borgerhoff, New York City, 1931.

Eggli, Edmond, *Schiller et le romantisme français,* 2 vols., Paris, 1927.

Eliot, T. S., *Poetry and Drama,* Cambridge, Mass., 1951.

El Nouty, Hassan, "Théâtre et anti-théâtre au dix-neuvième siècle," *PMLA,* LXXIX (Dec. 1964), 604-612.

Evans, David O., *Le Théâtre pendant la période romantique,* Paris, 1925.

Gastinel, Pierre, *Le Romantisme d'Alfred de Musset,* Paris, 1931.

Gaudon, Jean, *Victor Hugo, dramaturge,* Paris, 1955.

Ginisty, Paul, *France d'antan, Le Théâtre romantique,* Paris, 1923.

————, *Le Mélodrame,* Paris, n.d.

Glachant, Paul et Victor, *Essai critique sur le théâtre de Victor Hugo,* 2 vols., Paris, 1902-1903.

Glauser, Alfred, *Victor Hugo et la poésie pure,* Genève, 1957.

Gochberg, Herbert S., *Stage of Dreams, The Dramatic Art of Alfred de Musset (1828-1834),* Genève, 1967.

Grant, Richard B., *The Perilous Quest, Image, Myth, and Prophecy in the Narratives of Victor Hugo,* Durham, N.C., 1968.

Guillemin, Henri, *Victor Hugo par lui-même,* Paris, 1957.

Henriot, Emile, *Alfred de Musset,* Paris, 1928.

Hugo, Adèle, *Victor Hugo raconté par un témoin de sa vie,* 2 vols., Bruxelles, 1863.

Hugo, Victor, *Mangeront-ils?,* eds. Joubert et Robert, Cahiers Victor Hugo, publiés avec le concours du Centre National de la Recherche Scientifique, Paris, 1970.

————, Les Misérables, ed. Maurice Allem, Bibliothèque de la Pléiade, Paris, 1951.

————, *Oeuvres complètes*, ed. Paul Meurice, Gustave Simon, Cécile Daubray, 45 vols., Edition de l'Imprimerie Nationale, Paris, 1904-1952.

————, *Oeuvres poétiques*, ed. Pierre Albouy, Bibliothèque de la Pléiade, 2 vols., Paris, 1964-67.

————, *Théâtre complet*, ed. J. J. Thierry et Josette Mélèze, Bibliothèque de la Pléiade, 2 vols., Paris, 1963.

Jansen, Steen, "L'Unité d'action dans *Lorenzaccio*," *Revue Romane*, III (1968), 116-35.

Lacey, Alexander, *Pixerécourt and the French Romantic Drama*, Toronto, 1928.

Lafoscade, Léon, *Le Théâtre d'Alfred de Musset*, Paris, 1901.

Lebois, André, *Vues sur le théâtre de Musset*, Avignon, 1966.

Le Breton, André, *Le Théâtre romantique*, Paris, n.d.

Lefebvre, Henri, *Alfred de Musset dramaturge*, Paris, 1955.

Le Roy, A., *L'Aube du théâtre romantique*, Paris, 1904.

Lote, Georges, *En Préface à "Hernani,"* Paris, 1930.

Lyonnet, Henry, *Les "Premières" d'Alfred de Musset*, Paris, 1927.

————, *Les "Premières" de Victor Hugo*, Paris, 1930.

Matthews, Brander, *French Dramatists of the 19th Century*, New York, 1905.

Musset, Alfred de, *Oeuvres complètes*, édition dédiée aux Amis du Poète, Charpentier, 10 vols., Paris, 1865-66.

————, *Oeuvres complètes en prose*, ed. Maurice Allem et Paul Courant, Bibliothèque de la Pléiade, Paris, 1960.

————, *Poésies complètes*, ed. Maurice Allem, Bibliothèque de la Pléiade, Paris, 1957.

————, *Théâtre complet*, ed. Maurice Allem, Bibliothèque de la Pléiade, Paris, 1958.

Musset, Paul de, *Biographie d'Alfred de Musset, sa vie et ses oeuvres*, Paris, 1877.

Nebout, Pierre, *Le Drame romantique*, Paris, 1895.

Pendell, William D., *Victor Hugo's Acted Drama and the Contemporary Press*, Baltimore, 1947.

BIBLIOGRAPHY

Pommier, Jean, *Variétés sur Alfred de Musset et son théâtre*, Paris, n.d.

Poulet, Georges, "La Distance intérieure," *Études sur le temps humain*, II, Paris, 1952.

Rees, Margaret A., "Imagery in the plays of Alfred de Musset," *French Review*, XXXVI, No. 3 (Jan. 1963), 245-54.

Rickey, H. Wynn, *Musset shakespearien*, Bordeaux, 1932.

Riffaterre, Michael, "Un Exemple de comédie symboliste chez Victor Hugo," *L'Esprit Créateur*, III, No. 3, Fall (1965), 162-73.

Russell, Olga W., *Étude historique et critique des Burgraves de Victor Hugo, avec variantes inédites et lettres inédites*, Paris, 1962.

Sarcey, Francisque, *Quarante ans de théâtre*, IV, Paris, 1907.

Séché, Leon, *Alfred de Musset*, 2 vols., Paris, 1907.

Sessely, Annie, *L'Influence de Shakespeare sur Alfred de Vigny*, Berne, 1928.

Sices, David, "Musset's *Fantasio*: The Paradise of Chance," *Romanic Review*, LVIII, No. 1 (Feb. 1967), 23-37.

Smet, Robert de, *Le Théâtre romantique*, Paris, 1929.

Stendhal, *Racine et Shakespeare*, ed. Jean-Jacques Pauvert, Paris, 1965.

Treille, Marguerite, *Le Conflit dramatique en France de 1823 à 1830, d'après les journaux et les revues du temps*, Paris, 1929.

Vigny, Alfred de, *Oeuvres complètes*, ed. Fernand Baldensperger, Bibliothèque de la Pléiade, I, Paris, 1950.

Vigo-Fazio, Lorenzo, *I Drammi maggiori di Victor Hugo*, Catania, 1951.

——, *Il "Teatro in libertà" di Victor Hugo*, Lecce, 1953.

Weber, Jean-Paul, *Genèse de l'oeuvre poétique*, Paris, 1960.

Zola, Émile, *Oeuvres complètes*, ed. Henri Mitterand, Club du Livre Précieux, XI, Paris, 1968.

Zumthor, Paul, *Victor Hugo poète de Satan*, Paris, 1946.

Index

(Works by Hugo and Musset are listed alphabetically beneath their names.)

INDEX

In the nineteenth century, the French lyric poets imposed their diction on the theatrical genre and thus illuminated the essence of both poetry and theatre. Ten plays by Victor Hugo, the standard-bearer of the French romantic theatre, and Alfred de Musset, the romantic playwright most frequently performed in France today, are analyzed by Charles Affron to answer the question, "Can the dialetic form of the theatre accommodate the solitary élan of the lyric poet?"

As a functional point of departure, he considers those characteristics of lyric poetry—time, voice, and metaphor—which bring us closest to the singular attitudes of Hugo and Musset. Then, examining the texts of *Hernani, Les Burgraves, Torquemada, Fantasio,* and *Lorenzaccio* as well as several lesser-known plays, Mr. Affron discusses such topics as poetic time, the scope of analogy, theatrical and poetic rhetoric, the guises of the poet-hero, and the manner of sounding the poet's voice upon the stage.

In the conjunction of these romantic authors, Professor Affron provides criteria flexible enough to explain and preserve the originality of their hybrid creations—romantic dramas.

Charles Affron is Professor of Romance Languages and Literatures, New York University, and the author of *Patterns of Failure in "La Comédie humaine."*